T0205609

Progress in IS

"PROGRESS in IS" encompasses the various areas of Information Systems in theory and practice, presenting cutting-edge advances in the field. It is aimed especially at researchers, doctoral students, and advanced practitioners. The series features both research monographs that make substantial contributions to our state of knowledge and handbooks and other edited volumes, in which a team of experts is organized by one or more leading authorities to write individual chapters on various aspects of the topic. "PROGRESS in IS" is edited by a global team of leading IS experts. The editorial board expressly welcomes new members to this group. Individual volumes in this series are supported by a minimum of two members of the editorial board, and a code of conduct mandatory for all members of the board ensures the quality and cutting-edge nature of the titles published under this series.

More information about this series at http://www.springer.com/series/10440

Jorge Marx Gómez • Jantje Halberstadt •
Anna Henkel • Frank Köster • Jürgen Sauer •
Jürgen Taeger • Andreas Winter •
David M. Woisetschläger

Editors

Progress in Sustainable Mobility Research

Interdisciplinary Approaches for Rural Areas

 Springer

Editors

Jorge Marx Gómez
Department of Computing Science
Carl von Ossietzky University of Oldenburg
Oldenburg, Germany

Jantje Halberstadt
Chair of Economy of Sustainability
University of Vechta
Vechta, Germany

Anna Henkel
Chair of Sociology of Technology
University of Passau
Passau, Bayern, Germany

Frank Köster
Institute of Transportation Systems
German Aerospace Center (DLR)
Braunschweig, Germany

Jürgen Sauer
Department of Computing Science
Carl von Ossietzky University of Oldenburg
Oldenburg, Germany

Jürgen Taeger
Civil Law, Business Law, Legal Informatics
Information Law
Carl von Ossietzky University of Oldenburg
Oldenburg, Germany

Andreas Winter
Department of Computing Science
Carl von Ossietzky University of Oldenburg
Oldenburg, Germany

David M. Woisetschläger
Chair of Services Management
Technical University of Braunschweig
Braunschweig, Germany

ISSN 2196-8705   ISSN 2196-8713   (electronic)
Progress in IS
ISBN 978-3-030-70843-6   ISBN 978-3-030-70841-2   (eBook)
https://doi.org/10.1007/978-3-030-70841-2

This Springer imprint is published by the registered company Springer Nature Switzerland AG.
The registered company address is: Gewerbestrasse 11, 6330 Cham, Switzerland

Foreword

Climate change affects us all. Lower Saxony, as an agricultural and coastal state, will also be increasingly affected if the negative trend continues. Many ecosystems that are already heavily used by humans are no longer able to adapt to climatic conditions within the required framework.

These briefly described phenomena need to be addressed by politicians at all levels. Through their roles as advisors, science and research can contribute important insights. In doing so, science and research should be assured of support from research policy at European, federal and state levels. Because only in close cooperation can we succeed in solving this great challenge of our time.

With the "Science for Sustainable Development" funding programme, Lower Saxony's sustainability research has been brought into focus to a considerable extent. In three selection rounds so far (2013–2018), 18 projects have been selected, which will be funded for up to 4 years with a total of 28.1 million euros. One of them is the project "NEMo—Sustainable Fulfilment of Mobility Needs in Rural Areas".

The aim of the programme is to promote research projects that—oriented towards the key objective of sustainable social development—address current, socially significant questions and problems and work on them at the highest scientific level. The programme is thus open to all scientific disciplines and does not make any specifications with regard to concrete sustainability-related topics. This can be seen as a successful combination of social relevance and scientific freedom.

In addition, the programme was designed to enable the participation of non-scientists without specifying the form or intensity of this participation. This created the possibility for transdisciplinary research without making it a requirement for the projects.

In the field of climate and sustainability research, knowledge must continue to be generated within the framework of inter- and transdisciplinary research in order to achieve acceptance by as many participants as possible.

This is also very clear in project NEMo. I am pleased that scientists from the TU Braunschweig, DLR Braunschweig, the University of Oldenburg and the University of Vechta were involved in the project, that a scientist from the University of Passau also worked successfully in the project and that the population was involved to the highest degree.

In my opinion, the project is highly interesting because it combines existing mobile phone technology, apps and the Internet with existing offers such as collective taxis, call taxis, car-sharing agencies and women's night taxis in order to provide solutions for the mobility needs of rural areas with regard to infrastructural problems of public transport. The project is also highly relevant for Lower Saxony, since the results as well as the app could theoretically be applied in the wide rural areas of Lower Saxony (for example the Emsland, Wendland, South Holstein, Harz) besides the Wesermarsch district.

In the field of private transport in rural areas, the findings from the project can make a significant contribution to reducing carbon dioxide emissions. The NEMo mobility platform, which is also manifested in the "Fahrkreis" app, illustrates the contribution of the project beyond its usefulness in the scientific field. The publications, theses and three appointments resulting from the project as well as the following work will also disseminate the results achieved in the scientific landscape.

I was able to get a picture of the results of the project during my visit to the NEMo final event and was enthusiastic. I would be very pleased if the results of the research, the mobility platform and the app could be applied in other areas of Lower Saxony. I wish all the scientists involved every success in their further activities and the readers an informative reading of the following work!

Minister for Science and Culture of Lower Saxony   Björn Thümler
Hanover, Germany

Foreword

Something is wrong with our today's "mobility", which is sometimes appreciated and sometimes scolded but always required and often enough necessary. If we live in a big city, we appreciate the varied and colourful mobility offers in our area, which are easily accessible in many places by good public transport. At the same time, the density, noise and air pollution of private transport are a constant nuisance.

If we live in the countryside, less traffic, especially "thinned out" public transport, is an obstacle. The routes to work or training places, shopping, schools, day care centres, doctors or pharmacies and many leisure activities are difficult. The use of the individually available private car seems unavoidable to many. However, this individual option is associated with Ǔ- often underestimated – costs and is not even open to many citizens, for example, because he or she has no driver's license, or the ability to drive is no longer given for health or age-related reasons, or simply because there is insufficient money.

The now modern word "traffic turnaround (Verkehrswende)" often refers to the reduction of fossil fuels in favour of other resource-saving options such as electric mobility. These are certainly also worth striving for. But, even if every passenger car and every public transport vehicle were substituted by a technology described as sustainable, this would not change everything in the situations described earlier. But, the density of traffic in cities, on the one hand, and the undersupply in rural regions, on the other, remained exactly the same.

Around 47 million people in Germany, more than 50% of the German population, are living in rural areas. The question, therefore, arises why urban regions receive more attention than rural ones. Would it not be possible to increase the attractiveness of sparsely populated regions if the population staying there felt "better provided" with regard to mobility? Would life not be even more attractive if the way to work, to the doctor, etc. were easier?

This challenge, to ensure satisfactory mobility solutions in sparsely populated areas without increasing traffic density at the same time, is the main focus of project NEMo (Sustainable Fulfilment of Mobility Needs in Rural Areas). As existing and new, innovative providers of sustainable mobility working on—often competing— solutions, the NEMo approach links existing mobility capabilities with information and communication technologies. Instead of competing, project NEMo combines different public transport modes, mobility companies and voluntary private services. Thus, the static time schedule of public transport service is expanded by new virtual stops, dynamic routes and adequate timing and thus connects very different means of transport. It creates some kind of "Internet of real movement possibilities".

Research in the sustainability sciences has been long explained as very challenging due to its high degree of complexity, which can only be mastered by close cooperation of different research disciplines. A purely technical or scientific solution that is implemented by engineers, or a purely socio-political approach that regulates via enlightenment, guidelines and laws, or a purely economic approach that leaves the field to the "market" as the ultimate regulator does not seem to be sufficiently effective to most scientists.

For this reason, project NEMo is following an interdisciplinary and transdisciplinary approach that involves many different disciplines and perspectives. Computer science, sustainable entrepreneurship with corresponding business models, social and communication sciences, as well as legal experts worked closely together on the basis of their specific methods and from their point of view contributed to the success of the project through vital exchange over the entire duration of the project.

The results were not created in the so-called ivory tower. Scientific and practical knowledge were combined in a transdisciplinary sense. The pilot region Wesermarsch, from which more than 300 citizens actively participated, and the support from the local politicians and the public administration contributed to the success of project NEMo as well.

All this has resulted in an innovative mobility platform that is practically usable for citizens in rural areas. The former Federal President Horst Köhler said in a muchnoticed speech at the International Transport Forum in 2010:

> So, let's strip away old habits of seeing and thinking, let's at least try to question them. Let's look together for new ways to a mobility that is not a privilege for here and now, but that remains possible for everyone – also in the future.

From my personal view, the results of project NEMo are new in this sense and can be well transferred to other regions.

Lüneburg, Germany   Prof. Dr. Helmut Faasch

Acknowledgments

We want to thank Prof. Dr.-Ing. Benjamin Wagner vom Berg for his ideas and contributions in this project. Also, our thanks go to Benjamin Dietrich as interim project assistant.

The success of project NEMo is largely based on the willingness of the residents and local population to contribute to the interviews, surveys and field studies conducted during the project. We, therefore, thank all participants for their voluntary and unselfish commitment to project NEMo. Furthermore, we thank the Wirtschaftsförderung Wesermarsch and the City of Oldenburg for their help in recruiting the participants.

We want to thank Gunnar Barghorn, Prof. Dr. Helmut Faasch, Prof. Dr. Helmut Lessing and Prof. Dr. Katharina Manderscheid for their work and contributions in the scientific advisory board of project NEMo. Moreover, we thank the multitude of associated partners from municipalities, boards, businesses and research facilities for their support of project NEMo.

Project NEMo was enabled through the funding by the VolkswagenStiftung and the Ministry for Science and Culture of Lower Saxony. We, therefore, thank them for the confidence in the vision and objective of project NEMo, which led to the project results at hand.

Project NEMo was strongly embedded into research and teaching activities at the universities involved. More than 50 graduate students elaborated their final theses focusing on the research aspects of project NEMo. In addition, research assistants of the different departments contributed to the successful realization of the project idea. We would like to take this opportunity to express our appreciation to (or to thank) all (former) students who were part of project NEMo.

This work is part of the project "NEMo—Sustainable Fulfilment of Mobility Needs in Rural Areas". Further information are available on the following website: www.nemo-mobilitaet.de. The project is funded by the Ministry for Science and Culture of Lower Saxony and the Volkswagen Foundation (VolkswagenStiftung) through the "Niedersächsisches Vorab" grant programme (grant number VWZN3122).

Oldenburg, Germany   Jorge Marx Gómez
Vechta, Germany   Jantje Halberstadt
Passau, Germany   Anna Henkel
Braunschweig, Germany   Frank Köster
Oldenburg, Germany   Jürgen Sauer
Oldenburg, Germany   Jürgen Taeger
Oldenburg, Germany   Andreas Winter
Braunschweig, Germany   David M. Woisetschläger

Contents

Part IV   Technical Requirements and Implementations

Part V   Legal Considerations and Limitations

Contributors

Ali Akyol University of Vechta, Vechta, Germany

Ali Amin Rezaei Carl von Ossietzky University of Oldenburg, Oldenburg, Germany

Phillip Bühring Carl von Ossietzky University of Oldenburg, Oldenburg, Germany

Klaas Dählmann Carl von Ossietzky University of Oldenburg, Oldenburg, Germany

Jantje Halberstadt University of Vechta, Vechta, Germany

Martina Jahns Technical University of Braunschweig, Braunschweig, Germany

Dilshod Kuryazov Urgench Branch of Tashkent University of Information Technologies named after Muhammad al-Khwarizmi, Urgench, Uzbekistan

Jorge Marx Gómez Carl von Ossietzky University of Oldenburg, Oldenburg, Germany

Nadine Pieper Technical University of Braunschweig, Braunschweig, Germany

Johannes Rolfs Carl von Ossietzky University of Oldenburg, Oldenburg, Germany

Ute Samland Carl von Ossietzky University of Oldenburg, Oldenburg, Germany

Alexander Sandau Carl von Ossietzky University of Oldenburg, Oldenburg, Germany

Jürgen Sauer Carl von Ossietzky University of Oldenburg, Oldenburg, Germany

Ernst Schäfer Arbeitsgruppe für regionale Struktur- und Umweltforschung (ARSU) GmbH, Oldenburg, Germany

Ulrich Scheele Arbeitsgruppe für regionale Struktur- und Umweltforschung (ARSU) GmbH, Oldenburg, Germany

Johannes Schering Carl von Ossietzky University of Oldenburg, Oldenburg, Germany

Doris Schröder Landesinitiative Ernährungswirtschaft LI Food, University of Vechta, Vechta, Germany

Cedrik Theesen Carl von Ossietzky University of Oldenburg, Oldenburg, Germany

Andreas Winter Carl von Ossietzky University of Oldenburg, Oldenburg, Germany

Part I
Current State and Perspectives of Sustainable Mobility

Research Approaches and Objectives of Project NEMo

Ali Akyol, Klaas Dählmann, Martina Jahns, Dilshod Kuryazov,
Ali Amin Rezaei, Johannes Rolfs, Ute Samland, Alexander Sandau,
Johannes Schering, and Cedrik Theesen

Abstract NEMo is an inter- and transdisciplinary research project with the objective to improve mobility in rural areas through the holistic development of a sustainable, ICT-based mobility platform for carpooling, ridesharing, and public transportation services. This contribution details the research approaches and objectives as well as the general methodology. Moreover, it introduces the four relevant research modules of the project, consisting of the examination of the local communities, organizational aspects, suitable business models, and technical solutions. The relevance of the individual research modules is presented both on a theoretical level with regard to sustainability research in general and on an applied level with regard to specifics of project NEMo.

Keywords Carpooling · Mobility platform · Ridesharing · Rural areas · Sustainable mobility · Transdisciplinary research

A. Akyol
University of Vechta, Vechta, Germany
e-mail: ali.akyol@uni-vechta.de

K. Dählmann · A. Amin Rezaei · J. Rolfs · U. Samland · A. Sandau (✉) · J. Schering · C. Theesen
Carl von Ossietzky University of Oldenburg, Oldenburg, Germany
e-mail: klaas.daehlmann@uol.de; ali.amin.rezaei@uol.de; johannes.rolfs@uol.de;
ute.samland@uol.de; alexander.sandau@uol.de; johannes.schering@uol.de;
cedrik.theesen@uol.de

M. Jahns
Technical University of Braunschweig, Braunschweig, Germany
e-mail: martina.jahns@tu-bs.de

D. Kuryazov
Urgench Branch of Tashkent University of Information Technologies Named After Muhammad al-Khwarizmi, Urgench, Uzbekistan
e-mail: kuryazov@se.uol.de

© The Author(s), under exclusive license to Springer Nature Switzerland AG 2021
J. Marx Gómez et al. (eds.), *Progress in Sustainable Mobility Research*,
Progress in IS, https://doi.org/10.1007/978-3-030-70841-2_1

3

1   Introduction

In the Federal Republic of Germany, more than 50 million people live outside urban areas, with corresponding mobility and service needs. This corresponds to more than 60% of the total national population (Federal Statistical Office of Germany 2013). Due to the increasing concentration of medical and health care facilities and shopping centers, the demand for mobility in rural areas will further increase (Raabe et al. 2001). Last but not least, the accessibility of schools, health centers, leisure facilities, and jobs and training places will play a central role for companies when choosing a location (Zängler 2000; Institut für Mobilitätsforschung 2004, 2006). Therefore, mobility offers are an important location factor for the creation of corporate value and the basis for participation in social life (Beckmann et al. 2006; Rammler 2001). Nevertheless, in times of demographic change, it is becoming increasingly difficult to maintain a basic supply of mobility services without questioning social participation, regional value creation, and, of course, environmental protection goals. Mobility problems in rural areas will thus challenge society, politics, administration, and the economy in the future. It can be expected that mobility solutions that integrate traffic-optimizing coordination and organizational activities will be demanded increasingly by both public and corporate actors.

The objective of the project NEMo[1] is the sustainable and purposeful fulfillment of supply and mobility needs, considering the specific social structures in rural areas. These structures are the key to developing a mobility model based on social self-organization (community building). In this context, information and communication technology (ICT) in the form of socio-technical information systems play a crucial supporting role and can serve as a basis for a sustainable rural mobility supply.

Sustainability in its economic, social, and ecological dimensions should be taken into account. Especially the consideration of the last two dimensions requires a strategy of sufficiency II (Paech 2005). In this strategy, mobility should not be reduced overall, but rather in terms of its negative effects. Existing concepts such as function/purpose orientation, which focus on the shared mobility function instead of owning a vehicle, appear to be generally suitable for the implementation of such a strategy. This is particularly true for mobility in rural areas, as these are characterized by a high proportion of motorized private transport in the form of private cars and insufficient provision by local public transport (Heinze 2007).

The extreme condition of public transport in rural areas is mainly the result of a backlogged adaptation to the change of the spatial system environment. In rural areas the traditional public transport offer has shrunk considerably. Of the remaining demand for public transport, 70–90% of all transports in sparsely populated areas is now school transport. Despite its restrictions, school transport has thus become the generally accessible mobility basis and the minimum service offer for carless parts of the population. There are already places of residence without school transport,

---

[1] https://nemo-mobilitaet.de.

which are served only once a week or by stub trips as a call bus. For this reason, private mass motorization can be interpreted as a user-financed problem solution (Heinze 2007).

Solutions to limit the increasing mass motorization can be created by flexible forms such as shared call taxis (AnrufSammelTaxi), call buses, or carpooling. Some of these also act as feeders and distributors, which become more attractive due to their time flexibility (bus stop "front door") and have been proven to induce new traffic (also for later bus lines). The flexibility of carpooling can be achieved by transferring sharing and pooling concepts that are established in metropolitan areas and combining them with existing public transport services in rural areas. The particular challenge here is that private individuals are transformed into local mobility providers who offer their own vehicle capacities to other people. For instance, public transport stops could be served by private individuals. Furthermore, infrastructural, social and economic needs, and specifics of rural areas must be considered.

1.1 Research Methodology

For a long time, awareness of the mobility problems in rural areas had been relatively neglected in the focus of scientific research projects. Despite a large number of publications on the topic of mobility, rural regions are often excluded and cannot benefit from the research results, as they mainly address urban areas and adjacent areas. This leads to an increasing weakening of the rural areas and perpetuates the problematic situation. It is therefore necessary to focus research activities more on rural areas and their special conditions. Despite the knowledge about the problems and the advanced sensitization of the general public over the last years, measures to change the status quo have so far been insufficiently implemented and the solution of the rural problems associated with this question has been postponed. The following collective research question emerges from this:

Building on the social structures of rural areas, how can mobility needs be fulfilled under aspects of sustainability and purpose orientation?

In order to answer the collective research question, sub-areas were identified, which lead to desired transformation effects. Figure 1 shows the four sub-areas (hereafter referred as modules) community, organization, business models, and ICT, which are arranged according to the used research methodology of the Belief-Action-Outcome model.

The Belief-Action-Outcome model (Coleman 1986; Melville 2010), which was developed specifically for research in the context of sustainability, is used as the basic structure of the research project. This comprises the following three research steps.

Beliefs First, the central expectations of stakeholders in rural areas must be identified. This involves collecting requirements for the provision of new innovative

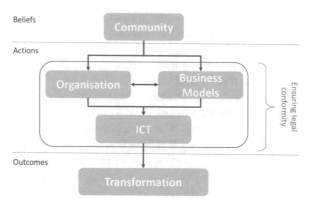

Fig. 1 Belief-action-outcome model applied to the NEMo research objective

mobility services that are optimally adapted to the needs of the rural population and foster sustainable mobility. These innovative mobility services must be accompanied by business models in which the roles of providers and consumers can be dynamically changed. The organization of all participants within the frame of the community should be largely autonomous based on already established social structures. The supporting ICT solution must consider the requirements of such a self-organized and self-optimizing community and help to make everyday mobility as seamless as possible without barriers.

Actions The analysis of the needs and capacities as well as the requirements of the community for the creation of new organizational forms serves as a starting point for the measures to be carried out. Through innovative business models, citizens are transformed into prosumers and thus enriched with real alternatives to the private car and public transport. New ways of bringing people together and to organize themselves in social structures are developed and introduced into existing rural areas. This integration is realized via self-organizing communication channels. Therefore, ICT is an important medium of communication, which eliminates information asymmetries and brings together consumers and providers.

Outcomes A significant impact results from the conception of exchange relationships within the frame of private mobility services within the community. A social transformation process is driven by the promotion of group-dynamic processes. This process is promoted by the development, piloting, and evaluation of a mobility platform that supports the organization of novel mobility services with special consideration of the existing mobility capacities, needs, and social structures in rural areas. The organization and consolidation of supply and mobility needs will be improved with simulations and optimization concepts. The development of long-term, periodically recurring organizational structures will lead to strong regional cohesion.

The social community with its requirements and mechanisms forms the basis for the development of new organizational concepts and business models for mobility in rural areas that are implemented with the help of ICT. On this basis, a transformation of mobility behavior in rural areas under sustainability aspects can be achieved as a result in the long term. The concepts developed in the sub-areas were implemented and used for a final evaluation. In the following, the four modules and their dependencies and relationships are presented in detail.

2 Sociological and Psychological Enhancement of the Community Idea (Module Community)

The module community is the starting point within the Belief-Action-Outcome model shown in Fig. 1. The actions and intended transformational processes of the project are therefore largely based on a thorough and successful analysis of the existing communities in rural areas.

2.1 Relevance

In order to be able to investigate the central research question of the formation of a sustainable and above all demand-oriented mobility offer in rural areas, the first step is to describe the social interaction in rural areas. These form the basis for the coordination and control of communities. Such a central coordination mechanism can be used, for example, to develop an initial concept for the use of various mobility offers (Wiesenthal 2000).

2.2 Theoretical Background

The core task of the sociological sub-project was to analyze the individual mobility patterns and routines of citizens in rural areas. The focus was on the practice of everyday mobility, the associated individual attitudes, and structural conditions, such as the use of public transport services or the advantages and disadvantages associated with the use of cars by only one person. With the focus on the daily execution of mobility—the doing (Reckwitz 2003)—routines can be described on the one hand, and on the other hand, a look at the daily repetitions of spatial mobility opens the view for their change.

Another important sub-area was the consideration of community mobility. Community mobility is meant here in the sense of carpooling, such as the joint journey to work (commuting), in order to drive children to school or to the nursery or to accompany other family members to the doctor or hairdresser. The main concern here was to find out how and in which situations community mobility already takes place or is organized, but also where there are barriers and reservations on the part of drivers and passengers. Finally, the attitude toward sustainability was enquired, i.e., what role sustainability plays in the organization and implementation of everyday mobility and what ideas of sustainability shape everyday mobility activities.

2.3 Applications and Practical Implications

These findings can then be applied to the development of a mobility platform, so that existing mobility practices, alone or in community, in a particular rural area can contribute positively to the development of an overall objective such as the mobility platform. The focus here is on lowering barriers to use community mobility and creating a sense of community that goes beyond existing forms of community mobility, as well as establishing a commitment to those who are mobile.

Building on this, the psychological drivers, such as feelings of responsibility, can then be investigated in greater depth, in order to use them as possible levers for the mobility concept (see chapter by Dählmann, Jahns, Pieper and Sauer in this volume). Findings on the sociological and psychological drivers and the barriers form the basis for the further development of an initial use concept (see chapter by Akyol and Halberstadt in this volume). By means of laboratory and real experiments (Eschweiler et al. 2007), these can be further developed into a holistic mobility concept in the next step. The focus here is on the integration of existing community capacities that were surveyed in the sociological part of the project. This also includes research into a non-monetary loyalty program, which should serve to increase ongoing use by emphasizing social norms. Summarizing the core results of the module community, respondents in the target communities show a predominantly positive attitude to the idea of online carpooling but with concerns about excessive coordination and coordination efforts as well as the safety of carpooling (see chapter by Samland in this volume).

3 Organizational Concepts for Sustainable Mobility Models and Social Self-Organization (Module Organization)

The social and psychological considerations and findings in Sect. 2 lead to a need for a systematic approach for an organizational model. Explanations and limitations of sustainable mobility are subsequently researched form a perspective of social self-organization.

3.1 Relevance of the Social Self-Organization Approach for Sustainable Mobility

For an ideal mobility provision under sustainability aspects, it is of central importance to organize all existing mobility capabilities in such a way that an efficient utilization is maximized. While their capacity utilization is often unproblematic in more urban areas, the rentability of "traditional" public transport services cannot always be ensured in rural areas due to the overall lower population density, resulting in reduced timing or canceled connections. This issue leads to an overall reduced accessibility and attractiveness of the public transport from the consumer's point of view. The organizational concepts for sustainable mobility models pursued in this project therefore envision to expand the available set of mobility capabilities by seamlessly integrating self-organized, dynamic ridesharing and carpooling opportunities offered by individual members of the community alongside the already existing public transport services. In this sense, the societal role of private persons must be extended to a prosumer-based notion not only consuming mobility capabilities but also providing those as well whenever possible. For this purpose it is necessary that mobility capacities owned and operated by individual private persons, such as the aforementioned dynamic ridesharing and carpooling resources, are brought together and made accessible to other members of the community.

3.2 Theoretical Background

The social self-organizing approach makes use of synergy effects of any trips taking place anyway (i.e., the driver would drive anyway and offers free capacities in the car to other people having the same destination and trip schedule; cf. definition of Furuhata et al. 2013, p. 28). This self-organizing approach includes elements from innovation research, which has been discussing social networks since the beginning of the twenty-first century as a new mode of producing something new (e.g., Rammert 2000). The core idea here is that innovation does not take place in individual companies or by individuals but has the best chances in a distributed, heterogeneous network, in which consumers, science, and economic companies work together at different stages of the exploitation chain. The approach chosen here also follows concepts of self-organization, as they have been elaborated in systems-theoretical organizational and management research (e.g., Luhmann 2000).

3.3 Application and Practical Implications of Social Self-Organization within the Context of the Project

As an instrument for supporting/enabling this self-organizational concept of mobility, a technical solution based on a ubiquitously available ICT-based platform seems appropriate because the coordination of private carpools with family and friends primarily via mobile apps indicates general acceptance of smartphone-based ICT solutions. Moreover, through the dissemination of mobile Internet, a relatively spontaneous matching of ridesharing/carpooling providers and consumers is possible with mobile ICT-based platforms. In general, the development of an ICT-based platform, which supports and fosters the self-organizational approach, requires appropriate organizational processes that enable the planning, booking, and billing of mobility services offered by private persons (see chapter by Bühring, Kuryazov, Sandau and Winter in this volume). Moreover, the approach proposed here is developed without organizational profit orientation, without formal membership, but instead by using dynamics of self-organization on basis of a common interest. For this purpose, appropriate business models must be developed in order to enhance mobility in rural areas as a whole (see chapter by Akyol and Halberstadt in this volume). Furthermore, within this framework, new contractual relationships emerge, within which legal implications regarding the conclusion of contracts with regard to performance, fulfillment of contracts, liability, etc. must also be considered (see chapter by Rolfs in this volume). Moreover, the simulative consideration of behavior in this self-organization approach needs to be considered as well (see chapter by Dählmann, Jahns, Pieper and Sauer in this volume). To enable general, more sustainable mobility, the developed platform must, first and foremost, provide an impetus for successful emergence of lasting social self-organization. This also means that a continuation of sharing rides with the same person(s) without the ICT platform through other means of private organization is in accordance with the idea of the project. Nevertheless, in line with the overarching objective of enhancing rural mobility, a long-term improvement might only be achieved once a critical mass of users regularly organize their mobility via the ICT platform, so that there is an attractive amount of offers and requests. In order to achieve this, an incentive system is integrated in the platform.

4   Development of Suitable Business Models (Module Business Models)

To enhance the mobility in rural areas, a rethink into new mobility solutions is necessary. Offering mobility services in rural areas is not lucrative enough for companies. Considering the demographic change shows that the lack of mobility services will increase. One of the main challenges is that rural areas have mostly monotonous mobility offers. This is a big challenge to find the gab and use the potentials of citizen.

4.1   Relevance of Business Model Development

Business management research has found evidence that the economic concept of the "tragedy of the commons" (Hardin 1968) also exists in shared mobility services (Bardhi and Eckhardt 2012). The perceived negative reciprocity and lack of connectivity lower the acceptance of mobility services and thus their economic success. Unfortunately, the positive influence of identification decreases with the increasing spread of larger providers (Pieper et al. 2013). When public transport is considered, it quickly becomes clear that different price and service models are offered between urban and rural areas. Rural areas are not sufficiently lucrative for many businesses because of their low population density and high operating costs. This is only one example of the numerous shortcomings of mobility in rural areas (Herget 2015).

The foregoing illustrates the need for research in the field of sustainable business approaches. Thus, the investigation and development of business models play an important role in the project in two respects. On the one hand, a business model must be developed by the company itself so that the concept is self-sustaining in the long term and, above all, motivates people to actively use it (see chapter by Akyol and Halberstadt in this volume). This is the only way to create a sustainable space for exchanging information on mobility concepts and requirements in rural areas. On the other hand, business models that contribute to improving mobility in rural areas must be examined. To this end, methods of diffusion, innovation, and entrepreneurship research are linked. A selection of suitable concepts can then be integrated into the concepts and evaluated.

4.2   Theoretical Background

Generating innovative and sustainable business ideas is considered to be a crucial precondition for developing successful business models and a key source of competitive advantage (Eppler et al. 2011; Mitchell and Coles 2003, 2004).

At the same time, it is one of the most challenging tasks, as it involves the complex interplay of a variety of factors such as the appropriate integration of knowledge and experience in different fields, awareness of challenges as a basis for business opportunities, team cooperation, and creativity (Chesbrough 2006; Briggs et al. 2003; Fay et al. 2006; Garfield et al. 2001). The core of our research area is the analysis of existing and development of new business models in the field of mobility, which considers the special needs of users in rural areas.

4.3   Using an Innovative Approach for the Structural Support of Idea and Business Model Generation for the NEMo Platform

In order to systematically generate business ideas and transform them into sustainable business models, it was necessary to develop an approach that supports focusing on a given situation and its specific requirements and therefore allows to integrate different perspectives and methods. This approach has been applied to the NEMo region and context. In close cooperation with other research groups and based on their previous results, various business ideas were developed, which have then been analyzed in detail and transferred into business models using a strategic selection process and (future) users' feedback. The first of these approaches has already been implemented.

Three main steps for generating business ideas within the context of project NEMo have been introduced. For each step, a general procedure has been developed and then applied in the project by example. Concrete business models are introduced and deliver insights into the selection process. Exemplary business models including the revenue model are then described in detail, and the challenges of pricing systems and policies as well as cost structures and resource management are discussed. As even the best technical solution is worthless if users do not adopt it, also the question of motivation and underlining the need for the early integration of future customers and creation of incentives for supporting mobility transformation in rural areas using the NEMo app were addressed. Integrating various offerings into the NEMo platform leads to a holistic approach that considers individuals' various needs, circumstances, and mobility options. By combining and optimizing these mobility options, a flexible and customized system that may lead to the sustainable improvement of mobility in rural areas via direct and indirect effects is provided.

The research results can be directly applied in practice by making selected offers from the different areas available on a platform. To make concrete offers available and enable exchange relations within the community, especially within the framework of private mobility services, appropriate IT infrastructure must be built and operated on a permanent basis.

The integration of different offers into the portal is essential for the acceptance of the overall platform by users, and this implies that the research results can be applied in practice to improve mobility in rural areas. In addition, the research results, business models, and associated offers can be evaluated, and usage behavior is examined. In this way, the platform is used as a research tool simultaneously.

5 Appropriate Support through Flexible, Adaptable, and Sustainable Software Architectures (Module ICT)

The ideas collected by social scientists and business model experts described above need to be implemented as a technical solution. Based on the demands of citizens in rural areas the development of the ridesharing app Fahrkreis was initiated. A selection of innovative business models was developed, e.g., to motivate the users to a frequent usage of sustainable mobility services and the application itself. The fundamental results act as a basis for the work of the Department for Business Informatics VLBA at the University of Oldenburg.

5.1 Relevance of Software Architectures for Sustainable Mobility

The establishment of the described community idea, business models, and organizational concepts poses special technical challenges. For the implementation, testing, and improvement of a technical solution to improve sustainable mobility in rural areas using the existing social structures, a flexible mobility platform is required that can be enhanced in the long term. The platform must be open regarding the participation of private, commercial, and public actors and has to support their different services and exchange relations. It must offer generic services to build up and stabilize a community, which requires mutual trust in the interaction of the individual players at "eye level" and pronounced equality as a stabilizing element. Software support for the formation and interaction within the community has to be suitable for coupling with services for the provision and billing of mobility services. In particular, existing heterogeneous mobility services that provide information (accessibility, costs, time, ecological burdens, etc.) about existing mobility services such as local bus companies, car-sharing services, long-distance transport, carpooling offers, taxis, etc. must be integrated and uniformly modeled. From the consumer's point of view, a homogeneous information offer on all relevant mobility offers must be created that supports not only door-to-door travel requests but also earmarked requests for specific transport and supply needs. Technical concepts must also be developed to enable the entire population (including older people, people with disabilities, etc.) in an affected (rural) area to participate in such a community—this results in high demands on the accessibility of the platform. Therefore, in addition to supporting access via the Internet and mobile devices, alternative accesses must be created (e.g., via display boards, terminals, or hotlines).

5.2 Theoretical Background

Independent of the scientific context, the application domain of novel mobility services also addresses to highly flexible software support. A continuous adaption of the mobility platform leads to more complex and less maintainable software systems (Lehman 1996). It should facilitate the recombination of existing mobility services to provide enhanced services, as well as completely new, unanticipated usage scenarios, and the development of corresponding business models (Combemale et al. 2016).

Finally, with the overall goal of NEMo being sustainability, it is only appropriate to strive for it in terms of software design. A rigid, monolithic software system would lead to high maintenance costs, and ultimately to its phase-out, close down (Rajlich and Bennett 2000), and forced replacement. To be sustainable, the NEMo mobility platform must make architectural provisions for sustainability, flexibility, and adaptability (Kateule and Winter 2018).

5.3   Application and Practical Implications of Software Architectures within the Context of the Project

The service consideration abstracts from specific implementations of the respective mobility service providers (service orientation) and thus allows the orchestration of these services to realize the application scenarios and business models of the mobility platform according to legal regulations (see chapter by Rolfs in this volume). Components implement mobility services according to their service specification within a component framework (e.g., SCA) and connect the existing IT systems of the mobility service providers (component orientation). Based on dependencies between components and services and their properties, concrete tool chains can be (partially) automatically orchestrated to support service orchestrations. The components of individual mobility service providers are based on different, heterogeneous data sets. These must be synchronized for the composition of the components. Model/transformation or ontology-based approaches are to be used for this purpose (data interoperability) (see chapter by Bühring, Kuryazov, Sandau and Winter in this volume). The overall research question is how to design, implement, and test a community-based interoperability platform for heterogeneous mobility services that supports data interoperability and legal requirements and implements high security requirements (see chapter by Sandau, Schering, Amin Rezaei, Theesen and Marx Gómez in this volume). In this context, the long-term evolution of this mobility platform with regard to the support of new mobility services and the integration of new technologies must be taken into account. In addition, high requirements in the area of reliability/availability and, if necessary, systematic degradation of functionality while guaranteeing a basic supply must be ensured.

6   Summary and Future Work

Project NEMo has shown how transdisciplinary research can be conducted successfully to understand and improve mobility needs in rural areas in a sustainable fashion. A general understanding of communities in the model region of the project was developed using both qualitative and quantitative surveys and interviews and leading to lasting exchange relationships and dialogue between rural communities. The results of the surveys and interviews were used to develop requirements to suitable business models and the optimal technical implementation for the improvement of rural mobility. Solution concepts for the back end and front end were developed and successfully applied leading to a functional NEMo platform and the Fahrkreis app. Performance, acceptance, and usability were evaluated both in the field and using appropriate simulation approaches and systems. Moreover, legal conformity of the concepts and solutions was ensured throughout the project. Core criteria of the resulting NEMo platform and Fahrkreis app were to incorporate multimodal mobility services such as carpooling and ridesharing, an operation at or below prices of comparable services, proper door-to-door route planning, real-time data of available services, and reliable data safety and security, especially with regard to the European General Data Protection Regulation GDPR.

Results of the project will be used both in future research projects and in practical applications. Subsequent research projects already use, adapt, and extend the developed concepts and infrastructures for new research objectives such as use cases based on ridehailing, corporate mobility, and bicycle use. Practical applications include the extension of the services to other districts and regions of Germany, the evaluation of further business and payment models, and the lasting establishment and operation of the NEMo platform and Fahrkreis app for years to come.

References

Bardhi, F., & Eckhardt, G. M. (2012). Access-based consumption: The case of car sharing. *Journal of Consumer Research, 39*(4), 881–898.

Beckmann, K. J., Hesse, M., Holz-Rau, C., & Hunecke, M. (2006). *StadtLeben, Wohnen, Mobilität und Lebensstil, Neue Perspektiven für Raum- und Verkehrsentwicklung [City life, housing, mobility and lifestyle, New perspectives for regional and traffic development].* Wiesbaden: Springer VS.

Briggs, R., van De Vreede, G.-J., & Nunamaker, J. (2003). Collaboration engineering with thinkLets to pursue sustained success with group support systems. *Journal of Management Information Systems, 19*(4), 31–64.

Chesbrough, H. (2006). *Open business models: How to thrive in the new innovation landscape.* Boston, MA: Harvard Business School Press.

Coleman, J. (1986). Social theory, social research, and a theory of action. *American Journal of Sociology, 91*(6), 1309–1335.

Combemale, B., Cheng, B. H., Moreira, A., Bruel, J. M. & Gray, J. (2016). Modeling for Sustainability. In *Modeling in software engineering 2016 (MiSE'16).*

Eppler, M. J., Hoffmann, F., & Bresciani, S. (2011). New business models through collaborative idea generation. *International Journal of Innovation Management, 15*(6), 1323–1341.

Eschweiler, M., Evanschitzky, H., & Woisetschläger, D. M. (2007). Ein Leitfaden zur Anwendung varianzanlytisch ausgerichteter Laborexperimente. [A guideline for the application of analytical variance-oriented laboratory experiments]. *WiSt Wirtschaftswissenschaftliches Studium, 36*(12), 546–554.

Fay, D., Borrill, C., Amir, Z., Haward, R., & West, M. (2006). Getting the most out of multidisciplinary teams: A multi-sample study of team innovation in health care. *Journal of Occupational and Organizational Psychology, 79*(4), 553–567.

Furuhata, M., Dessouky, M., Ordóñez, F., Brunet, M.-E., Wang, X., & Koenig, S. (2013). Ridesharing: The state-of-the-art and future directions. *Transportation Research Part B, 57,* 28–46.

Garfield, M. J., Taylor, N. J., Dennis, A. R., & Satzinger, J. W. (2001). Research report: Modifying paradigms—individual differences, creativity techniques, and exposure to ideas in group idea generation. *Information Systems Research, 12*(3), 322–333.

Hardin, G. (1968). The tragedy of the commons. *Science, 162*(3859), 1243–1248.

Heinze, G. W. (2007). Öffentlicher Verkehr und demographischer Wandel: Chancen für Nordostdeutschland [Public Transport and Demographic Change: Opportunities for Northeast Germany]. In: S.Beetz (ed.): *Die Zukunft der Infrastrukturen in ländlichen Räumen [The future of infrastructures in rural areas]* Materialien Nr.14 (pp. 21–30). Berlin: Berlin-Brandenburgische Akademie der Wissenschaften.

Herget, M. (2015). *Mobilität von familien im ländlichen raum: Arbeitsteilung, routinen und typische bewältigungsstrategien*. Springer-Verlag.

Institut für Mobilitätsforschung (ed.) (2006). *Öffentlicher Personennahverkehr – Herausforderungen und Chancen [Local public transport—challenges and opportunities]*. Berlin: Springer.

Institut für Mobilitätsforschung (ed.) (2004). *Erlebniswelten und Tourismus [Worlds of experience and tourism.]*. Berlin: Springer.

Kateule, R., & Winter, A. (2018). Architectural design of sensor based environmental information systems for maintainability. In *Nachhaltige Betriebliche Umweltinformationssysteme* (pp. 87–96). Berlin: Springer.

Lehman, M. M. (1996). Laws of software evolution revisited. In *European Workshop on Software Process Technology* (pp. 108–124). Berlin: Springer.

Luhmann, N. (2000). *Organisation und Entscheidung. [Organization and decision.]* Wiesbaden: Westdeutscher Verlag GmbH.

Melville, N. (2010). Information systems innovation for environmental sustainability. *MIS Quarterly, 34*(1), 1–21.

Mitchell, D., & Coles C. (2004). Business model innovation breakthrough moves. *Journal of Business Strategy, 25*(1), 16–26.

Mitchell, D., & Coles, C. (2003). The ultimate competitive advantage of continuing business model innovation. *Journal of Business Strategy, 24*(5), 15–24.

Paech, N. (2005). Nachhaltigkeit zwischen ökologischer Konsistenz und Dematerialisierung: Hat sich die Wachstumsfrage erledigt? [Sustainability between ecological consistency and dematerialization: Has the growth question been resolved?]. *Natur und Kultur, 6*(1), 52–72.

Pieper, N., Heußler, T., Woisetschläger, D., & Backhaus, C. (2013). Relevanz der Intermodalität für CarSharing-Konzepte. In: *Schritte in die künftige Mobilität* (pp. 379–399). Wiesbaden: Springer Gabler.

Raabe, T., Mattern, U., & Zielstorff, H. (2001). Nachfragepotenziale mit Mobilitätspaketen ausschöpfen – Limit-Conjoint-Analyse von ÖPNV-Nutzern in der Region Hannover [Exploiting demand potential with mobility packages – Limit-conjoint analysis of public transport users in the Hannover region]. *Der Nahverkehr, 19*(10), 7–11.

Rajlich, V., & Bennett, K. (2000). A staged model for the software life cycle. *Computer, 33*(7), 66–71.

Rammert, W. (2000). Auf dem Weg zu einer post-schumpeterianischen Innovationsweise. Institutionelle Differenzierung, reflexive Modernisierung und interaktive Vernetzung im Bereich der Technikentwicklung. [On the way to a post-Schumpeterian way of innovation. Institutional differentiation, reflexive modernization and interactive networking in the field of technology development.] In Rammert, W. (Ed.), *Technik aus soziologischer Perspektive 2. [Technology from a sociological perspective 2]* (pp. 157–173). Wiesbaden: Westdeutscher Verlag GmbH.

Rammler, S. (2001). *Mobilität in der Moderne: Geschichte und Theorie der Verkehrssoziologie [Mobility in the Modern Age: History and Theory of Transport Sociology]*. Berlin.

Reckwitz, A. (2003). Grundelemente einer Theorie sozialer Praktiken. Eine sozialtheoretische Perspektive [Basic Elements of a Theory of Social Practices. A Perspective in Social Theory]. *Zeitschrift für Soziologie, 32*(4), 282–301.

Statistisches Bundesamt (Federal Statistical Office of Germany) (2013). *Grad der Verstädterung nach Fläche, Bevölkerung und Bevölkerungsdichte am 31.12.2013 [Degree of urbanization by area, population and population density on December 31, 2013]*. Retrieved December 12, 2020 from https://www.destatis.de/DE/Themen/Laender-Regionen/Regionales/Gemeindeverzeichnis/Administrativ-Nicht/33-verstaedterung.html

Wiesenthal, H. (2000). Markt, Organisation und Gemeinschaft als "zweitbeste" Verfahren sozialer Koordination [Market, Ogranization and Community as "secondbest" procedure of social coordination] In *Gesellschaftliche Komplexität und kollektive Handlungsfähigkeit* (pp. 44–73). Campus. Frankfurt am Main.

Zängler, T. (2000). *Mikroanalyse des Mobilitätsverhaltens in Alltag und Freizeit [Micro analysis of mobility behavior in everyday life and leisure]*. Berlin: Springer.

The Future of Mobility in Rural Areas: Participation and Co-creation in a Real-World Laboratory

Ulrich Scheele and Ernst Schäfer

Abstract The article describes the special challenges for ensuring sustainable mobility in sparsely populated rural regions under the conditions of demographic change. Based on the postulate of the principle of "equal living conditions" potential strategies for action are presented and evaluated. Using the example of a coastal community in north-western Lower Saxony that is heavily influenced by tourism, it is shown how locally adapted mobility solutions can be developed and implemented using the real-world laboratory approach in a co-creative process.

Keywords Rural areas · Mobility · Demographic change · Real laboratory · Co-creation

1 Introduction

The transport policy debate is currently characterized by the catchphrase of a mobility transition. A restructuring of the mobility system can be seen particularly in cities and urban areas. The strengthening of local public transport, new business models, the digitalization of transport, new sharing concepts, the promotion of active mobility, and new drive technologies are core components of new mobility solutions. But still in Germany—depending on the definition—approx. 90% of the area is characterized as rural and over 50% of the people live here. As a rule, they have very specific mobility needs and the regions have special framework conditions for the mobility sector. How will the mobility of the future be shaped in rural regions, especially under the conditions of demographic change, but also in view of the increasing challenges of an ambitious climate protection policy? Countless research projects and pilot projects deal with this question, but the question of mobility is also the subject of programs and initiatives that deal more

U. Scheele (✉) · E. Schäfer
Arbeitsgruppe für regionale Struktur- und Umweltforschung ARSU GmbH, Oldenburg, Germany
e-mail: scheele@arsu.de; schaefer@arsu.de

© The Author(s), under exclusive license to Springer Nature Switzerland AG 2021
J. Marx Gómez et al. (eds.), *Progress in Sustainable Mobility Research*,
Progress in IS, https://doi.org/10.1007/978-3-030-70841-2_2

fundamentally with the future of rural areas. There are interesting approaches and mobility concepts that have developed out of niches, but what (Weiss 2020) aptly describes still applies: In the mobility transition in rural regions, not even the indicator for the turning maneuver is set. When you turn to an indicator, you at least already know in which direction to go. This cannot be seen for transport policy, especially for rural regions. It is quite obvious in all considerations that there will be no "one size fits all" solution, but that solutions must be adapted locally. A prerequisite for this, however, is the more active involvement of local and regional stakeholders. In the following, the perspectives of such participatory solutions, but also the specific challenges, are described using the example of a rural region in which initial experiences were made with the approach of real-world laboratories. Section 2 first briefly outlines the current status of the mobility debate with a focus on rural areas under the postulate of equivalence of living conditions. Based on this, in Sect. 3, new mobility concepts are presented and their suitability for rural areas is assessed. Section 4 describes the background, methodological approach, and results of a real-world laboratory in a rural municipality in northwest Lower Saxony. The conclusions and recommendations are set out in Sect. 5.

2 The Postulate of Equivalence of Living Conditions and the Implications for Mobility

The polycentric settlement and economic structure of Germany has grown historically. In the development of rural areas there are disparities both in comparison to the urban areas but also between the differently structured rural areas. (Küpper 2016) As the numerous regional rankings make clear, there are growing rural regions that have good prospects due to their location, a strong medium-sized industry, and an increasing number of inhabitants. In addition, there are regions that are affected by structural change, which due to their peripheral location are not or only insufficiently affected by general economic developments and in which demographic change often made itself felt through declining population numbers, aging of the population, and emigration processes. In these regions, municipal financial problems then intensify and make necessary adjustment measures more difficult (Hesse et al. 2019; Hünnemeyer and Kempermann 2020; Oberst and Voigtländer 2020; Prognos 2019).

However, this classic city–country dichotomy between prosperous urban centers and structurally weak rural areas does not stand up to detailed analyzes. Overall, a very differentiated picture emerges in which different trends overlap and manifest themselves spatially (Wolff et al. 2020). At the same time, the differences between the living conditions and lifestyles of the population in rural and urban areas are increasingly converging, with mobility and the new possibilities of digital communication also contributing. Rural, peripheral regions can also offer their residents and immigrants attractive job and life prospects. A crucial prerequisite for this, however, is digital infrastructures and, above all, mobility offers that are widely available, efficient, affordable, sustainable, and user oriented. But there are still many underserved areas, especially in rural areas.

In many rural regions and villages, basic supply facilities for everyday goods and services, such as grocery stores, bakeries and butchers, hairdressers, post offices, and bank branches, have withdrawn or given up their livelihoods. Citizens have to travel significantly longer distances to reach these central infrastructures and public services. This has a very significant impact on people's lives and quality of life and also has a decisive influence on the choice of means of transport. Many of the facilities are then only accessible by car. This is particularly problematic for the growing number of residents who do not have a private car or are no longer able to use their own vehicle due to their age.

Information about the distribution of services of general interest and their accessibility as well as information about access to central infrastructures is provided by several information portals, including the "infrastructure atlas"[1] (Bundesministerium für Wirtschaft und Energie BMWi 2020), the "broadband atlas"[2] (Bundesministerium für Verkehr und digitale Infrastruktur BMVI 2019a,b), the "Landatlas",[3] or the "Daseinsvorsorgeatlas Niedersachsen"[4] (Innovations gruppe UrbanRural SOLUTIONS 2019). The picture that is drawn is not always clear, but it does the need to deal in detail with the specific conditions on site.

With a view to the demands on mobility, the development of commuter relations is also of interest. Not only has there been an increase in the number of commuters in recent years but also a significant increase in commuter distances (Buthe et al. 2018; Dauth and Haller 2018). For workers from rural regions, this also means that private motor vehicle remains the only option.

In Germany there has been a very long discussion about the question of equality of living conditions. The focus is not only on the potential instrumental design of spatial planning and regional policy, on the question of measuring equivalence, but also on the question of whether the principle is valid or needs to be adapted (Bundesinstitut für Bau- Stadt- und Raumforschung BBSR im Bundesamt für Bauwesen und Raumordnung BBR 2020; Milbert 2019; Ragnitz and Thum 2019; Steinführer and Küller 2020; Winkler-Kühlken 2019).

In 2018, this discourse was the trigger for the establishment of a commission to deal with the topic of "Equal living conditions" in the regions. Various ministries, the federal states, and the central municipal associations were represented in the commission. On the basis of a common understanding of equivalent living conditions, the commission has developed recommendations for action with a view to different regional developments and demographic changes in Germany. The recommendations are very comprehensive and broad, but safeguarding mobility in rural

---

[1] https://www.breitband-monitor.de/infrastrukturatlas.

[2] https://www.bmvi.de/DE/Themen/Digitales/Breitbandausbau/Breitbandatlas-Karte/start.html.

[3] https://www.landatlas.de.

[4] Atlas of Services of general interest. https://www.ideen-fuer-das-land.de/urbanruralsolutions.php.

areas is of central importance (Bundesministerium des Innern für Bau und Heimat, Bundesministerium für Ernährung und Landwirtschaft, & Bundesministerium für Familie Senioren Frauen und Jugend 2019). The Federal Government has taken up the recommendations and has summarized its plans in a package of measures. Rural structurally weak regions will be able to fall back on more than 20 funding programs (Bundesregierung 2020a).

The Federal Government particularly emphasizes the question of mobility and names two aspects that are of particular relevance for the following analyses:

- Mobility policy can no longer just be transport policy; adjustments in the settlement structure, securing local supplies but also the challenges of environmental and climate protection must also be taken into account.
- Every region is different and there is also no one size fits all option: the very specific conditions and problem areas also require locally adapted, flexible, and need-based solutions (Bundesregierung 2019).

3 Mobility Turnaround: The Status of the Discussion

Germany has also committed itself to ambitious climate policy goals within the framework of international agreements. Greenhouse gas emissions are to be reduced by at least 55% by 2030 compared to 1990 levels, and by 2050 the aim is to be largely climate neutral. Achieving these goals is a particular challenge, especially with regard to the transport sector, which is responsible for around a fifth of greenhouse gas emissions and where emissions have even increased in recent years. The Federal Government has planned a CO_2 reduction in the transport sector of 40 to 42% by 2030. Measures to reduce emissions from the transport sector are of eminent importance for the achievement of the climate goals (Expertenkommission zum Monitoring-Prozess "Energie der Zukunft" 2020; Haas and Sander 2020; Prognos et al. 2020).

However, open societies are associated with a high degree of mobility; if the ecological limits are to be adhered to at the same time, then both adjustments in the mobility pattern and new forms of transport will be necessary (Schneidewind 2018; Agora Verkehrswende 2017). In transport research, a distinction is made between three central levers.

Avoidance of Traffic   Reduction of the volume of traffic, for example, through the development of compact settlement structures or through the optimization of goods transport.

Relocation   All measures that aim to relocate traditional modes of transport based on fossil fuels to more ecologically compatible forms of transport (public transport, train, bicycle traffic, pedestrians, etc.).

Improve   Includes all measures aimed at either using less energy per person/ton-kilometer (increased efficiency, better utilization, etc.) or generating less CO_2 per unit of energy used and reducing other emissions (e.g., e-mobility, use of hydrogen, or synthetic fuels).

Images of the mobility of the future are summarized as:

Networked Vehicles will be connected to each other and to the Internet.

Electrified The electric motor will establish itself as a drive technology.

Shared Mobility is increasingly becoming a service that can also be used in shared and collective forms.

Automated In the long term, vehicles will be able to drive more and more independently.

The transport turnaround is a very complex process and requires changes at different levels and the interaction of numerous private, public, or semi-public actors. Adjustments are not only necessary at the technical level, but must be accompanied by a cultural change, behavioral changes among users, and appropriately adapted incentive systems (Bormann et al. 2018).

In the meantime, this process of transformation has begun in cities and urban areas. Here, the problem pressure from motorized traffic is high and is not only reflected in emissions, but also in noise pollution and high land consumption. New mobility concepts in urban areas also benefit from the existing scientific and technical know-how on site and from numerous research programs (Agora Verkehrswende 2020a,b,c; Canzler and Knie 2018, 2019; Koska et al. 2020; Ruhrort 2020; Umweltbundesamt 2020).

What does the situation look like in the rural regions? Here the low population density, financial problems of the municipalities, declining population numbers, and changing population structures pose new challenges. Both at the national level and at the level of the federal states and regions, there are countless programs and projects that deal with mobility solutions for rural regions, with a focus on digitization, different approaches to networking the transport systems, sharing concepts, and strengthening of cycling (Bitkom 2020; Hergert et al. 2020; InterLink Consulting 2020; Kabinettsausschuss Ländlicher Raum 2018). The core of many of the suggestions is also to supplement existing offers with voluntary or cooperative solutions. The projects and initiatives are often the results of research projects and receive financial and personnel support accordingly. The concepts are not always integrated into higher-level planning. In addition, there is often a particular challenge in stabilizing the offers after the end of the project.

The starting point for the considerations for securing mobility in the regions is the statement that private motor vehicles cannot be completely replaced in the future either.[5] Against this background, of course, e-mobility also plays a role, although this does not significantly change the mobility pattern (Starre 2019). Autonomous driving is also seen as offering special opportunities in rural regions (Fitte et al. 2019; Fleischer and Schippl 2018; Huber 2019; Klementschitz et al. 2019; Maurer et al. 2015; Meyer et al. 2016; Perret and Fischer 2019; Rosser and Ribi 2019; von

---

[5]The role that private cars play in the everyday life of residents is also shown in the results of surveys, according to which the respondents showed a high level of satisfaction with mobility (ADAC 2018).

Mörner and Boltze 2018). However, these technical solutions may be feasible on a large scale in the medium or long term.

The expansion of local public transport in rural regions is part of many regional development concepts and funding programs, but due to the specific framework conditions in these regions, local public transport will only be able to play a very limited role from an economic point of view (Verband Deutscher Verkehrsunternehmen 2020).

The question that remains is how the need for mobility can be reduced. Short-term effective solutions are seen primarily in the improvement of local supplies in rural areas in villages. Village shops operated by the residents are classic examples here, but also new delivery systems for food (Kokorsch and Küpper 2019). In the long term, coordinated spatial planning, especially in regional planning or municipal land-use planning, will also influence the location of facilities of general interest and thus their accessibility. The well-known restrictions of municipal and regional planning then apply here.

With a view to the potential for decentralization, great expectations are associated with teleworking, which has recently received a new boost in connection with the Corona pandemic. Numerous studies that deal with the post-Corona phase assume that there will be no return to normalcy and that new work and business models will also exist in the long term (Klös 2020; Sneader and Singhal 2020a,b). There is particular potential here, especially for rural areas, (Bertelsmann Stiftung 2020; Bundesministerium für Bildung und Forschung BMBF 2020; Grunau et al. 2020; Möbert and Schattenberg 2020). However, primarily rural areas in the vicinity of larger cities and less peripheral regions will benefit. In principle, however, the potential can only be realized if long-term regional and local strategies form the basis (Bundesministerium für Bildung und Forschung BMBF 2020; Fischedick and Schneidewind 2020). With the expansion of teleworking, there is also hope for a reduction in the volume of traffic and thus also in environmental pollution. However, previous studies that have dealt more systematically with these questions do not come up with clear results (Belzunegui-Eraso and Erro-Garcés 2020; Hook et al. 2020).

This cursory overview of the planning and approaches to guarantee sufficient mobility in rural regions also highlights the need for solutions that are more closely adapted to local conditions. Just as there is no such thing as "rural areas," the mobility models will also be as diverse and differentiated.

4   Local Adapted Mobility Solutions: Working in a Real-World Laboratory

The challenges in developing and implementing a locally adapted mobility concept should be shown using the example of a rural region that is particularly affected by demographic change.

4.1 The Project "wat nu"

Demographic change is changing the image of many cities, municipalities, and regions. Rural communities in particular are faced with a variety of challenges. In response to this, the Federal Ministry of Education and Research (BMBF) launched a funding measure called "Kommunen Innovativ," which supports associations of municipalities, science, and civil society in looking for solutions to these challenges and using experimental spaces in dealing with demographic change (Bundesregierung 2020b).

One of the funded projects is the joint project "Demographic Change in the Wadden Sea Area. Real laboratories and governance approaches as the nucleus for sustainable strategies and measures in tourism communities (wat nu)" in which two islands and two mainland communities in the North Sea Region are supported in developing new ways of dealing with the consequences of demographic change. The focus of the conceptual work was on the municipality of Wangerland. The community is in a spatially very exposed location and is part of the National Park, the Biosphere Reserve, and the UNESCO World Natural Heritage "Lower Saxony Wadden Sea." On the one hand, natural capital creates the basis for positive regional development; on the other hand, it also creates restrictions for future development strategies.

With approx. 176 km^2 the community counts as one of the largest municipalities in Lower Saxony, and the number of inhabitants is slightly more than 9100. The number of inhabitants has decreased in recent years, and the forecasts also indicate a further decline in population. Comparable to the general trend, the population structure is changing; the number of older residents is increasing.

The main characteristics of the municipality are the very low population density and, above all, the dispersed settlement structure with a total of 16 small villages. Over 50% of the population lives outside of these villages. The uneven distribution is exacerbated by the fact that the population is largely concentrated in the immediate coastal area, while the main town with the municipal administration is in the hinterland.

The particular challenge for the municipality arises from its function as one of the most important vacation spots on the German North Sea coast (Vorwig 2020). In 2019, the community recorded over 2.1 million overnight stays and over 330,000 tourists. For the municipality, tourism is, therefore, the most important economic sector that generates income and employment. This also means that the municipality has to maintain and finance a municipal infrastructure and public services of general interest that are dimensioned in such a way that it can meet demand during the main holiday periods. As a small municipality, it therefore has to maintain the infrastructure of a large city.

Retirement migrations and a growing number of second home owners increase the demands on the infrastructure in the long term. The increase in the number of apartment owners, who are often only there for a certain period of the year, also contributes to the change of the social structures in the community.

In its planning and investment measures, the municipality also has to take its tight financial situation into account. The coastal region and the municipalities have recognized these special challenges in recent years, have launched numerous initiatives and projects and organized themselves in different ways in formal and informal networks, and this way have broken new ground. However, these activities are not always sufficiently coordinated and sustainable: different spatial reference levels, planning periods, and technical responsibilities and objectives make cooperation more difficult.

In addition, there is the coexistence of numerous research projects and funding programs that address comparable issues in rural areas. Against this background, the starting point of the joint project "wat nu" is the question how the resulting and scattered system and transformation knowledge can be used to develop and test appropriate options for action and measures in dealing with the consequences of demographic change using new techniques and forms of cooperation. The project draws on the methodical approach of real-life laboratories, in which different stakeholders from the economic, scientific, and political–civil society sectors work together with citizens in order to develop joint solutions to real problems in a specific spatial context.

4.2   Real-World Laboratories: Concepts and Features

The concept of real-world laboratories is booming; it is currently playing an important role in the implementation of the great transformation (e.g., energy transition). But it is not always sufficiently clear what is actually hidden behind it. In general, real-world laboratories refer to specific spatial units in which cooperation between science (universities and organizations for applied research and development services), practice (e.g., politics, administration, public and private companies), and civil society (citizens, initiatives, NGOs) occurs. For example, in a region, a city, a quarter, or even in a neighborhood, an experimental environment is created in which the actors design and initiate real change and adaptation processes. The aim of real-world laboratories is to offer unconventional solutions that serve social welfare a real space to try out. The cooperation between science, practice, and civil society should at the same time ensure that the solutions are not developed detached from people's everyday lives and that they diffuse into everyday life as quickly as possible. It will then not only be about organizational, technical or regulatory solutions, but also, for example, about the initiation of new behaviors or the breaking of habitual patterns. When describing real-world laboratories, a comparison is often made with a classic laboratory: While experiments are carried out there under defined and controlled framework conditions, in a real-world laboratory they are embedded in social contexts and are guided by these to a certain extent. Real-world laboratories cannot, therefore, be equated with experiments or projects that are strictly defined in terms of time and content. The work in a real laboratory can develop in very different, unpredictable directions and take a lot of time. Classic research projects, which run for around 3 years, clearly fall short in these social contexts. In the meantime, there is an almost unmanageable number of publications that deal with the different facets of real-world laboratories and name the essential framework and conditions for success (Hahne and Kegler 2016; Klötzke et al. 2018; Kronsell and Mukhtar-Landgren 2018; Meurer et al. 2015; Parodi et al. 2016; Reiter et al. 2016; Roggema and Scheele 2014; Schneidewind 2014; Schneidewind and Scheck 2013; Schneidewind and Singer-Brodowski 2015; Wagner 2017) . The central features can be summarized as follows.

Real Social Challenges   The starting point for work in a real laboratory is very specific problems, usually in a very specific spatial context.

Active User Involvement   The users of a product or service are actively involved and encouraged to influence the innovation process.

Co-creation   Users develop and design together in a real laboratory.

Multi-stakeholder Approach   All relevant stakeholders are involved; in addition to potential users, these can also be technology and service providers, government institutions, companies, NGOs, etc.

Exploration   New trends, changed user behavior, and new market opportunities are continuously recorded and incorporated into the process.

Experimenting in a Real-life Setting   Users experience products and services in real situations, i.e., also uncertainties and failures are central elements of a real laboratory process.

Methods and Evaluation   Different methods and concepts are used.

4.3   Implementation of the Real-World Laboratory Approach in the Study Community

An important goal of the project was to activate the community's endogenous potential, i.e., the know-how, resources, and interests of the citizens of the community, politics, and administration and other stakeholders. At the same time, however, exogenous potential should also be exploited, i.e., the experience and willingness to cooperate, for example, the tourists who often visit the community regularly and have a special interest in the sustainable development of the region. The measures and methods implemented as part of the project can be roughly assigned to three components:

- contextualization and problem identification,
- development and implementation of experiments, and
- consolidation and evaluation of the project.

4.3.1 Identify Problems

The work in a real-world laboratory begins with a joint analysis of the initial conditions and the creation of a common understanding of the problem. In the wat nu project, various formats were used in this step, each of which involved very different groups of actors:

- coordination meetings and future talks with politics and administration;
- kick-off event in a demography cafe;
- citizens' workshop with residents of the community and second home owners;
- short films and interviews;
- activation of tourists via mental maps;
- photo competition;
- student study projects;
- master theses and bachelor theses.

This process was continuously supported and documented by the scientific project partners. From the point of view of the actors involved, the central challenge of the future turned out to be the long-term security of mobility. The complex interrelationships and also the realization that the mobility issue must be seen in a close connection with the future of local supply and can only be solved together were clearly worked out jointly. Together with the actors from politics and administrations and the citizens, it was therefore decided to initially work on the issue of mobility as a priority.

4.3.2 Develop and Implement Experiments

In this module, together with the actors, solutions for the specific problems mentioned are developed and implemented, in the case of the municipality of Wangerland, that is, the question of how the mobility offers can be improved. Again, very different formats were used here:

- Citizens workshops on the connection between mobility and local supply and on the instrument of citizens' buses. A total of six community workshops were held in which over 140 people took part and work together in small groups.
- Information events with external speakers on car sharing concepts in rural regions.
- Student projects and supervision of master theses and bachelor theses.
- Household survey on the citizens' bus: There was a lack of reliable information bases for the development of the mobility strategy in the municipality of Wangerland. A comprehensive household survey on the subject of citizens' buses was, therefore, carried out jointly. The questions asked included the mobility habits, the potential routes, the willingness to pay, and also the willingness of the citizens to get involved in such a project. The results of the survey were documented, graphically processed, and put up for discussion in community workshops. A relatively high participation of over 450 citizens indicates the high level of interest in the issue.

4.3.3 Consolidation

The central feature of a real-world laboratory is the concrete testing and implementation of the developed concepts. The community workshops gave rise to an interest in promoting the topic of mobility and local supply. With the support of the project team, a "Mobility Association Wangerland" was founded. As a first project, the association has planned the establishment of a citizens' bus. The association organizes a get-to-know tour with the citizens' bus of a neighboring association. In the meantime, the plans for the implementation of the idea have made further progress, especially thanks to the corresponding support from the municipality. Important legal framework conditions have been clarified as well as the financing of a bus and its integration into the local transport plan. The project had the opportunity to bring the results of the household survey into the discussion about updating the local transport plan for the district of Friesland.

The establishment of the mobility association creates the framework for the development of further problem solutions. More concrete ideas for the problem of securing local supplies were developed, and initial considerations for the development of a crowd-funding platform to support local initiatives and micro-projects were developed.

The project was able to establish itself as a problem solver in the region. There is an interest in continuing the initiated initiatives, even if the scientific support is no longer available after the end of the project. With the Wadden Sea Forum, an organization could be found that has agreed to offer a certain institutional framework for these future processes.

5 Conclusions and Recommendations

In order to ensure sufficient and sustainable mobility in rural regions, it is increasingly necessary to rely on locally and regionally adapted strategies and solutions. The "wat nu" project has shown that it is possible to bring users and other relevant actors into a co-creative process and use their knowledge, experience, and commitment and to initiate social innovations (Christmann and Federwisch 2019). The experience from the project allows some conclusions and recommendations that are not only, but above all, important for the mobility sector.

5.1 Activation of the Actors

- A mix of formats and methods is required to activate the actors; they are to be determined according to functional criteria and designed appropriately (e.g., outreach participation).
- Allow sufficient time to activate the actors. The activation effort differs according to the actors.

- Participation processes are expedient and successful if they help actors to bridge old habits and leave their "comfort zones."
- The number of participants is not always decisive for the success of participation processes. It is not necessary to win over all or as many participants as possible for a particular format.
- Participants must always have the option of entering or exiting a format or entering it again after a certain period of time. This flexibility increases the actors' willingness to participate and often also suits their personal circumstances.
- The activation of pulse generators is of crucial importance. These can be individual, highly motivated citizens, or representatives of cooperative organizations or voluntary initiatives.
- In all participation processes, the limits of voluntary work and, above all, the time-limited resources of interested citizens must be given greater consideration.
- The wishes and sensitivities of the actors must be addressed more explicitly.
- A particular challenge is to clearly highlight the scope and limits of participation. In this way, it must also be clearly communicated that not every solution developed can be implemented by the municipality.

5.2   Communication and Open Questions

- It turned out to be particularly important to address the actors in a target-group-specific manner. A mix of methods is essential for communication.
- When activating for citizens, care must be taken to "translate" the terms that have arisen in the scientific context into everyday language.
- The project homepage is not sufficient for communication. Citizens are often not aware of its existence, and not every citizen has sufficient knowledge of dealing with digital media. Press work and the early and active involvement of the local media in particular have proven to be an important information tool.
- Support from local politics is an important factor for the success of a project in which it creates legitimacy and which promotes acceptance. At the same time, however, one has to counteract the dangers that local politics will take over the process politically and that the participation procedures will follow a certain political agenda.

In the course of the project a number of unanswered questions arose, which were addressed in the various formats, but for which no final solutions have (yet) been found: Where are the limits of volunteering in the area of tension between compulsory municipal tasks and entrepreneurial solutions? How can the appreciation of voluntary work be improved and which innovative financing models are conceivable in this context? Is it necessary to (re)establish an entrepreneurial culture in rural areas as a counterpart to voluntary solutions? Do we need start-up and innovation centers in and for rural areas and strengthen the identification of young scientists with the region?

5.3   The Changed Understanding of Roles within the Real-World Laboratory

The various process levels result in different roles for actors in a real laboratory, in which they play actively, consciously, and unconsciously. The construction of the real-world laboratory can also change the classic understanding of the roles of individual groups of actors.

This applies above all to the self-image with which science works in this context. In real-world laboratories, scientists are no longer just "objective" and "reflective" observers, but rather they become designers and participants in the process. This begins with the active provision of information and analyses, extends beyond the moderation, organization, and conception of working meetings and workshops, and can also include the initiation and implementation of specific measures. This changed basic understanding and the new form of relationships with actors outside the scientific scene make it possible to work between science and practice on an equal footing. Success depends very much on the ability and willingness of science to design attractive and meaningful co-creation spaces and to get involved in the process.

But new role models are also emerging on the practical side. Here, too, there must be a corresponding basic willingness to get involved in such processes. It will no longer be sufficient if the municipal and regional partners merely submit an expression of interest and then wait for the next steps. Rather, municipalities and regions must offer specific spaces, both for the implementation of interventions and at the process level. This includes, for example, the provision and making available of rooms for regular cooperation, the provision of intervention areas and necessary infrastructures, the participation of committed and interested staff, and, above all, the openness to the results.

The role of civil society will also change. While in the past civil society was often more or less confronted with facts and had to deal with the solutions proposed by developers and planners and developed on the drawing board, it now has the opportunity to actively intervene in the process within the framework of real-world laboratories. Participants from civil society can help scientists, planners, and designers to sharpen their understanding of the problem, to get new perspectives or to understand why certain habits manifest themselves. The goal is then to develop better solutions or to show ways in which new contributions can be made if one is prepared to leave the habitual patterns of thought and action. Based on citizen science concepts, civil society can also take on the role of supporting field researcher through certain formats and methods and thus also contribute to the generation of knowledge.

Acknowledgments Thanks to the Carl von Ossietzky University as the lead partner and to the "Gemeinde Wangerland" for supporting the project.

This work is part of the project "Demographic change in the Wadden Sea region. Real-world laboratories and governance approaches as germ cells for sustainable action strategies and measures in tourism communities (wat nu)." Further information are available on the following website http://www.wat-nu-im-watt.de. The project is funded by the German Federal Ministry of Education and Research (grant number 033L178B).

References

ADAC. (2018). *ADAC Monitor "Mobil auf dem Land". Gesamtbericht.* München.

Agora Verkehrswende. (2017). *Mit der Verkehrswende die Mobilität von morgen sichern. 12 Thesen zur Verkehrswende.* Berlin

Agora Verkehrswende. (2020a). *Ein anderer Stadtverkehr ist möglich. Neue Chancen für eine krisenfeste und klimagerechte Mobilität.* Berlin.

Agora Verkehrswende. (2020b). *Städte in Bewegung. Zahlen, Daten, Fakten zur Mobilität in 35 deutschen Städten.* Berlin.

Agora Verkehrswende. (2020c). *Technologieneutralität im Kontext der Verkehrswende. Kritische Beleuchtung eines Postulats.* Berlin.

Belzunegui-Eraso, A., & Erro-Garcés, A. (2020). Teleworking in the context of the Covid-19 crisis. *Sustainability, 12*(9), 3662.

Bertelsmann Stiftung (Hrsg.). (2020). *Coworking im ländlichen Raum. Menschen, Modelle, Trends.* Gütersloh.

Bitkom. (2020). *Klimaschutz durch digitale Technologien – Chancen und Risiken. Kurzstudie.* Berlin.

Bormann, R., Fink, P., Holzapfel, H., Rammler, S., Sauter-Servaes, T., Tiemann, H., et al. (2018). Die Zukunft der deutschen Automobilindustrie – Transformation by Disaster oder by Design?. Friederich Ebert Stiftung (Ed.), *WISO Diskurs* 03. Bonn.

Bundesinstitut für Bau- Stadt- und Raumforschung (BBSR) im Bundesamt für Bauwesen und Raumordnung (BBR) (Hrsg.). (2020). Regionale Lebensverhältnisse – Ein Messkonzept zur Bewertung ungleicher Lebensverhältnisse in den Teilräumen Deutschlands *BBSR-Online-Publikation* 06. Bonn.

Bundesministerium des Innern für Bau und Heimat, Bundesministerium für Ernährung und Landwirtschaft, & Bundesministerium für Familie Senioren Frauen und Jugend. (2019). *Unser Plan für Deutschland. – Gleichwertige Lebensverhältnisse üerall - Schlussfolgerungen zur Arbeit der Kommission "Gleichwertige Lebensverhältnisse".* Berlin.

Bundesministerium für Bildung und Forschung (BMBF). (2020). *Für eine suffiziente und resiliente Entwicklung von Städten und Regionen. Memorandum Post-Corona-Stadt.* Berlin.

Bundesministerium für Verkehr und digitale Infrastruktur (BMVI). (2019a). *Aktuelle Breitbandverfügbarkeit in Deutschland (Stand Ende 2019).* Berlin.

Bundesministerium für Verkehr und digitale Infrastruktur (BMVI). (2019b). *Bericht zum Breitbandatlas Teil 1: Ergebnisse. (Stand Ende 2019).* Berlin.

Bundesministerium für Wirtschaft und Energie (BMWi). (2020). *Verfügbarkeit von Infrastruktureinrichtungen in Deutschland – Infrastrukturatlas zu Fahrzeiten und lokalen Knappheiten.* Berlin.

Bundesregierung. (2019). *Maßnahmen der Bundesregierung zur Umsetzung der Ergebnisse der Kommission "Gleichwertige Lebensverhältnisse".* Berlin.

Bundesregierung. (2020a). *Das gesamtdeutsche Fördersystem für strukturschwache Regionen.* Berlin.

Bundesregierung. (2020b). *Dritter Bericht der Bundesregierung zur Entwicklung der ländlichen Räume. Unterrichtung durch die Bundesregierung.* Berlin.

Buthe, B., Pütz, T., & Staats, J. (2018). Verkehrsbild Deutschland: Raumordnerische Beurteilung von Verkehrsinfrastrukturprojekten. In Bundesinstituts für Bau-Stadt- und Raumforschung (Ed.), *BBSR-Analysen kompakt* 04. Bonn-Bad Godesberg.

Canzler, W., & Knie, A. (2018). Die Zukunft urbaner Mobilität: Ansätze für eine ökologische Verkehrswende im digitalen Zeitalter. Heinrich-Böll-Stiftung (Ed.), *böll.brief – Grüne Ordnungspolitik* No 6. Berlin.

Canzler, W., & Knie, A. (2019). *Autodämmerung. Experimentierräume für die Verkehrswende. Strategiepapier.* Berlin: Heinrich-Böll-Stiftung.

Christmann, G., & Federwisch, T. (2019). Soziale Innovationen in Landgemeinden – wie sie entstehen und was sie begünstigt. In Akademie für Raumforschung und Landesplanung (Ed.), *Nachrichten der ARL: Ländliche Räume* pp. 26–38. Hannover.

Dauth, W., & Haller, P. (2018). Klarer Trend zu längeren Pendeldistanzen. Berufliches Pendeln zwischen Wohn- und Arbeitsort *IAB Kurzbericht* 10. Nürnberg.

Expertenkommission zum Monitoring-Prozess "Energie der Zukunft". (2020). *Klimaschutz vorantreiben, Wohlstand stärken – Kommentierung zentraler Handlungsfelder der deutschen Energiewende im europäischen Kontext.* Berlin, Münster, Nürnberg, Stuttgart.

Fischedick, M., & Schneidewind, U. (2020). *Folgen der Corona-Krise und Klimaschutz – Langfristige Zukunftsgestaltung im Blick behalten.* Wuppertal Institut für Klima Umwelt Energie gGmbH. Wuppertal.

Fitte, C., Berkemeier, L., Teuteberg, F., & Thomas, O. (2019). Elektromobilität in ländlichen Regionen. In J. Marx Gómez, A. Solsbach, T. Klenke, & V. Wohlgemuth, (Eds.), *Smart Cities/Smart Regions – Technische, wirtschaftliche und gesellschaftliche Innovationen. Konferenzband zu den 10. BUIS-Tagen* (pp. 37–52). Wiesbaden.

Fleischer, T., & Schippl, J. (2018). Automatisiertes Fahren. Fluch oder Segen für nachhaltige Mobilität? *TATuP – Zeitschrift für Technikfolgenabschätzung in Theorie und Praxis, 27*(2), 11–15.

Grunau, P., Steffes, S., & Wolter, S. (2020). Homeoffice in Zeiten von Corona: In vielen Berufen gibt es bislang ungenutzte Potenziale. *IAB Forum*. Nürnberg.

Haas, T., & Sander, H. (2020). Decarbonizing transport in the European Union: Emission performance standards and the perspectives for a European Green Deal. *Sustainability, 12*(20), 8381.

Hahne, U., & Kegler, H. (2016). *Stadt und Region – Reallabore der resilienzorientierten Transformation.* Frankfurt/M.

Hergert, M., Neumeier, S., & Osigus, T. (Eds.). (2020). *Mobilität – Erreichbarkeit – Ländliche Räume und die Frage nach der Gleichwertigkeit der Lebensverhältnisse.* Wissenschaftliche Konferenz 17.–18. März 2020. Braunschweig.

Hesse, M., Starke, T., Jänchen, I., & Glinka, P. (2019). Prosperierende Städte, abgehängte Regionen? *Wirtschaftsdienst, 99*(10), 703–710.

Hook, A., Court, V., Sovacool, B. K., & Sorrell, S. (2020). A systematic review of the energy and climate impacts of teleworking. *Environmental Research Letters, 15*, 093003.

Huber, T. (2019). *Mobilität im ländlichen Raum. Entwicklungschancen für E. Mobilität, autonome Busse und on demand mobility.* DB Regio Bus Bayern. Ingolstadt.

Hünnemeyer, V., & Kempermann, H. (2020). Ländliche Regionen in Deutschland – Ergebnisse des IW-Regionalrankings 2020. *IW-Trends* 2. Köln: Institut der deutschen Wirtschaft.

Innovationsgruppe UrbanRural SOLUTIONS. (2019). *Der Daseinsvorsorgeatlas Niedersachsen. Kurzinformation zum digitalen Planungstool.* Hamburg.

InterLink Consulting. (2020). *Potenzialstudie zu ländlicher Mobilität.* Studie im Auftrag der Fraktion Bündnis 90/DIE GRÜNEN im Bundestag. Berlin.

Kabinettsausschuss Ländlicher Raum. (2018). *Mobilitätsprojekte der Landesregierung Baden-Württemberg erfasst im Rahmen der Interministeriellen Arbeitsgruppe "Mobilität im Ländlichen Raum".* Stuttgart.

Klementschitz, R., Angerer, M., Bauernfeind, A., Haider, T., & Haydn, P. (2019). Potenziale für den Einsatz gemeinschaftlich genutzter autonomer Fahrzeuge im ländlichen Raum. *REAL CORP 2019 Proceedings/Tagungsband* (pp. 553–562). Karlsruhe.

Klös, H.-P. (2020). *Nach dem Corona-Schock: Digitalisierungspotenziale für Deutschland* IW-Policy Paper No 14. Köln: Institut der deutschen Wirtschaft.

Klötzke, M., Brost, M., Fraedrich, E., -M., Gebhardt, L., Karnahl, K., Kopp, G., et al. (2018). Reallabor Schorndorf. Bürgernahe Entwicklung eines haltestellenlosen Quartiersbussystems. In H. Proff, & T. M. Fojcik, (Eds.), *Mobilität und digitale Transformation* (pp. 295–309). Wiesbaden.

Kokorsch, M., & Küpper, P. (2019). Trends der Nahversorgung in ländlichen Räumen. *Thünen Working Paper* 126, Braunschweig.

Koska, T., Jansen, U., Reuttler, O., Schäfer-Sparenberg, C., Spitzner, M., & Ulrich, A. (2020). Praxis kommunale Verkehrswende. Ein Leitfaden. Band 47 der *Schriftenreihe Ökologie*. Berlin: Heinrich Böll Stiftung.

Kronsell, A., & Mukhtar-Landgren, D. (2018). Experimental governance: the role of municipalities in urban living labs. *European Planning Studies, 26*(5), 988–1007.

Küpper, P. (2016). Abgrenzung und Typisierung ländlicher Räume. Thünen-Institut für Ländliche Räume. *Thünen Working Paper* 68. Braunschweig.

Maurer, M., Gerdes, H. C., Lenz, B., & Winner, H. (Eds.). (2015). *Autonomes Fahren. Technische, rechtliche und gesellschaftliche Aspekte*. Berlin/Heidelberg.

Meurer, J., Erdmann, L., von Geibler, J., & Echternacht, L. (2015). *Arbeitsdefinition und Kategorisierung von Living Labs. Arbeitspapier im Arbeitspaket 1 des INNOLAB Projekts*. Universität Siegen Wirtschaftsinformatik und Neue Medien. Siegen.

Meyer, J., Becker, H., Bösch, P. M., & Axhauen, K. W. (2016). *Autonomous Vehicles: The next Jump in Accessibilities?*. Zürich: ETH Zurich – Institute for Transport Planning and Systems.

Milbert, A. (2019). Wie misst man "Gleichwertige Lebensverhältnisse"? *Aus Politik und Zeitgeschichte, 46*, 20–29.

Möbert, J., & Schattenberg, M. (2020). Arbeitswelt der Zukunft. Ist das Homeoffice wirklich das Ei des Kolumbus? *Deutschland-Monitor*. Frankfurt/M: Deutsche Bank Research.

Oberst, C., & Voigtländer, M. (2020). Aufsteigerregionen in Deutschland: Go east. Eine empirische Analyse der Entwicklung deutscher Kreise. *IW Report* 20. Köln: Institut der deutschen Wirtschaft.

Parodi, O., Albiez, M., Beecroft, R., & Meyer S. (2016). Das Konzept "Reallabor" schärfen: Ein Zwischenruf des Reallabor 131: KIT findet Stadt. *GAIA – Ecological Perspectives for Science and Society, 25*(4), 284–285.

Perret, F., & Fischer, R. (2019). Denkbare Anwendungen und Effekte des automatisierten Fahrens. Herausforderungen und Handlungsoptionen für Städte und Agglomerationen. *Strasse und Verkehr* (1–2) (pp. 18–29).

Prognos, Öko-Institut, & Wuppertal-Institut. (2020). *Klimaneutrales Deutschland. Zusammenfassung im Auftrag von Agora Energiewende, Agora Verkehrswende und Stiftung Klimaneutralität*. Berlin

Prognos AG. (2019). *Prognos Zukunftsatlas 2019. Das Ranking für Deutschlands Regionen*. Berlin.

Ragnitz, J., & Thum, M. (2019). Gleichwertig, nicht gleich. Zur Debatte um die "Gleichwertigkeit der Lebensverhältnisse". *Aus Politik und Zeitgeschichte* 46 (pp. 3–10).

Reiter, D., Parodi, O., & Seebacher, A. (2016). *Gemeinsam Nachhaltigkeit gestalten: Quartier Zukunft*. Labor Stadt Reallabor 131 – KIT findet Stadt. Institut für Technikfolgenabschätzung und Systemanalyse (ITAS). Karlsruhe.

Roggema, R., & Scheele, U. (2014). *Klimaanpassung im Reallabor: Integrative Raumstrategien*. Winschoten: Präsentation.

Rosser, S., & Ribi, F. (2019). *Elektromobilität: Planungsgrundlagen für Marktaktivitäten und Verteilnetz*.

Ruhrort, L. (2020). Reassessing the role of shared mobility services in a transport transition: can they contribute the rise of an alternative socio-technical regime of mobility? *Sustainability, 12*(19), 8253.

Schneidewind, U. (2014). *Urbane Reallabore – ein Blick in die aktuelle Forschungswerkstatt*. pnd online.

Schneidewind, U. (2018). *Die große Transformation. Eine Einführung in die Kunst gesellschaftlichen Wandels*. Frankfurt am Main.

Schneidewind, U., & Scheck, H. (2013). Die Stadt als "Reallabor" für Systeminnovationen. in Rückert-John, J., (Ed.), *Soziale Innovation und Nachhaltigkeit: Perspektiven sozialen Wandels* (pp. 229–248). Wiesbaden.

Schneidewind, U., & Singer-Brodowski, M. (2015). Vom experimentellen Lernen zum transformativen Experimentiere. Reallabore als Katalysator für eine lernende Gesellschaft auf dem

Weg zu einer Nachhaltigen Entwicklung. *Zeitschrift für Wirtschafts- und Unternehmensethik* 16/1(2015) (pp. 10–23).

Sneader, K., & Singhal, S. (2020a). *From thinking about the next normal to making it work: What to stop, start, and accelerate. As businesses step into the post-Coronavirus future, they need to find a balance between what worked before and what needs to happen to succeed in the next normal.* McKinsey & Company.

Sneader, K., & Singhal, S. (2020b). *The future is not what it used to be: Thoughts on the shape of the next normal.* McKinsey & Company.

Starre, S.-J. (2019). Elektromobilität für den ländlichen Raum? Ja. bitte. Erneuerbare Energien, Retrieved December 7, 2020 from https://www.erneuerbareenergien.de/elektromobilitaet-fuer-den-laendlichen-raum-ja-bitte

Steinführer, A., & Küller, P. (2020). Daseinsvorsorge in ländlichen Räumen. *Informationen zur politischen Bildung* No. 43 (pp. 16–25).

Umweltbundesamt. (2020). *Verkehrswende für ALLE. So erreichen wir eine sozial gerechteund umweltverträglichere Mobilität Position.* Dessau-Roßlau.

Verband Deutscher Verkehrsunternehmen e. V. (2020). *Gute Mobilität in ländlichen Räumen – Gemeinwohlorientierung und Lebensqualität vor Ort.*

von Mörner, M., & Boltze, M. (2018). Sammelverkehr mit autonomen Fahrzeugen im ländlichen Raum. Zur Zukunft des ÖPNV in dünn besiedelten Gebieten. *Der Nahverkehr*(11) (pp. 6–12).

Vorwig, W. (2020). Tourismusintensität in Niedersachsen. *Statistische Monatshefte Niedersachsen* No. 8 (pp. 376–382).

Wagner, F. (2017). Reallabore als kreative Arenen der Transformation zu einer Kultur der Nachhaltigkeit. In J.-L. Reinermann, & F. Behr (Eds.), *Die Experimentalstadt. Kreativität und die kulturelle Dimension der Nachhaltigen Entwicklung* (pp. 79–94). Wiesbaden.

Weiss, C. (2020). Stand der Mobilitätswende in ländlichen Regionen. Retrieved December 7, 2020 from https://www.zukunft-mobilitaet.net/171427/analyse/laendliche-regionen-mobilitaetswende-zukunft-der-mobilitaet-auf-dem-land/

Winkler-Kühlken, B. (2019). Standards in der Raumordnung auf dem Prüfstand? *Aus Politik und Zeitgeschichte* 46 (pp. 11–19).

Wolff, M., Haase, A., & Leibert, T. (2020). Mehr als Schrumpfung und Wachstum? Trends der demographischen Raumentwicklung in Deutschland nach 2011. *UFZ Discussion Papers.* Leipzig

Part II
Social Reasoning and Models

The Social Practice of Community Mobility in Rural Areas

Ute Samland

Abstract Social participation and the flexible accessibility of goods and services for daily needs, the workplace, school, or leisure facilities are essential reasons to use a car in rural areas. By means of the theoretical approach of social practices, routine mobility behavior in everyday life is investigated with special emphasis on community mobility. The result is that community mobility in the form of carpooling takes place in a variety of ways, both within the family context, e.g. as accompanying mobility, and among friends and colleagues. At the same time, there are regular journeys, especially to and from work, which are made singularly by car because it is used as a space for retreat or contemplation. The car—whether it is used only by one person or collectively—is utilized to deal with tight schedules on a daily basis and to implement efficient travel routes. The aim is to make the best possible use of rigid daily structures and flexibility depending on the day's events. The taking along of strangers is particularly emotionally charged and perceived as a particular security risk. However, online portals for carpooling are seen as an option to minimize this insecurity.

Keywords Community mobility · Ridesharing · Daily mobility · Social practice · Ridesharing

1 Introduction

Driving in rural areas is a feature of quality of life. Compared to urban areas with good accessibility and a well-developed public transport system, automobiles play a vital role in providing food, realizing cultural and recreational activities, pursuing a job, and providing education and training in rural areas. Securing social participation is, for the most part, linked to the availability of an automobile and

U. Samland (✉)
Carl von Ossietzky University of Oldenburg, Oldenburg, Germany
e-mail: ute.samland@uni-oldenburg.de

© The Author(s), under exclusive license to Springer Nature Switzerland AG 2021　　　37
J. Marx Gómez et al. (eds.), *Progress in Sustainable Mobility Research*,
Progress in IS, https://doi.org/10.1007/978-3-030-70841-2_3

corresponding transport infrastructures (Kirchesch 2013; Neu 2009; Canzler and Knie 2005). Yet, this kind of everyday mobility is by no means natural, but rather a result of decades of transport policy based on the model of automobility. Now, with regard to the development of ecologically sustainable mobility options, the great dependency on the automobile becomes particularly clear. Because from an ecological point of view, car traffic still accounts for the largest share of CO_2 emissions. At the same time, the quality of life in rural areas needs to be maintained, so the creation of alternative mobility services through the formation of carpools as an option to complement existing public transport services in the development of regional development approaches is increasingly being considered (Beauftragter der Bundesregierung für die Neuen Länder 2011; NMELV 2012; BMVI 2018). However, it seems difficult to establish new forms of community mobility, because so far all possible projects have failed. In the context of sustainable regional development in times of demographic, social, and climate changes, the development of new forms of community mobility is increasingly seen as an option to complement public transport services and reduce overall traffic. This also is against the background that in the city well-functioning alternatives to the own car, such as car sharing in some very sparsely populated areas, do not provide meaningful application for economic actors. Therefore, citizens should take the increasingly important role to support the public service function of mobility. However, the focus on the application level reveals a lack of understanding or knowledge of community mobility and related individual and collective tendencies toward persistence and how behavioral changes can be achieved in the interplay between individual attitudes and structural framework conditions (cf. also Knie et al. 2016). So far, there is neither extensive knowledge about (community) mobility behavior nor possible political strategies of operationalization. The idea of alternative ways of being mobile is by no means new. Historically, ride-sharing, especially in the form of hitchhiking, is as old as the car itself (Schlebecker 1958, p. 305). Even in the rural area, hitchhiking has been widespread, especially in close ranges, which was justified among other things with already poorly developed public transport (Fiedler et al. 1989, p. 76). Ridesharing agencies not only as a safe and organized form of hitchhiking but also as the current revival of ride-sharing banks (Mitfahrbänke) are other forms of catching a ride.

This raises the question of what kinds of community mobility can be found in rural areas—especially against the background of their functionality as a basic service (Daseinsvorsorge). The aim is to work out the limits and potentials of community mobility from a sociological perspective by considering community mobility as a social practice. Community mobility should be understood as a broad concept here. Rather than limiting the focus on carpools, all forms of communal being-on-the-move in everyday life should be considered (Neoh et al. 2015; Sonnberger and Gallego Carrera 2012). As the automobile plays a key role in rural everyday mobility, however, it requires a certain amount of focus, although other forms of community mobility may be considered, too. Thus, in addition to the usual carpooling to work or picking up small children from or dropping them off at day care and other activities, a variety of community mobility that takes place in the wider family, in the neighborhood, or in the circle of friends must be considered.

2 Spatial Mobility from a Practice Theory Perspective

Before considering mobility from the perspective of practice theory, a distinction between mobility and traffic is necessary, since while traffic only accounts for the actually realized paths and routes, the concept of mobility focuses on the possibility of spatial movement (Canzler 2013, p. 922).

Including existing options for mobility (nature of the transport system, access to public transport, and possibilities for virtual mobility) sheds light on how they are used or not. By looking at social practices, these mechanisms, which routinely lead to covering distances as well as movement in space, can be considered (Manderscheid 2013, p. 55).

In this way, practice theory offers the possibility to go beyond the usual rational decision models of mobility studies (Sheller 2004; Dangschat and Segert 2011; Manderscheid 2012) and to elaborate theretofore missing motives (Canzler and Knie 2002; Canzler et al. 2016) that lie beneath decision structures. The works of Bourdieu, Giddens, Foucault, and Wittgenstein are regarded as central forerunners of the newer practice theory movement (Reckwitz 2003; Schatzki 2016; Schäfer 2016; Schmidt 2017). The concept of social practice is centralized as the "place of the social," anchored in the body and characterized by behavioral patterns manifested by collective and implicit knowledge (Reckwitz 2016). On the one hand, in the execution of the practice of competently appropriated patterns of action and movements of the body (Reckwitz 2004, p. 321), which refer to "implicit, sequentially used forms of knowledge and understanding, [...] without which the actors would not be capable of producing the corresponding uniformity of body movements" (Reckwitz 2004, p. 321). Thus, "the social world is composed of very concrete, identifiable, individual, interrelated practices" (Reckwitz 2003, p. 290). On the other hand, social practices are not only material in terms of their embodied execution, also essential to the realisation of social practice are material artifacts, such as technologies, media, and images, which are dealt with in practice (Schäfer 2019, p. 12). In this sense, not only the patterns of action of the actors are relevant for the consideration of the everyday mobility practice as well as the community mobility but also which things they use for it. Furthermore, mobility cannot be understood in isolation from other everyday practices, since spatial movement is a prerequisite for coping with everyday life (Manderscheid 2019, p. 165), which means that in addition to material execution and use of objects, other practices that incorporate mobility practices must also be considered. In the following sections, these elements are described, and some specific aspects in their context are highlighted. The main purpose of this is to explore the social practices of everyday mobility and community mobility within their social boundaries.

3 The Social Practice of Everyday Mobility with Regard to Community Mobility

These findings outlined in this section are based upon empirical data raised in project NEMo[1] (sustainable fulfillment of mobility needs in rural areas).

Mobility is firmly anchored in the daily lives of those interviewed. Depending on age and occupation, community mobility practices tend to be mobility within family structures, job mobility, and mobility with colleagues or during leisure time. Your own car is usually at the center of all these practices. According to the individualized automotive culture, the private car is a guarantee for flexibility and autonomy. This value is shared by all participants. For example, a teacher informs:

> Yes, well the loss of flexibility, my flexibility is paramount for me, since I'm the type of person that is very erratic, very spontaneous, one who spontaneously changes her mind and changes what was initially planned. (Anja, 590)

The quality of driving alone is taken as a justification for limiting mobility in community. Driving solo is also referred to as "luxury" (Patrick), where "you have no-one to answer to except yourself" (146). Also, in this context, the body of the car is referred to as an "enclosed space" (Angela, 260), in which one can act freely, listen to music, or keep the window open or closed. At the same time, there arises, for those outside, a certain unavailability regarding the person driving the car. The moment a person gets into a car, they become only partially accessible to the outside world. Johannes, who occupies a public office in a small town, understands the public space of the city as a place of communication and exchange and finds it "incomprehensible" (148) why the neighbors voluntarily withdraw from this space by using their car to cover the minutest distances, such as a visit to the bakery (148). By driving to the bakery by car, the people he recognizes as neighbors deny themselves their ability to enter public space as active communication partners.

4 Accompanying Mobility (Begleitmobilität)

The automobile continues to be seen as a boundary to public space in the planning and execution of community mobility. However, despite claims of flexibility and autonomy, community mobility takes place in certain contexts and events. Within the family, community mobility is mainly characterized by accompanying mobility, which is characterized by tight schedules, efficient pathways, and a combination of rigid daily structures and flexibility depending on the circumstances of the day,

---

[1]https://nemo-mobilitaet.de.

especially in families with small children. The kindergarten administrator Ruth describes her observations as follows:

> A lot of organization, there's just the organization around the family. Whether it's grandmother or grandfather picking up the children from the crèche, after-school care or something, or from school. Or there are acquaintances, friends, with whom the children play in the afternoons, that pick up the children (Ruth, 416)

Especially, mobility with small children is closely related to the use of specific items. Social practices point to the "interaction of skilled bodies, representational artefacts, natural things as well as socio-material and technical infrastructures" (Schmidt 2017, 338). Child car seats for children of different ages are permanently installed in the car. Taking other people with you is only possible under certain circumstances, according to the interviewed parents. So, Nadine says, "I have a big car [...] a Sharan, so actually enough space, but with two child seats, which are quite wide, I could perhaps fit a thin person in the middle, but no-one beyond that" (114). In addition to the child seats, strollers and groceries also require space in the car (Herget 2013, p. 134).

The use of strollers in public spaces is also discussed. Here, barriers play an important role, which tend to lead to a dominant use of the automobile. High entrances in buses and barriers in public spaces, such as curbs, stairs, and missing elevators, are addressed: "As far as barrier-free expansion is concerned, there is still a lot of catching up to do" (Natascha, 29). These examples show that families develop fixed mobility routines that are significantly shaped by discrete child-specific items and the structure of the material environment. In contrast to the few practical conditions and options that characterize public transport in the rural area under investigation here, the car has an established place in the household and family life. The use of the car manifests itself through both everyday repetitive routines and the associated activities as well as the material conditions that accompany them.

Routines also develop alongside repetitive leisure activities. This is how Pierre, father of two children, reports about his routine practice of carpooling:

> Regarding ourselves, definitely where the children are concerned. Especially when it comes to sports or something. Carpools are formed in principle, because at the moment we also live in such a way that we have many families in the new development area, where you pick up the children and drop them all off again in the evening after sports. (Pierre, 381)

This shows that organizational practices are closely related to spatial conditions. In this case, it is a self-contained residential area made up of single-family houses. Only an access road and a bike path lead to this settlement on the outskirts of the small town, which separates the area from the rest of the city. The spatial limitation and the fact that most of the residents are in a similar stage of life (family phase) leads to particularly strong networking among the residents. This relates not only to mobility requirements but also to other neighborly support practices, such as borrowing equipment. The practice of carpooling can be seen as an element of an entire network of support practices. The location of the residential area with the available options of being mobile means that the children are driven frequently.

However, it also shows that the practice of accompanying mobility changes with the age of the children. Anja, whose daughter soon goes to school and therefore has to go to the next largest city, reports:

> Of course we form a car pool and then drive to school together in the morning. (Anja, 375)

Children learn how to move independently, i.e. they learn about public transport and cycling practices and gain knowledge of spatial distances and the geographic environment. This acquired knowledge and the associated practices of the children lead to a change in the practice of carpooling within the family. On the one hand, this means that mobility is trained and practiced as a necessity at an early stage, and on the other hand, that it is treated as a possibility and, by the increasing demand for independence, valued as individual mobility, which in turn points to the social mobility that benefits from spatial mobility. The spatial expansion of independent everyday mobility also increases with age. This is particularly determined by the structuring of rural areas: while a primary school is still located close to a child's place of residence, the next larger city must be reached upon enrollment in the secondary school. This relocation and extension of routes mean that new, different mobility routines have to be designed, which in turn are influenced by the accessibility to alternative mobility options such as public transport (timetables, distance to the stop, accessibility).

5 Carpooling in the Context of Family, Friends, and Colleagues

As soon as the driver's license is acquired, which is currently happening in rural areas when the child reaches legal age, and a vehicle is available, carpools are formed. This happens in the circle of friends or within the family. Katharina, a student, reports:

> Last year I commuted from [city A] to [city B] to school and was lucky that my mother worked in the hospital which was right next to my school in [city B]. That means we could mostly drive one route together and then alternate the other one so that [...] she somehow took the car back. She was on shift duty. [...] Sometimes I went back by car. (Katharina, 47)

With the acquisition of a driver's license, the car available in the family is increasingly being integrated into the everyday life of the new driver as a mobility option: Katrin, the mother of an adult son, reports:

> Our son goes to school in [city D]. He drives with the said [name of the bus line] and is happy that they now drive every hour. Before that, it only drove every 2 h. [...] Sometimes it just doesn't fit at all in terms of time or [he] wants to go to [city D] for sports and then he takes a car. Or if it rains, routes that he previously cycled [...] or that he still wants to visit someone, then [he] asks if he can have the car. (Katrin, 122)

There are three aspects of note here: first, the so-called "cuckoo effect" (Canzler 2016, p. 345) can be observed, in the sense that previously established modes of transport, such as the use of bicycles or buses, are increasingly being replaced by the car, and, furthermore, destinations are being chosen that can only be easily reached by car. Second, mobility is organized around the availability of the car, which means that the number of car users increases, which increases efforts in organization and communication. Third, the increasing use of the car also shows that it is understood as a matter of course, since there is an unspoken understanding among adults to make the car available. In addition, the acquired mobility practice of driving is performed by the driving of friends. The inclusion of automotive practice not only opens up possibilities for the actor but also influences the mobility practices of the wider environment by offering automotive flexibility as part of friendship-based mobility services. In this context, a mother continues to report that the son occasionally "plays taxi" (Katrin, 142–144).

The delivery and collection services, dubbed "taxi" trips, are mentioned several times in the discussions. One acts "more or less as a taxi" (Leo, 110) in joint activities, for example, in which the consumption of alcohol is also involved. The driver who agrees to function as "taxi" not only has the task of picking up the passengers but also has to refrain from drinking alcohol. Another reason to "play taxi" is if the passengers have not yet reached maturity and/or if there is no car available. In these cases, too, "people are collected" during leisure events (Patrick, 131).

The practice of community mobility basically materializes along the automobile. Although other options, such as bicycles or buses, are used in parallel, the use of these options is mostly subordinate to the possibility of automobility. Within the circle of friends, larger detours are sometimes made in order to do a favor for the person who has been picked up. Monetary remuneration plays a role here, as in the example above, but it is also important that the value of friendship is paramount. Patrick reports that it is always important to him "that this is not so precise [. . .] but that it always happens on such a friendly basis that both benefit from it" (Patrick, 146).

Mutuality is valued in circles of friends. In the area of community mobility, it means that attention is paid to compensation, for example, by everyone "driving" or, if this option is not available, the best possible balance between travel expenses and a material equivalent. As indicated by Patrick, this can be generalized reciprocal, i.e. no direct compensation of performance is expected (Stegbauer 2011). In this context, Stegbauer states that "in the case of reciprocity, which has been generalized over a long period of time, individual gifts lose their importance; there is no exact offset" (Stegbauer 2011, p. 68). In return, it means that the more directly a reciprocal relationship is established, the less extensive it is embedded in the network of social friendship and family relationships. This is the case, for example, in professional commuting mobility: there is a great need for financial compensation, particularly among trainees. This is achieved either through multimodal and intermodal mobility in everyday life or by taking others with you. The willingness to take along is pronounced and helps to reduce financial burdens. So, there is "no problem taking people with you, not even in the morning or anything" (Marco, 424). Rather, the driver surveyed "actually doesn't really care" (Marco, 424), because the passenger regularly pays "so and so much money for it" (Marco, 424), and the meeting point "is exactly on the way" (Marco, 424). Important things and artifacts in trainee mobility are the availability of a driver's license and an automobile, but also fuel (Sprit) and money for fuel (Sprit Geld) when carrying out the practice. At the same time, the time frame for community mobility has been established with the actors having the same working hours. Since the passenger is located directly on the driver's route, no additional detour is necessary. However, the description of this practice by the actor suggests that there are no other binding factors regarding the shared trip to the same employer. This becomes clear when Marco reports that carpooling only works if certain rules are followed: punctuality and reliability. In addition to financial relief, these rules are essential for the functionality of community mobility. If these are not adhered to several times in succession, the practice of taking people along will disintegrate: "Well, I'm actually always open to everyone, so I'm actually always the one who tries everything, I give everyone a chance (but if the individual does) not manage to take the chance, then (that's their problem)" (Marco, 478). This form of taking someone along can be summarized with the aforementioned term "direct reciprocity" (Stegbauer 2011), which means ride for money. This fact in turn suggests that this form of community mobility is rather fragile. In short, renumeration is gladly accepted, but not at any price. If community mobility takes place among a group of colleagues and within the context of work, carpools are organized according to practical aspects. The number of cars, the number of participating colleagues, the destination, and the place of residence of the driver who makes their car available are the aspects of the material structures on which the practices of community mobility are based. The aim is that drivers do not have to travel an additional route and that passengers can also get home or get to their own car without any problems.

6   The Car as Retreat

With the consolidation of the professional career, fixed mobility routines emerge, with the automobile at the center. The automobile is increasingly being viewed here as a retreat. Stacy shares in the focus group discussion:

> I'm selfish now, so that's the other side. I find it nice in my enclosed space sometimes. I can decide freely: open the window, turn on the radio or CD player, just pursue my thoughts. It's nice sometimes. (Stacy, 257)

The spatial structuring of the social "is composed of the location of bodies and artifacts, which thus arrange a space in relation to each other, which is simultane-ously interpreted in a certain way by participants and observers" (Reckwitz 2016, p. 165). The situation of the driver in the "encased space" of the automobile indicates a demarcation in two ways: on the one hand, the driver disassociates himself/herself from everyday requirements from the time he/she gets into the car. Driving in a private automobile provides a space for contemplation, equipped with certain relaxing elements, such as an audio CD, and driving time is perceived as qualitative time in which "thoughts can be pursued". The space within the car thus serves as a kind of "world in between" and describes a "third space next to the here and there" that brings with it independent qualities (Hilti 2013, p. 213). The time in the car as a "world in between" is used here for a short, but repeatedly recurring intermediate period of intellectual leisure. On the other hand, the "encased space" of the car also serves to delimit it from public space. Within the enclosure of the car cabin, the driver limits his or her contact to outside world. There is an expansion of the private space. The spatial arrangement is thus divided into public space and the moving private spaces of the automobiles that connect different places.

7 Age and Mobility

With living in the same place long term, integration into different social contexts (through hobbies or voluntary activities) and changes in the family constellation (in which the children have moved out and, for example, through widowhood), the actors with increasing age increasingly open up to their local neighborhood and the local population in general. Wilde (2014), for example, notes that older people in rural areas regularly move within two social contexts: in the family, whose members meet in everyday life and whose processes are interwoven, and in regular meetings with neighbors and friends (Wilde 2014, p. 88f.). Meetings with neighbors and friends take place randomly, for example, at the market, where a short conversation is planned or regular meetings take place in fixed groups (Wilde 2014, p. 88). The types of encounters mentioned by Wilde can also be found here. For example, Elvira reports that "on our street we still talk to each other" (694). Overall, there is the impression that seniors are integrated in a stable support network that also takes mobility needs into account, and the mobile persons help the less mobile persons again and again spontaneously. It is about being taken along as well as taking along. Adele, a very active 71-year-old senior citizen, integrates neighborly help into her own mobility. She tells how, when she is driving around town, she offers her help to "known" people. The joy and gratitude felt by the helpers seem important to her. As mentioned above, public space is an important place for exchange. In a conversation, needs can be determined and help can be offered. Spontaneity and temporal flexibility are essential. There is also a certain selflessness with this form of support. Stegbauer describes this as a relationship-creating reciprocity. Selfless giving intersects here with the aim of being liked and experiencing the joy of the recipient (Stegbauer 2011, p. 65). Stegbauer describes that the acceptance of a selfless gift for the recipient is combined with the expectation of a gift. This is often associated with a perceived hesitation in accepting the help. According to Adele, it is a great pleasure for her to bring joy to others by spontaneously offering her help in situations in which others appear to be in need of help. The preservation of independence and self-reliance are also desired aims in old age. The capabilities of your own body play an important role in this. Health-related restrictions on mobility are reported in detail in the interviews. In addition to the walker, wheelchair, and bicycle, the car is an essential mobility aid. The goal is to use the car far into old age. For example, Adelheid (82 years), when she was allowed to drive a car again after an illness-related failure, reports that "older people should use the car every day so that they are always in traffic [...] even if they drive not so long distances" (Adelheid, 401–405). Mutual aid for supply purposes also takes place at the intergenerational level, as Wilde (2014) has stated. Particularly, family members living in the neighborhood help to meet mobility and care needs. Delivery services are offered, and the delivery of purchases is also taken care of.

Overall, it can be said that community mobility takes place in a variety of ways within a spatial framework. Although the independence and autonomy associated with the automobile are in the foreground, carpools are formed again and again for economic and social reasons. Ecological motives play a role, especially in the case of mobility among colleagues to and from work. Taking strangers with you has clear limits. As this form of transport differs significantly from the other forms of community mobility, this will be dealt with separately in Sect. 8.

8 Taking Along Strangers

The picking up of strangers is largely viewed with skepticism or even dislike. This refers, on the one hand, to a planned pick up as well as to the so-called hitchhiking (Schmauks 2003). For instance, the refusal to take strangers along is justified with a concern that potential passengers might not show the car sufficient care: Katharina, who has permission to drive one of her father's cars, reports the following:

> under no circumstance would I take along a stranger, because I know that my father is that kind of person who protects the car door with his hand so it doesn't connect with anything [...] after every ride the floor mat is knocked free of dirt, so: no. that's too risky for me. When I drive to friends it's all about 'be careful', 'don't get dirt everywhere' and so on... (Katharina, 245)

First of all, the decided refusal ("under no circumstances") signifies that no distinction is made here between who should be taken along. "A stranger" suggests that neither the clichéd old woman in need of help nor a young homeless person would be invited into the car. The use of the term "stranger" displays a general decision that all unknown people generally show a lack of care. One's own handling of the car is a large enough challenge in their own rights. Taking someone else or even strangers would mean losing control of the condition of the car and cost extra effort. On the other hand, the idea of Ruth shows the responsibility that arises when taking other people with you. She sees them as equal partners and guests whose needs she helps to meet. Since the automobile represents a private space, like apartments, this is also subordinate to the primary territory of the owner (Schmauks

2003). In this sense, people who enter this territory are treated accordingly as guests, and an appropriate service is offered, e.g. by accepting detours or paying costs in the event of an accident. This perspective motivates them to invite or take certain people on a shared trip. She therefore sees the need to know insurance issues beforehand in order to be legally covered in the event of an unexpected event. Taking along hitchhiking strangers is highly contentious. Martin, a trainee, reports:

> To me, it simply doesn't look good standing by the side of the road. That's something completely different of course if you have a breakdown, but in that case you have the ADAC or something. But if you, alone, stand by the road with a sign or an outstretched thumb? Well, I don't know but that just isn't done anymore, in my view. (Martin, 623)

The reasons for the decreasing social acceptability of hitchhiking lie in the aforementioned possibilities provided by online carpooling portals. Mentioned mostly is the lack of security that comes with the entry of one or more strangers into your own vehicle. The safety concerns relate to yourself or the car. The female participants, with one exception (Anja), are very skeptical, even anxious about this topic, although positive experiences were made, too. At the same time, family members of Ursula actively advised her against taking strangers with her: "I have taken someone with me and my sons scolded me afterwards. I'd rather not have that ... I mean, there was nothing ... but ... it was said, stop that, it's not necessary ..." (1173).

In the interviews, the term "stranger" is ramped up, increased by using terms such as "complete stranger" (Helga) "totally unknown" (Katrin), or "male stranger" (Ursula, Marco). According to Simmel, the stranger is always an element of the group, since only when "the stranger is close" can a social relationship be constructed. This closeness has a spatial point of reference. Simmel writes, that the stranger "is fixed within a particular spatial group [...] [b]ut his position in this group is determined, essentially, by the fact that he has not belonged to it from the beginning [...]" (Simmel 2013, p. 765; Translated by Wolf, Kurt 1950). Inviting the stranger into your car is connected to a certain level of perceived imposition, which is not overcome easily. With the ramping up of the term "stranger" to "complete stranger" or "totally unknown," the social distance that is created becomes apparent. Thomas Winkelkotte, the founder of the carpooling initiative "mobil in MOL," states in his report that the "intimate character of the interior of the automobile" is characteristic, particularly in rural areas (Winkelkotte 2015, 45). He states that the crossing of a stranger into the interior of the car tends to be felt as transgressive (Winkelkotte 2015, p. 45).

In this context, the interviewees use the word "fear" to explain why no unknown people are taken along. Although this fear is attributed to prejudices, media reports, and socialization ("Never go with strangers"), there is some intense dislike. In this context, Marco formulates, "No, over my dead body, no" (668). Another problem is being picked up from the side of the road. The senior citizen Adelheid comments on the topic of being picked up from the side of the road as follows: "So I would not stand on a street and say I want to go there" (1009). Winkelkotte comments on the "shame to be on the side of the road" that the need of being picked up from the side of the road is often interpreted as "neediness that is to be pitied" (Winkelkotte 2015, p. 44).

On the other hand, the focus group participants are open to taking along others if this is organized via online carpooling portals. Information about the driver provides security in advance and replaces the lack of trust. Overall, the spectrum of picking up or taking along strangers is characterized by skepticism on the one end and dislike on the other. One possibility is the use of online portals, but this is only relevant for certain usage groups and routes. There is fundamental uncertainty in insurance and liability issues.

9   Conclusion: The Potential of Changing Mobility Practices

Rural areas are shaped by the natural use of automobiles. It is the normal means of transport with which all needs are met. The guarantee of social participation can usually only be met by covering longer distances. Community mobility is widely used. Taking others along in one's car is a widespread practice among older school children, trainees, and students and offers the possibility of optimizing scarce financial resources. The transport of others is understood to bear a certain vulnerability which increases in old age. On the one hand, the loss of automobile independence is delayed as long as possible. Nevertheless, an increasingly limited autonomy in mobility is perceived, which leads to an increased engagement with mobility in the form of agreements, support, and communication. In addition, due to the neighborhoods that have grown over the years, there are spontaneous supportive mobility services.

A revival of this practice in younger generations can be observed using the social medium "WhatsApp." Families are less willing to take other people with them. Here, the space of the automobile constitutes, on the one hand, a space that is firmly structured by child seats and, on the other hand, a retreat due to the many tasks to be carried out in the family context. There is a concrete unwillingness to form carpools. Generally, taking strangers along is considered problematic. This affects both one's own safety as that of those close to one and the cleanliness and integrity of the car. However, the lack of trust can be countered by using online carpooling websites. Numerous studies on digital trust building show that trust can be generated through the use of easily manageable groups (source), through rating systems (source), and through shared interests (source). Trust is even considered to be a basic requirement for participation in collaborative consumption, such as shared driving in a private car (Möhlmann 2015).

Establishing trust online, and thus enabling drivers to take other people, including strangers, with them, is one way of increasing the potential for increased communal mobility at least in the vulnerable social groups of trainees, students, and older schoolchildren. Among senior citizens, it seems important to create situations in which personal contact can be made and needs can be discussed. In conclusion, it can be said that the car is perceived as not only a flexible and individual means of covering distances but also a retreat, an enclosed space away from public space. The fact that the automobile is considered a matter of course means that it serves as a benchmark when it comes to the nature of public space and public transport: poor accessibility, in the form of lowered curbs, stairs, missing or inoperable elevators, and narrow entrances to buses and trains. All of these aspects can be circumvented or avoided with the use of the car through the direct accessibility that the road traffic infrastructure and the technical equipment of the automobile offer, for example through family parking spaces, large luggage compartments for groceries and strollers, and high car entrances for those with restricted mobility. The spatial restrictions of cities, such as the lack of parking space, are practically non-existent in rural areas. In addition to the spatial conditions, automobility is also the measure of flexibility and autonomy in rural areas.

To maintain automotive practice, various forms of carpooling are considered acceptable. The limits lie solely in the individual availability of temporal, spatial, and economic scope and neighborly familiarity. By taking along others, social relationships with specific people or groups of people are created, consolidated, or avoided. A question still to be answered would be how, due to the high density of cars in rural areas, drivers and owners occasionally do without their own vehicle and can still be sure that they can meet their needs within a reasonable timeframe.

References

Beauftragter der Bundesregierung für die Neuen Länder. (2011). *Daseinsvorsorge im demografischen Wandel zukunftsfähig gestalten. Handlungskonzept zur Sicherung der privaten und öffentlichen Infrastruktur in vom demographischen Wandel besonders betroffenen ländlichen Räumen.* Retrieved December 12, 2020 from https://www.demografie.sachsen.de/ Langfassung_2_Handlungskonzept_NBL_barrierefreie_PDF.pdf

BMVI. (2018). *Sicherung von Versorgung und Mobilität. Strategien und Praxisbeispiele für gleichwertige Lebensverhältnisse in ländlichen Räumen.* Bundesministerium für Verkehr und digitale Infrastruktur. Berlin. Retrieved December 12, 2020 from https://www.bmvi.de/ SharedDocs/DE/Publikationen/G/abschlussbericht-versorgung-mobilitaet-laendlicher-raum. pdf?__blob=publicationFile

Canzler, W. (2013). Verkehr und Mobilität. In: Mau, S., & Schöneck-Voß, N. M. (Eds.): *Handwörterbuch zur Gesellschaft Deutschlands* (3rd ed., pp. 922–935). Wiesbaden: Springer VS.

Canzler, W. (2016). Räumliche Mobilität und regionale Unterschiede. Art und Umfang der räumlichen Mobilität. In: *Datenreport 2012.* Ein Sozialbericht für die Bundesrepublik Deutschland (pp. 341–346). Bonn: BpB (Schriftenreihe der Bundeszentrale für Politische Bildung).

Canzler, W., Dienel, H.-L., Götz, K., Kesselring, S., Knie, A., Lanzendorf, M., Rammler, S., et al. (2016). *Beharrung und Wandel in der Mobilität. Die Verkehrswende als Ausgangspunkt für eine neue Forschungsagenda.* Positionspapier.

Canzler, W., & Knie, A. (2002). "New Mobility"? Mobilität und Verkehr als soziale Praxis. In: Bundeszentrale für politische Bildung (Eds.), *Aus Politik und Zeitgeschichte: Mobilität – Verkehrspolitik.* Retrieved December 12, 2020 from http://www.bpb.de/apuz/25355/ newmobilitymobilitaetundverkehralssozialepraxis.

Canzler, W., & Knie, A. (2005). Wie die Bahn schrumpfen wird. *WZB-Mitteilungen* Heft 107 (pp. 29–32). Wissenschaftszentrum Berlin.

Dangschat, J. S., & Segert, A. (2011). Nachhaltige Alltagsmobilität – soziale Ungleichheiten und Milieus. *ÖZS, 36*(2), 55–73.

Fiedler, J., Hoppe, R., Berninghaus, P., & Lenhart, A. (1989). *Anhalterwesen und Anhaltergefahren unter besonderer Berücksichtigung des "Kurztrampens"*. Wiesbaden: BKA Forschungsreihe.

Herget, M. (2013). *Verkehrsverhalten und Mobilitätsstrategien von Familien in ländlichen Räumen Deutschlands unter besonderer Berücksichtigung rollentypischer Arbeitsteilung*. Dissertation. Technische Universität Berlin.

Hilti, N. (2013). *Lebenswelten multilokal Wohnender. Eine Betrachtung des Spannungsfeldes von Bewegung und Verankerung*. Wiesbaden: Springer VS.

Kirchesch, M. (2013). Mobilität als Basis der Daseinsvorsorge in ländlichen Räumen. In: Bundesanstalt für Landwirtschaft und Ernährung under collaboration of Ortwein, S., Hercksen, H., Kirchesch, M., & Schulz-Hönerhoff, B. (Eds.), *Daseinsvorsorge in ländlichen Räumen unter Druck. Wie reagieren auf den demografischen Wandel?* (pp. 13–16). Bonn.

Knie, A., Rammler, S., & Zimmer, W. (2016). Mut zur Zukunft. Der Wandel zur neuen Mobilitätsgesellschaft – Ansätze für einen Politikwechsel. *Internationales Verkehrswesen, 68*(3), 10–12.

Manderscheid, K. (2012). Mobilität. In: Eckardt, F. (Ed.), *Handbuch Stadtsoziologie* (pp. 551–570). Wiesbaden: VS Verlag für Sozialwissenschaften.

Manderscheid, K. (2013). Mobilität als relationale Aushandlung. In: M. Hömke (Ed.) *Mobilität und Identität* (pp. 51–77). Wiesbaden: Springer Fachmedien.

Manderscheid, K. (2019). Auto-logische Kopplung. eine quantitativ-praxistheoretische Perspektive auf Mobilität. *Swiss Journal of Sociology, 45*(2), 161–183.

Möhlmann, M. (2015). Collaborative consumption. Determinants of satisfaction and the likelihood of using a sharing economy option again. *Journal of Consumer Behaviour, 14*(3), 193–207.

Neoh, J. G., Chipulu, M., & Marshall, A. (2015). What encourages people to carpool? An evaluation of factors with meta-analysis. *Transportation, 44*(2), 423–447.

Neu, C. (Ed.) (2009). *Daseinsvorsorge. Eine gesellschaftswissenschaftliche Annäherung* (1st ed.). Wiesbaden: VS Verlag für Sozialwissenschaften.

NMELV. (2012). *Mobilität in ländlichen Räumen in Niedersachsen. Ergebnisbericht*. Niedersächsisches Ministerium für Ernährung, Landwirtschaft, Verbraucherschutz und Landesentwicklung. Hannover. Retrieved December 12, 2020 from http://www.ml.niedersachsen.de/download/67431

Reckwitz, A. (2003). Grundelemente einer Theorie sozialer Praktiken. Eine sozialtheoretische Perspektive. *Zeitschrift für Soziologie, 32*(4), 282–301.

Reckwitz, A. (2004). Die Entwicklung des Vokabulars der Handlungstheorien: Von den zweck- und normenorientierten Modellen zu den Kultur- und Praxistheorien. In: M. Gabriel (Ed.), *Paradigmen der akteurszentrierten Soziologie* (pp. 303–328). Wiesbaden: VS Verlag für Sozialwissenschaften.

Reckwitz, A. (2016). Praktiken und ihre Affekte. In: H. Schäfer (Ed.), *Praxistheorie. Ein soziologisches Forschungsprogramm* (1st ed., pp. 163–180). transcript (Sozialtheorie). Bielefeld.

Schäfer, H. (2016). Praxis als Wiederholung. Das Denken der Iterabilität und seine Konsequenzen für die Methodologie praxeologischer Forschung. In: H. Schäfer (Ed.), *Praxistheorie. Ein soziologisches Forschungsprogramm* (1st ed., pp. 137–162). Bielefeld. transcript (Sozialtheorie).

Schäfer, H. (2019): Praxistheorie als Kultursoziologie. In: S. Moebius, F. Nungesser, & K. Scherke (Eds.), *Handbuch Kultursoziologie. Band 2: Theorien – Methoden – Felder*. (1st ed.) Wiesbaden: Springer Fachmedien Wiesbaden GmbH; Springer VS (Springer Reference Sozialwissenschaften).

Schatzki, T. R. (2016). Praxistheorie als flache Ontologie. In: H. Schäfer (Ed.), *Praxistheorie. Ein soziologisches Forschungsprogramm* (1st ed., pp. 29–44). transcript (Sozialtheorie). Bielefeld.

Schlebecker, John T. (1958). An informal History of Hitchhiking. *The Historian, 20*(3), 305–327.

Schmauks, D. (2003). Nonverbale Interaktion zwischen Trampern und Autofahrern. *Psychosozial, 94*, 119–127.

Schmidt, R. (2017). Praxistheorie. In: R. Gugutzer, G. Klein, & M. Meuser, (Eds.), *Handbuch Körpersoziologie. Band 1: Grundbegriffe und theoretische Perspektiven* (pp. 335–344). Wiesbaden: Springer VS.

Sheller, M. (2004). Automotive emotions. *Theory, Culture & Society, 21*(4–5), 221–242.

Simmel, G. (2013). *Soziologie. Untersuchungen über die Formen der Vergesellschaftung*. In: O. Rammstedt (Ed.) *Gesamtausgabe in 24 Bänden – Band 11*. Suhrkamp Taschenbuch Wissenschaft. Frankfurt am Main.

Sonnberger, M., & Gallego Carrera, D. (2012). *Konzepte des kollektivierten Individualverkehrs*. Literaturbericht. Universität Stuttgart, Stuttgart. Internationalen Zentrum für Kultur- und Technikforschung der Universität Stuttgart (ZIRN).

Stegbauer, C. (2011). *Reziprozität. Einführung in soziale Formen der Gegenseitigkeit* (2nd ed.). Wiesbaden: VS Verlag für Sozialwissenschaften/Springer Fachmedien Wiesbaden GmbH.

Wilde, M. (2014). *Mobilität und Alltag. Einblicke in die Mobilitätspraxis älterer Menschen auf dem Land*. Dissertation. Universität Jena. Wiesbaden: Springer VS (Research, 25).

Winkelkotte, T. (2015). *gut finden oder mitmachen. Erkenntnisse regionaler Mitfahrinitiativen*. Reichenow.

Wolf, K. (1950): *The Sociology of Georg Simmel*. (pp. 402–408). New York: Free Press.

From Empirical Data to Operational Models: An Approach for the Development of a Decision-Making Component for an Agent-Based Mobility Simulation from Quantitative Survey Data

Klaas Dählmann, Martina Jahns, Nadine Pieper, and Jürgen Sauer

Abstract This contribution illustrates a holistic approach to determine and implement a decision-making component for an agent-based mobility simulation framework based on empirical data. The decision component uses a generic fuzzy inference concept developed for a flexible simulation framework for mobility scenarios, the variables and rule base of which are acquired from quantitative survey data of 194 participants. Using a minimal example case of ridesharing intention, it is shown how such a survey can be analyzed using structural equation modeling to subsequently derive a decision-making model of relevant, empirically estimated determinants for the subsequent implementation as a fuzzy inference system. The fuzzy inference system is applied in a simulation scenario to compare survey results and simulative behavior. The similar overall results of both survey and simulation regarding the used determinants indicate a general feasibility of the approach.

Keywords Agent-based simulation · Empirical data · Fuzzy inference · Ridesharing · Travel mode choice

1 Introduction

In Germany, rural areas are challenged by demographic change due to the aging population, which is not compensated by a corresponding population growth, e.g. by birth and immigration rates (Maretzke 2016, p. 177, p. 180 and p. 184). While

K. Dählmann (✉) · J. Sauer
Carl von Ossietzky University of Oldenburg, Oldenburg, Germany
e-mail: klaas.daehlmann@uol.de; juergen.sauer@uol.de

M. Jahns · N. Pieper
Technical University of Braunschweig, Braunschweig, Germany
e-mail: martina.jahns@tu-bs.de; n.pieper@tu-bs.de

© The Author(s), under exclusive license to Springer Nature Switzerland AG 2021   53
J. Marx Gómez et al. (eds.), *Progress in Sustainable Mobility Research*,
Progress in IS, https://doi.org/10.1007/978-3-030-70841-2_4

this phenomenon is less crucial in more attractive rural areas with productive and service factors, structurally weaker regions struggle with this in a greater extent due to higher emigration and lesser immigration rates (Maretzke 2016, p. 181 and p. 184). A share of 12.6% of the German population (resp., 39.4% of the rural population) live in these structurally weaker regions (Maretzke 2016, p. 174ff.).

These structurally weaker regions face several mobility-related challenges: caused by factors like decreasing population density, a car ownership rate of 90% of households in rural areas (Follmer and Gruschwitz 2019, p. 6), and therefore a lower number of potential users, the public transport is getting economical unviable in these areas. This, in turn, leads to increasingly insufficient public transport operation times (Steinrück and Küpper 2010, p. 18 and p. 25). Furthermore, this poor public transport system in combination with a greater effort for securing livelihood induced by scaling-down processes of local (public) infrastructure (Winkel 2008, p. 44) poses serious mobility problems, especially for people without access to a car (Holz-Rau 2009, p. 797).

In general, for rural regions the development of efficient mobility solutions is important for **economic** (e.g. accessibility of workplaces strengthens the local economy), **social** (e.g. higher quality of life due to security of supply, especially for immobile people), and **ecological** reasons (e.g. avoidance of unnecessary traffic volume) (Riesner 2014, p. 42f.).

Demand-responsive mobility concepts—partly based on the voluntary engagement of citizens in rural areas, e.g. "citizen bus" (Riesner 2014, p. 45)—already try to bridge the largest supply bottlenecks. An additional transportation concept based on a self-organizing approach of citizens is ridesharing, which is defined as *"a mode of transportation in which individual travelers share a vehicle for a trip and split travel costs such as gas, toll, and parking fees with others that have similar itineraries and time schedules."* (Furuhata et al. 2013, p. 28). The dissemination of mobile internet and information and communication technologies enables a more flexible and short-term matching of people (Amey et al. 2011, p. 103). Ridesharing appears to be a suitable enhancement of mobility due to **economic** (e.g. shared travel costs; Agatz et al. 2011, p. 534; Amey et al. 2011, p. 103), **social** (e.g. connection of people), and **ecological** benefits (e.g. fewer CO_2 emissions per passenger; Chan and Shaheen 2012, p. 96).

Nevertheless, the introduction of technology-enabled peer-to-peer ridesharing in rural areas comes along with various challenges: In line with the previously mentioned high amount of car ownership (Follmer and Gruschwitz 2019, p. 6), there are only a few households without a car, even though their demand for mobility options contributing to an improvement of their mobility situation is urgent.

In order to achieve an operable concept, a certain number of users ("critical mass"; Amey et al. 2011, p. 107) as well as a balanced proportion of demander (i.e. passengers) and suppliers (i.e. drivers) of ridesharing services are required. Although people appreciate the basic idea of ridesharing (Meurer et al. 2014, p. 1930; from qualitative study with elderly people), this peer-to-peer concept is also connected to several barriers, e.g. the concerns of getting stranded due to no available return trip for dynamic ridesharing (Deakin et al. 2010, p. 132) or regarding prerequisites like not having enough users in sparsely populated rural areas. This aspect of achieving a balanced "critical mass" of users poses several challenges for the initial establishment of ridesharing but can be facilitated through a well-designed app with an adequate operating dynamic routing algorithm.

In order to further estimate the overall performance of the collaborative mobility concepts as well as their reach of the target audience, an agent-based simulation framework was developed during the project NEMo[1] ("sustainable fulfillment of mobility needs in rural areas") to analyze and evaluate representative mobility use cases. It has been designed to explicitly consider any soft beliefs and opinions that facilitate or inhibit the acceptance and use of new mobility concepts such as dynamic peer-to-peer ridesharing. This decision component of the simulation framework is based on a flexible template for a fuzzy inference system, and the variables and rule base of which must be determined through qualitative or quantitative field research. The framework therefore provides an experimental environment to make otherwise static field research results applicable and executable in a simulative context for the ex ante analysis of use cases that represent different contexts of use for the business models and ridesharing services of the entire project NEMo.

Project NEMo aims at the development of sustainable mobility services. Therefore, the mobile app "Fahrkreis" has been developed and tested in the pilot regions in and around Oldenburg as well as in the district of Wesermarsch (both in Germany)— the latter is typed as a structurally weaker region (Maretzke 2016, p. 172). The app "Fahrkreis" consists of three components:

1. mobility information and planning by combination of different means of transport,
2. development of (mobility-related) business models for strengthening the community in rural areas,
3. platform for peer-to-peer ridesharing offers and requests in order to better utilize vacant car capacities and also improve mobility for people without access to a car.

This contribution showcases our approach of using empirical data in order to develop and implement a fuzzy inference system for the aforementioned simulation framework using the exemplary application context of a ridesharing simulation. The empirical data was collected via an online questionnaire in the model regions of project NEMo. Primary contribution of this contribution is the holistic method from the design and evaluation of an empirical survey to the development and implementation of a fuzzy inference system that reflects the constructs and relationships of the empirical model.

The contribution is structured as follows: in Sect. 2, we briefly examine the state of the art in traffic and mobility simulation to further point out the research gap addressed in this contribution. Section 3 then illustrates the simulation framework and its decision-making component, in particular, to familiarize the reader with the

---

[1] https://nemo-mobilitaet.de.

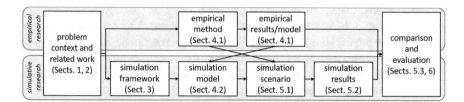

Fig. 1 Overview of the relationship between the interdisciplinary, methodological approach of this contribution, and the structure of this contribution

underlying architecture, design decisions, and assumptions of the full simulation system. Subsequently, Sect. 4 presents the development of a fuzzy inference system for ridesharing decisions for the agents within the simulation system from the underlying quantitative research to the technical fuzzy inference system. In Sect. 5, the inference system is evaluated through a simulation scenario that mimics the context of the original empirical study to compare stated intention of the participants of the survey and simulated behavior of the agents within the simulation framework. Section 6 concludes this contribution with a brief summary and an outline of our planned future research. The overall relationship between the approach and the structure as well as the dependencies between the sections of this contribution is summarized in Fig. 1.

2 State of the Art in Traffic and Mobility Simulation

The underlying issue of modeling mobility and traffic behavior has been tackled in many works from up to several decades ago. For this contribution, we reduce the overall body of contributions to the field according to several constraints: first, we purposely only consider works that provide not only an explanatory model but also the technical environment for the computational execution and simulation of said models. Moreover, the state of the art for such systems is to pursue a microsimulation approach using both agent-based (Wooldridge 2009, 2013) and activity-/tour-based models (Bowman and Ben-Akiva 2000, p. 3; Ortúzar and Willumsen 2011, p. 473f.) as opposed to the outdated 4-step method of traffic generation (Cascetta 2009, p. 172–175). With regard to the scope of this contribution, we especially emphasize the chosen decision-making approach and the underlying data set for each related work.

ALBATROSS (A Learning Based Transportation Oriented Simulation System) is an activity-based simulation system built on a model of activity and modal choice (Arentze et al. 1999; Arentze and Timmermans 2004). ALBATROSS generates complete tours by chaining one or more trips connecting individual activities on a household basis. The data set used for this generation is based on a travel diary survey from two regions of the Netherlands. Using this data set, the decision-making component within the system is based on a decision tree that can be applied in the system to generate feasible tours and pick an appropriate mode of transport. In subsequent applications, Bayesian networks have also been explored as an alternative to the initially proposed, rule-based decision tree approach (Janssens et al. 2004, 2006). The fundamental tour scheduling approach used for ALBATROSS has recently been expanded into FEATHERS (Forecasting Evolutionary Activity-Travel of Households and their Environmental Repercussions) (Bellemans et al. 2010). The system is based on a multidimensional data set containing GPS and social network data as well as information from questionnaires/interviews and stated preference experiments in the Flanders region of Belgium.

The TAPAS (Travel Activity Pattern Simulation) system for the calculation of travel demand on a microscopic level (Heinrichs et al. 2016, 2017). The simulation model consists of four consecutive modules to generate traffic assignments. An artificial population is first synthesized from statistical data, which then leads to activity generation for the population and subsequently plausible location and modal choice. The modal choice is based on household constraints such as car availability as well as time and budget where the probability of choosing a particular mode of transport is calculated with a multinomial logit model. The system has been applied with a synthetic agent population based on various statistical data of the German capital Berlin.

MATSim-T (Multi-Agent Transport Simulation Toolkit) offers a general framework to model and simulate travel demand and traffic flow (Balmer et al. 2008). The generation of the agent population and their personal, household, and activity is probabilistic and has been applied based on swiss census data. The system divides the complete daily tours of the agents into subtours starting and ending at the same location, for which the modal choice is based on a probabilistic multinomial logit model.

The agent-based C-TAP (Continuous Target-based Activity Planning) system emphasizes the dynamic pursuit of activities through the calculation of the increasing, perceived discomfort when typical recurring local activities are not pursued regularly (Märki et al. 2014). The approach has been evaluated using swiss travel diary data and further adapted for long-distance travel (Janzen and Axhausen 2018).

TASHA (Travel and Activity Scheduling for Household Agents) is a household-based microsimulation system that generates and schedules activities and subsequently performs modal choice to determine trip chains and traffic assignments for its agents (Roorda et al. 2006). A genetic algorithm is used to estimate the parameters for the modal choice component, which among common private and public transport options also includes ridesharing options. The system has been successfully applied using survey data from the Greater Toronto Area in Canada.

Most existing technical systems are based on measured traffic data or quantitatively evaluated travel information on already established modes of transport. Main purpose is usually to model the current state and capacity of large-scale traffic systems with thousands up to several hundred thousands of agents. Therefore, plausible population synthesis and activity generation play an integral role for those systems. Because of this macroscopic level of analysis, the agent's decision-making for individual modes of transport is often based on few and easily quantifiable factors. Overall, those systems ideally reach a state of equilibrium close to the actual modal split and travel times within the modeled systems. In contrast, when attempting to conduct an ex ante simulation of potentially new modes of transport, the reasoning plays an integral role in the quality of the simulation. We therefore emphasize a flexible decision-making component that must respect soft beliefs and opinions as much as it has to be able to include conventional decision factors. Hence, the simulation framework of project NEMo pursues a scenario-based approach where the viability of the available services and modes of transport is evaluated regarding separate use cases. This way, the individual simulation scenarios representing different parameter combinations of the use case, such as agent population and activities, available vehicles, and decision model, can be completely separated from the simulation framework providing the runtime environment for the scenarios.

3   Description of the Simulation Framework

The underlying simulation system has been implemented as a simulation framework that enables the systematic exploration and evaluation of different mobility scenarios through a flexible, modular design. Dählmann and Sauer (2019) show the generalized conceptual derivation of the simulation framework and discuss the social theories and models the framework is based on in detail. Moreover, implementation alternatives to fuzzy inference from the field of computational intelligence are discussed.

The framework utilizes several state-of-the-art simulation principles from the fields of both computer science and transportation research: fundamentally, it is based on a multiagent system (Wooldridge 2009, 2013), where each agent represents a single person. All logic and reasoning are encapsulated in the agents, which use information from the simulation environment to generate and decide on potential solutions to their mobility needs. Moreover, all internal processes of the agents are designed to be completely deterministic, based on the assumption that reasoning and decision-making on an individual micro-level usually are not probabilistic according to macroscopic probability distributions but rather based on the individual and contextual determinants of the situation. To generate the underlying mobility needs, the framework is based on an activity-based simulation approach (Bowman and Ben-Akiva 2000; Ortúzar and Willumsen 2011, p. 473f.), where each agent has a set of activities which forces them to be at specific places, at specific times, and for specific durations. Currently, the framework only supports tours consisting of only two trips, that is, an outward trip to an activity and a return trip back home. Lastly, the framework is based on a discrete event simulation system (Banks et al. 2005, p. 60f.; Train 2003, p. 15), with a time resolution of 1 min. Each step in the simulation therefore represents 1 min of real time. This fine time resolution allows the representation of any activity and trip durations, from several hours at work to a short trip to the mailbox.

A simulation step consists of two stages for each agent, a planning stage and an action stage. Within the planning stage, an agent schedules any upcoming trips and decides on the best mode of transport for each trip. Within the action stage, an agent executes one of the three possible states: the agent is either idle at home waiting to depart for an activity, in transit to or from an activity, or currently pursuing an activity until it ends.

Figure 2 shows an abstract and simplified representation of the internal process of an agent during the planning stage. The process may be canceled at any time, for example, if all current activities have already been successfully scheduled in any previous step. The details of the action stage are not shown any further.

Beginning at the scheduling component, an agent does not schedule all activities at once. Instead, the always progressing simulation time and date may cause an agent to plan how to get to and from an upcoming activity when the activity enters the agent's planning horizon. This is done by recognizing that there must be an outward and a return trip to the activity and back home after the activity has ended. These trips are initialized with the desired arrival and departure time based on the activity to be planned.

The subsequent routing component attempts to gather any available mobility options for each of the outward and return trips. The number and quality of the found mobility option are based on the vehicles the agent has access to as well as the specific routing and transportation sources the simulation is connected to. These routing can be done by using the simulation-internal street network, by retrieving information from web-based interfaces for individual or public transportation or by connecting to other available mobility services such as ridesharing networks. After all possible mobility options for the outward and return trips have been gathered, the agent trims these options to include only valid pairs of trips. In particular, a valid pair must return the agent's vehicles if they have been used for the outward trip and may not use the agent's vehicles for the return if they have not been used for the outward trip as well.

The final decision-making component is used to determine the best possible tour based on all identified valid pairs of trips. This is done by calculating a normalized utility score for each mobility option of each trip individually. By adding the utility scores of the outward and return mobility options for each pair, the pairs can be compared, and the best pair can be chosen as the optimal tour for the activity at hand. The decision-making component is based on a fuzzy inference system that can be configured to use any number of available input values, such as the agent's attributes, information on the mobility option and activity, or global simulation attributes along the rule base used for the agent's decision-making.

After the agent has determined the best possible pair of outward and return trips for the activity, this tour is handed over to the action stage where it may be immediately executed or stored until the departure time of the outward trip. Moreover, should the agent have decided to use its car for the tour, it may add the tour to any ridesharing services the simulation is connected to so that other agents may consider those unique and temporary offers along their available individual and public transport options.

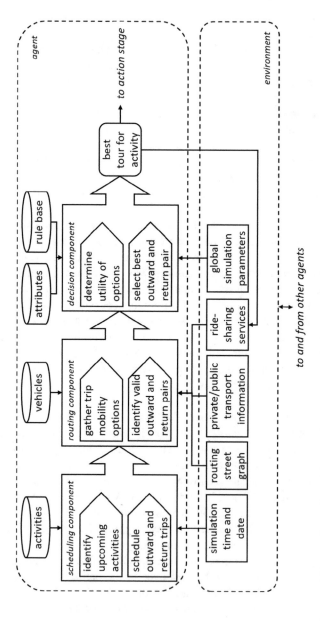

Fig. 2 Abstract architectural overview of the overall behavior of the agents within the NEMo simulation framework

3.1 General Fuzzy Inference Concept for Decision Component

This section describes the general structure of any fuzzy inference system that is used for the calculation of the utility scores within the decision-making component of any agent of the simulation system, as mentioned in Sect. 3. An earlier version of the concept has been introduced by Dählmann and Sauer (2018) and further applied by Dählmann et al. (2019).

This general concept may serve as a generic template that is to be filled in with the reasoning information from any quantitative model for travel mode intention or travel mode choice in order to design an implementable fuzzy inference system. It can be used as a systematic guideline to transform epistemic model data into a technical implementation for the application in the computational agent-based simulation. The primary functional purpose of any fuzzy inference system implemented using this concept is to process the parameters of a decision situation in the simulation in order to calculate a normalized utility score for a given mobility option. In essence, it works like a funnel taking in all available contextual information on the mobility decision at hand, evaluating the attitudes toward all modes of transport in that mobility option, and then determining a single utility score for comparison with other, competing decision options to identify the best option. This contextual information can be potentially multidimensional and diverse such as an agent's individual attributes (e.g. age, gender, or other sociodemographic factors), information on the mobility option (e.g. distance, duration, or waiting times during transit using public transportation), information on the pursued activity (e.g. the purpose, or the desired start and end time of the activity), or global information (e.g. the current or expected weather). The general fuzzy inference concept is shown in Fig. 3. The general concept is divided into four stages, each serving a specific purpose during the calculation of the utility of a given mobility option from the available input information.

Stage 0 is the fuzzification of all available input values. A fuzzy variable must be defined for each input value to be used in the decision-making, each variable in turn containing suitable linguistic terms to fuzzify the input. For example, when deciding between walking and going by car, the exact distance might not of particular interest. Rather, one might just be interested in whether the distance is a short or a long one or maybe "somewhere in between." This mapping between all crisp input values and their counterparts as fuzzy linguistic terms is the result of stage 0.

Stage 1 is the operationalization of intermediate constructs that cannot be immediately represented as simulation parameters and linguistic terms, respectively. In some decision models for travel mode choice, not all attitudes toward the modes of transport can be easily and directly tied toward one piece of contextual information. For example, the perceived feeling of safety can be a major influence in the use of ridesharing (Amey et al. 2011), yet this subjective feeling of safety cannot be easily represented as a parameter of a computational simulation. Instead, it must be operationalized from potentially any number of contextual factors. This stage is therefore an optional step that might be helpful or even necessary for the implementation of some decision models.

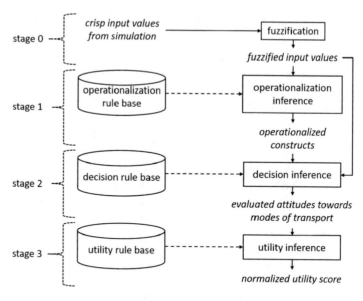

Fig. 3 Stages of the general fuzzy inference concept to be used for the development of the decision-making component of the NEMo simulation framework based on Dählmann and Sauer (2018)

Functionally, this stage introduces additional fuzzy variables, each representing a required subjective construct (e.g. perceptions or opinions). Each variable uses fuzzy singleton terms to represent the value of the variable. For example, a variable representing the feeling of safety might contain two singleton terms, a term representing a bad feeling with a term value of −1 and a good one being represented by a value of 1. The rules of the operationalization rule base represent the facilitating and inhibiting beliefs that influence the perceived opinion represented by the variable and its terms. The activation of each term is based on the aggregated activation degrees of each applying rule. The result of stage 1 is the finished operationalization of all required, intermediate constructs for the subsequent reasoning on the modes of transport.

Stage 2 is the actual decision-making toward the individual modes of transport within a given mobility option. Because a mobility option may be an intermodal chain on different modes of transport, it is necessary to evaluate each mode of transport within the option individually. For example, an intermodal trip consisting of a bike to the bus stop, the bus ride itself, and a short walk at the end contains three different modes, and each mode might be evaluated differently. These different and potentially conflicting attitudes must be represented.

Functionally, this stage contains a fuzzy variable for each mode of transport within the decision option. Each variable again contains two fuzzy singleton terms representing the attitude toward that mode of transport: a contra term with a value of −1 and a pro term with a value of 1. The rules of the decision rule base then determine the opinion on the modes of transport based on either the fuzzified input values directly or the activation of the terms of the operationalized constructs. The result of stage 2 is the attitudes toward the individual modes of transport within the mobility option.

Stage 3 is the calculation of the normalized utility score from the pros and cons of each mode of transport. This stage uses only one fuzzy variable representing the utility. The variable also contains two singleton terms that represent the lower and upper bounds of the range of the utility score, from bad (term value of -1) to good (term value of 1) utility.

Functionally, the operationalization rule base maps simply between the terms of stage 2 and stage 3, a pro attitude regarding a mode of transport translates to a good utility and a contra attitude to a bad one, respectively. As the inference system only uses singleton terms in its output stage, the crisp utility value is calculated using the weighted sum of the value and the activation of both terms of the utility variable. This results in a single score to assess and compare the mobility option at hand with others using the principle of Takagi–Sugeno inference (Sugeno 1985).

4 Data Acquisition and Development of a Fuzzy Inference System for Ridesharing

A deeper understanding of realistic beliefs and attributes is a key prerequisite to generate valid outcomes for the decision-making process. Since survey data is based on people's perceptions and beliefs, this kind of data seems to be suitable for the decision component. We therefore describe how this survey data was collected and analyzed. Afterward, the results are transferred to fuzzy rules for the decision component.

4.1 Data Acquisition and Analysis

In this section, the conceptual model for analyzing the survey data is introduced, followed by a description of the data collection, analysis, and an interim discussion of the results.

4.1.1 Conceptual Model and Hypotheses

In order to show the process of the derivation of fuzzy rules based on survey data, we conceptually developed a basic illustrative model (Fig. 4) using one usage motive as representation of a positive influence factor (promoter) and one usage barrier as an exemplification of a negative influence factor (inhibitor). In line with the objective of project NEMo, a positive influence factor is represented by perceived environmental benefit, as the grouping of journeys results in positive environmental effects such as lesser CO_2 emissions (Chan and Shaheen 2012, p. 96).

As an exemplary negative influence factor, our model contains concerns of potential users regarding the unavailability of a sufficiently large ridesharing community, and thus the lack of a satisfactory amount of ridesharing offers and requests. Therefore, this barrier represents concerns regarding a fundamental prerequisite of ridesharing: the existence of a "critical mass" (Amey et al. 2011, p. 107). This aspect is especially in peer-to-peer (ride)sharing essential, as no guarantee of getting a suitable offer exists.

Therefore, we assume that perceived environmental benefit positively and availability concerns negatively affect the intention to use ridesharing:

H1 Environmental benefit positively affects ridesharing usage intention.
H2 Availability concerns negatively affect ridesharing usage intention.

Furthermore, we assume that perceived environmental benefit and availability concerns as well as the ridesharing usage intention are affected by demographic attributes. Regarding the background of project NEMo, we consider the (rural vs. urban) living environment. For people living in rural areas with a lower population density, traffic-related environmental issues like congestions or emissions are not as present in their direct consequences as for people living in more urban areas (e.g. Brereton et al. 2011, p. 217 and p. 21, for rural areas in Ireland and Umweltbundesamt 2009, p. 5f., for urban vs. rural fine dust pollution in Germany). Therefore, we hypothesize

H3a A rural living environment negatively affects environmental benefit.

Additionally, we assume that in sparsely populated rural areas, concerns regarding a low likelihood of matching people with similar journeys are prevalent:

H3b A rural living environment positively affects availability concerns.

In line with the specified challenges of rural areas (see Sect. 1), we assume that in rural areas, there is a lower ridesharing usage intention:

H3c A rural living environment negatively affects the ridesharing usage intention.

We include age as a second demographic attribute, as elderly people might be potential target groups of ridesharing. In a qualitative study with elderly people, a positive attitude regarding ridesharing was shown (Meurer et al. 2014, p. 1930). However, the study of Meurer et al. (2014, p. 1928f) also revealed that the passengers' dependency from the driver seems to be incompatible with the demand regarding autonomy and independence in mobility of elderly individuals. We assume that this feeling of dependency can be considered as a consequence of the perception that there are lacking alternative ridesharing offers available (i.e. higher availability concerns) or difficult to organize. Furthermore, a meta-analysis revealed a relationship between elderly individuals and particular areas of pro-environmental behavior like attempting to avoid environmental pollution and more active protection of nature (Wiernik et al. 2013, p. 843). Based on that, we assume:

H4a Age positively affects environmental benefit.
H4b Age positively affects availability concerns.
H4c Age positively affects the ridesharing usage intention.

4.1.2 Method and Sample Description

The data was collected via an online questionnaire[2] in summer 2017 in the region of Wesermarsch in Lower Saxony, Germany. In total, 338 residents participated in the survey. The respondents are on average 40.17 years old ($SD = 16.74$), and almost half of them are female (47.3%).

Approximately, half of the respondents had to put themselves in the perspective of a driver ($n = 144$) and the other half in the perspective of a passenger ($n = 194$) while answering the questions. The allocation to these two perspectives occurred randomly for car owners. To increase external validity, respondents without access to a car were directly assigned to the passenger's perspective. Since offering a ridesharing supply as a driver compared to requesting a ridesharing demand as a passenger operates on different technical levels, in this study we only focus on analyzing the passenger's perspective (i.e. $n = 194$ respondents).

To introduce the purpose of project NEMo, respondents saw a short newspaper article at the beginning of the survey. This article summarizes the project's subgoal "social mobility" by shortly explaining the concept of peer-to-peer ridesharing between residents of a local region as a self-organizing approach.

For the measurement of the dependent and independent variables, validated constructs are used, which are adapted to the study context (see Table 1). The operationalization of living environment bases on population-based categories of city and community types/sizes (Bundesinstitut für Bau-, Stadt- und Raumforschung 2015).

4.1.3 Empirical Results

Before testing our hypotheses, we conducted a confirmatory factor analysis (CFA) in MPlus 7.4 (Muthén and Muthén 2012). All quality criteria (indicator, factor, and scale reliability as well as discriminant validity) are fulfilled (see Table 1). Results of the CFA show good global fit indices (CFI = 0.988; TLI = 0.980; RMSEA =

---

[2]This questionnaire is a refined version of a previous survey conducted in 2016 with most of the respondents living in the project's pilot region, Oldenburg (Pieper et al. 2017). The purpose of this follow-up survey is the explicit consideration of residents living in Wesermarsch, representing another pilot region of project NEMo. Descriptive results of the Wesermarsch survey are published on the NEMo homepage (Jahns and Woisetschläger 2017, p. 9).

Table 1 Results of the confirmatory factor analysis

Scale/item	λ	α	CR	AVE	M	SD
Environmental benefit (adapted from Hamari et al. 2016)		0.826	0.826	0.704		
... I can contribute to lower traffic volume	0.817	–	–	–	6.03	1.22
... I contribute to environmental protection	0.860	–	–	–	5.98	1.20
Availability Concerns (conceptually based on Lamberton and Rose 2012)		0.803	0.811	0.592		
... I think it will be difficult to find people with similar mobility needs and rhythms in my area	0.894	–	–	–	5.05	1.66
... I think it will be difficult to get enough people in my environment enthusiastic about the concept of ridesharing	0.722	–	–	–	4.74	1.76
... The probability is high that a ride is not available when I need it	0.674	–	–	–	5.14	1.42
Ridesharing intention (adapted from Lamberton and Rose 2012)		0.938	0.938	0.835		
... I would intend to take up this offer	0.946	–	–	–	4.43	2.04
... It is likely that I will actually let the other person take me	0.904	–	–	–	4.32	2.01
... I would consider booking such a ridesharing offer	0.891	–	–	–	4.53	2.03

λ Factor loading, α Cronbach's, *AVE* Average variance extracted, *CR* Composite reliability, *M* Mean, *SD* Standard deviation
Note: All items are measured on a 7-point Likert scales anchored at 1 = "does not apply at all" and 7 = "fully applies"

0.057; SRMR = 0.043),[3] as CFI and TLI are higher than 0.95 and RMSEA and SRMR are lower than 0.06 and 0.08, respectively (Hu and Bentler 1999, p. 27).

Structural equation modeling (SEM) is used for analyzing the data. The indices (CFI = 0.989; TLI = 0.982; RMSEA = 0.039; SRMR = 0.037) allocate the overall adequacy of the structural model, since the empirical data fits the hypothesized model (Hu and Bentler 1999, p. 27).

The results show a significant positive influence of perceived environmental benefit on the intention to use ridesharing as a passenger ($\beta = 0.278$, $p < 0.001$), providing support for H1. In line with H2, results reveal a significant negative influence of availability concerns on ridesharing usage intention ($\beta = -0.198$, $p = 0.011$). The living environment of the respondents has a positive influence on availability concerns ($\beta = 0.255$, $p = 0.001$). As a rural living environment is accompanied by stronger availability concerns, this result lends support for H3b. Moreover, H3c can be accepted, as living environment negatively affects ridesharing

---

[3]Comparative Fit Index (CFI), Tucker–Lewis Index (TLI), Root Mean Square Error of Approximation (RMSEA), and Standardized Root Mean Square Residual (SRMR).

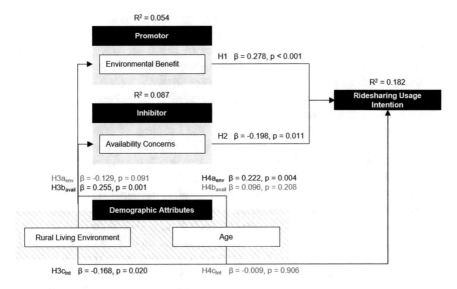

Fig. 4 Conceptual model with empirical results

usage intention, meaning that the ridesharing usage intention is lower of residents living in rural than in urban areas ($\beta = -0.168$, $p = 0.020$). H3a has to be rejected due to a non-significant effect of living environment on the perceived environmental benefit ($\beta = -0.129$, $p = 0.091$). As age is positively related to the perceived environmental benefit ($\beta = 0.222$, $p = 0.004$), this provides support for H4a. Due to non-significant effects of age on availability concerns ($\beta = 0.096$, $p = 0.208$) and on ridesharing usage intention ($\beta = -0.009$, $p = 0.906$), respectively, H4b and H4c are rejected.

Overall, the variables explain 18.2% of the variance of the dependent variable ridesharing usage intention as well as 5.4% and 8.7% of the perceived environmental benefit and availability concerns, respectively. Figure 4 shows the conceptual model and empirical results of the survey.

4.1.4 Discussion of Empirical Results

In line with existing literature, the results of structural equation modeling show a positive effect of perceived environmental benefit on ridesharing usage intention (Chan and Shaheen 2012, p. 96). Accordingly, people considering environmental benefits like mitigating traffic congestions, conserving fuel, and therefore reducing air pollution are more willing to use ridesharing. Moreover, the results also confirm the negative effect of availability concerns on ridesharing usage intention. So, if people are sceptical about getting a suitable amount of ridesharing offers, it lowers their behavioral intention (Amey et al. 2011, p. 107). Especially, people living in rural areas are concerned about the sufficient amount of ridesharing offers and requests ("critical mass"), providing evidence for the hypothesized positive effect of rural living environment on availability concerns.

Although we found no significant effect of the living environment on the perceived environmental benefit, it might be that in rural areas there is also a demand for reducing the traffic volume, but not primarily for sustainability issues as it might be a positive side effect only: people living in rural areas need to travel longer distances for securing their livelihood, leading to demands of reducing or pooling them (e.g. in order to save time). The bundling of trips might also be realized through, e.g. neighbors bringing each other groceries and such. This refers to the social aspect of the "Fahrkreis" app. And this is accompanied by positive environmental effects, which project NEMo intends.

Additionally, our results confirm that a rural living environment negatively affects the ridesharing usage intention. This might be influenced by the overall higher amount of car ownership in rural areas (Follmer and Gruschwitz 2019, p. 6). This and further variables like the urgency of lacking mobility options (e.g. if no car is available) as well as mobility satisfaction in general should be investigated in further research models (e.g. based on our approach or data set). They might consider more aspects, as we did in our illustrative model for the purpose of showing the integration of user data in the decision process of a software agent. Furthermore, the (moderating) influence of sharing affinity and (ride)sharing familiarity in general should be investigated in further research.

In line with our expectations and in accordance with the meta-analysis of Wiernik et al. (2013), the results show that age positively affects perceived environmental benefit. This finding might be explained by a different understanding of sustainable behaviors, especially of sustainable mobility, of people of younger vs. older age. Maybe younger people have a more critical attitude toward the effectiveness of sustainability issues. Regarding the influence of age on availability concerns and on ridesharing usage intention, we found no statistical significance.

To sum it up, the results of this model point out the availability challenge in rural areas. These availability concerns might be reduced through a communication about the approach of ridesharing with dynamic routing algorithm in general. Moreover, when encouraging more people to participate, these concerns decrease in consequence. For reaching these encouragements, incentive systems might be useful as well as communication measures for introducing the app.

4.2 Derivation of Operational Fuzzy Inference System

In this section, we apply the general fuzzy inference template introduced in Sect. 3.1 to the constructs and dependencies of the empirical model determined in Sect. 4.1 to construct a working fuzzy inference system. This fuzzy inference system can then be used for the decision-making of the agents in a simulation scenario on potential ridesharing use. The empirical results can be used to model stage 0 to stage 2 within the general fuzzy inference template. The fuzzification of the input values for living environment and age is stage 0, the relationships between living environment/age and environmental benefit/availability concerns is stage 1, and the relationships between living environment/age/environmental benefit/availability concerns and ridesharing intention is stage 2. The calculation of the utility score from the ridesharing intention follows in stage 3. For the design of this particular fuzzy inference system, we only consider the significant dependencies between the constructs of the empirical model, as indicated by the bold face font of some of the dependency labels in Fig. 4.

For stage 0, the empirical model contains two independent constructs that eventually determine the ridesharing intention: the living environment and the age. Both constructs must therefore be represented as fuzzy linguistic input variables to be used for fuzzification of any actual input value for living environment and age during the simulation. Because the empirical model assumes a linear dependency between all of its related constructs, it is sufficient to define only one linguistic term for each input variable. Moreover, the empirical model is only valid within the scope of its underlying questionnaire data, but input values to the variable could of course exceed the ranges used for the construction of the empirical model. This issue is particularly tangible when looking at possible input values of the age variable. The empirical model is based on the age distribution of all participants, in this case ranging from 16 to 77. People obviously can be younger or older than that, but the empirical model is based on this sample. The range of the living environment was encoded with values 1 (large city with a population of 100.000 or more) to 6 (small hamlet with a population of less than 50). To accommodate potentially smaller or larger input values than those the empirical model is built on, the domain of the input variables is not limited to the given scope. Instead, the functions associated with the linguistic terms have a constant output when outside the explanatory scope of the empirical model. The ruralness of a given living environment encoding x is therefore defined as shown in Eq. (1):

$$\text{rural}(x) = \begin{cases} 0, & x < 1 \\ \dfrac{x}{5} - \dfrac{1}{5}, & 1 \le x \le 6, \\ 1, & x > 6 \end{cases} \tag{1}$$

Accordingly, the oldness of a given age x is defined in Eq. (2):

$$\text{old}(x) = \begin{cases} 0, & x < 16 \\ \dfrac{x}{61} - \dfrac{16}{61}, & 16 \le x \le 77. \\ 1, & x > 77 \end{cases} \tag{2}$$

This way, the degree of membership only changes within the scope of the original empirical model, but the inference system may also handle input values outside this scope.

For stage 1, the relationships between the input variables and the environmental benefit/availability concerns must be modeled. First, both the fuzzy variables for environmental benefit and the availability concerns are defined through two singleton terms each, as mentioned in Sect. 3.1: The terms for both environmental benefit and availability concerns used in this particular inference system are "not existing" with a value of -1 and "existing" with a value of 1. The rule base for stage 1 is then defined as

```
IF livingEnvironment IS rural
THEN availabilityConcerns IS existing WITH 0.255

IF livingEnvironment IS not rural
THEN availabilityConcerns IS notExisting WITH 0.255

IF age IS old
THEN environmentalBenefit IS existing WITH 0.222

IF age IS not old
THEN environmentalBenefit IS notExisting WITH 0.222
```

As mentioned above, only significant dependencies in the empirical model are considered, and the rule base for stage 1 therefore only contains the shown relationships. Each significant relationship is divided into two rules, the first one being the relationship directly shown in the empirical model, and the second one being the inverse of that relationship, where the inverse of the input maps to the inverse of the output. The weights of the rules are based on the β-coefficient denoted along each relationship in Fig. 4. In the empirical model, the β-coefficient between two variables represents the influence strength of an independent variable on its dependent variable. Since the ranges of all fuzzy variables are standardized between 0 and 1, the β-coefficients can be used as multiplicative rule weights for the corresponding fuzzy rules. We therefore use the β-coefficients to calibrate the weight of influence of different relationships within this fuzzy inference system.

For stage 2, the remaining relationships between independent or intermediate constructs and the final ridesharing intention must be modeled. For the fuzzy variable representing the ridesharing intention, we again use the same two singleton terms: the ridesharing intention can be "not existing" (-1) or "existing" (1). The rule base for stage 2 is defined as

```
IF environmentalBenefit IS notExisting
THEN ridesharingIntention IS notExisting WITH 0.278

IF environmentalBenefit IS existing
THEN ridesharingIntention IS existing WITH 0.278

IF availabilityConcerns IS notExisting
THEN ridesharingIntention IS existing WITH 0.198

IF availabilityConcerns IS existing
THEN ridesharingIntention IS notExisting WITH 0.198

IF livingEnvironment IS rural
THEN ridesharingIntention IS notExisting WITH 0.168
```

```
IF livingEnvironment IS not rural
THEN ridesharingIntention IS existing WITH 0.168
```

This rule base again contains only the significant dependencies and is designed in the same way as for stage 1.

For stage 3, the calculation perceived utility of a ridesharing offer is very simple because according to the empirical model, the ridesharing intention is the only major indicator for ridesharing use. The fuzzy variable for the utility again contains two singleton terms that define the range of the utility from bad (-1) to good (1) utility. The rule base for this last stage is also very straight forward:

```
IF ridesharingIntention IS notExisting THEN utility IS bad
IF ridesharingIntention IS existing THEN utility IS good
```

As described in Sect. 3.1, the calculation of the crisp utility score is done using the weighted sum of the utility variable, that is, weighing the degree of activation of each of its terms (bad and good) with their respective weights (-1 for bad and 1 for good).

5   Application to the Simulation Framework

In this section, we showcase the application of the fuzzy inference system designed in Sect. 4.2 within the context of the agent-based simulation framework illustrated in Sect. 3. The purpose of this application is to compare the stated ridesharing intention of the participants of the original study with the behavior of their agentic counterparts within the simulation.

For this application, the simulation framework was connected to the backend system of the mobile app "Fahrkreis" developed during project NEMo. The backend not only integrates routing and public transport information but also offers a ridesharing service for its users. The agents of the simulation are given access to the system through an interface that provides the same mobility options and additional information on the options as the actual mobile app developed in project NEMo.

5.1   Agent Population and Simulation Scenario

We initialized a population of 194 agents for the simulation based on the data set used for the calculation of the original empirical model in Sect. 4.1. Each agent was therefore given the age and approximate living environment of one of the participants in the study. Each of the agents was given a means to conduct private transport. To create mobility needs, the agents have to pursue random activities in nearby municipalities. To ensure that the agents will be offered a ridesharing option for each trip, a second set of dummy agents has been added to the simulation solely to artificially generate and provide ridesharing offers within the connected

"Fahrkreis" backend. This set of dummy agents is of course not considered for the simulation results. Moreover, since we only designed a fuzzy inference system for the calculation of a utility score for ridesharing options but not for private transport, a dummy inference system for the intention toward private transport has been implemented which always immediately defaults to a utility score of 0 for any private transport option.

5.2 Simulation Behavior and Results

During the simulation, each agent decided between using their own means of private transport and accepting one of the ridesharing options provided by the dummy agents through the connected "Fahrkreis" service. Among the agent population, 115 agents decided to use the ridesharing options, while 79 agents decided to use private transport. These numbers can be compared with the original data set, as the stated ridesharing intention of the participants was analyzed through three items in the questionnaire directly, as shown in Table 1. Each of these items was rated on a 7-point Likert scale, and the average of which is used in this comparison. In the original data set, 103 participants have a stated positive ridesharing intention with an average score of 5 or higher, while 54 participants rejected ridesharing with a score of 3 or lower. 37 participants have an average ridesharing intention between 3 and 5 and cannot be classified clearly. When the number of undecided participants is forcefully reduced further by courting any intention above or below a value of 4 toward ridesharing acceptance and rejection, respectively, these numbers change to 120 participants in favor of ridesharing and 61 participants rejecting it. 13 participants remain undecided with a ridesharing intention of exactly 4 on the scale. Overall, the average ridesharing intention of the participants of the study and their corresponding simulated utility correlate statistically significant ($r = 0.242, p = 0.001$).

To compare intention of the participants and behavior of their agent counterparts further, the stated intention and simulated behavior are compared based on the age and living environment of the participants and agent population, respectively. Because the utility score of the fuzzy inference system is calculated on a range from -1 to 1, yet the stated intention is represented on a range from 1 to 7, the utility score is scaled toward the 7-point scale of the stated intention by multiplying the utility with 3 to expand the range and then adding 4 to move the center of the scale.

Figure 5 shows the stated intention and simulated behavior based on the age of the participant, respectively, and agent. Additionally, linear regression lines are shown for both the stated intention and the simulated behavior to illustrate the overall trend in ridesharing throughout the range of age.

It is apparent that the stated intention of the original data set has significantly larger dispersion along the full range of the scale, while the simulated behavior remains within approximately 1 unit of the center of the scale. Yet, the overall change in intention and behavior represented by the regression lines throughout

age vs. intention/behavior

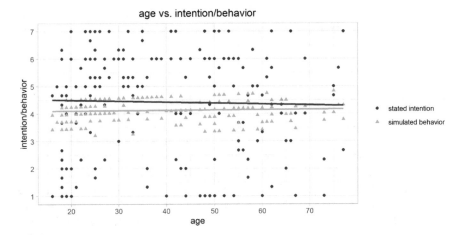

Fig. 5 Stated intention and simulated behavior with regard to age

living environment vs. intention/behavior

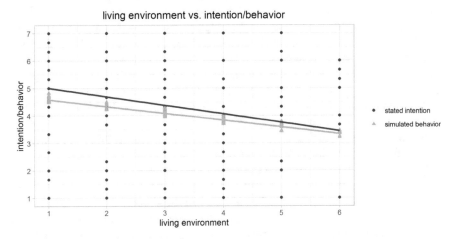

Fig. 6 Stated intention and simulated behavior with regard to living environment

the age range remains relatively steady and is comparatively similar as indicated by their similar slopes and y-intercepts. As the dependency between the independent variable age and the stated ridesharing intention is not significant (cf. Sect. 4.1.3), the regression lines do not have an obvious slope.

Figure 6 again shows intention and behavior, this time, based on the living environment of the participants and agent. Again, linear regression lines are also shown to illustrate the overall trends.

The dispersion in the stated intention is again stronger than in the simulated behavior, but the trends indicated by the regression line are similar, but this time showing a decline in ridesharing with increasing ruralness of the living environment. Opposed to the relationship between age and intention/behavior in Fig. 5, there is a significant dependency between the independent variable living environment and the stated ridesharing intention (Sect. 4.1.3), and the regression lines do have a clearly visible slope.

5.3 Discussion of the Simulation Results

Section 5.2 has shown the results of the execution of the simulation scenario developed in Sect. 5.1 using the empirically developed fuzzy inference system. In order to evaluate the behavior of the agent population of the simulation scenario, its ridesharing intention based on the simulated data vs. the survey data was regressed on age and living environment. A comparison of the resulting regression lines shows only slight differences, indicating a good fit between the survey data and the simulated behavior, improving with increasing age and ruralness of the living environment. The clear difference in dispersion within the empirical data on the one hand and simulated behavior on the other can be explained by the fact that the simulation model is based on already aggregated values through the structural equation modeling approach, thereby reducing the gap within the original data set.

Similarly, the slight difference between the two regression lines also originates from the circumstance that the simulated behavior is based on the complete empirical model containing not only the ridesharing intention itself but also the variables and constructs influencing the intention indirectly. In a sense, the full empirical model underestimates the ridesharing intention compared to the items concerning only ridesharing intention directly. Also, the more detailed comparisons of the study data and the simulated behavior in both Figs. 5 and 6 regard only one independent variable at a time, not the entire model at once.

Moreover, the evaluation only relates to the fit between the survey data and the simulated behavior of the agents. The fit between the simulated behavior/forecasts and reality will most likely be lower, as the simulation scenario used for the evaluation represented the best-case situation of perfect and limitless availability of ridesharing options for all agents.

Furthermore, the overall explanatory power of the analyzed empirical model is rather low, as the (reduced set of) analyzed influence factors and attributes only explain 18.2% of the variance of ridesharing intention. The evaluation in this contribution therefore only addresses the fit between the empirical results and their application in the simulation.

Additionally, the simulated 194 agents represent only a small fraction of the Wesermarsch population. Due to the method of an online survey, only people with internet access participated in the online survey, but as the app "Fahrkreis" focuses on technology-enabled ridesharing, this kind of self-selection bias should not have severe effects.

On a general note, it should be remembered that a model is only a simplification of reality (Stachowiak 1973, p. 132) and that not every factor or a combination of factors influencing the mobility behavior is precisely measurable and subsequently correctly simulatable, inevitably leading to imperfect simulation behavior. For example, the SEM approach taken in this contribution assumes linear dependencies and relationships between all considered variables. This of course is a simplification of reality for the sake of a manageable model with its complexity reduced to the prominent features.

6 Conclusion

This contribution has illustrated our approach of developing an empirically grounded fuzzy inference system for application as the decision-making component in an agent-based mobility simulation. Based on our simplified application example, the approach seems to be a promising general method to obtain empirical information on intended behavior regarding mobility options. Therefore, the development of a more complex inference system based on a larger empirical model with more explanatory power seems to be a promising way of developing a meaningful decision component for the simulation framework shown in this contribution.

Simulation systems and models like the one presented in this contribution are useful for e.g. policy makers that are concerned with developing and improving the traffic systems and overall mobility situations. For example, such ex ante simulations may be useful to evaluate whether a specific proposed solution to mobility issues does in fact reach the target audience or to estimate the required critical mass of users for a successful ridesharing service. Of course, the quality of such simulations is significantly improved by considering local peculiarities in the design of the studies used to derive the simulation models.

Further studies leading to such better models might include additional factors influencing ridesharing intention or contain further items regarding not only ridesharing but also other, potentially competing means of transport such as walking, (e-)bikes, car, or public transportation.

Moreover, results of the passenger's perspective might be contrasted to a driver's perspective regarding ridesharing. By integrating findings from the driver's perspective, the "dummy agents," which were implemented in our passenger-focused simulation to generate the ridesharing suppliers, can be foregone in favor of more complex agents that not only consume ridesharing offers but also provide them. This could potentially increase the dynamics and interplay during the simulation, as agents can dynamically participate in ridesharing as either driver or passenger, provided that a car is available for the agent.

Furthermore, the approach shown in this contribution might be extended to additional data sources such as representative census data or qualitative travel diary data, as done by some of the simulation systems shown in Sect. 2. Based on this mixed-methods approach, forecasts of the synthesized agent population might be even more valid.

References

Agatz, N. A. H., Erera, A. L., Savelsbergh, M. W. P., & Wang, X. (2011). Dynamic ride-sharing: A simulation study in Metro Atlanta. *Procedia Social and Behavioral Sciences, 17*, 532–550.

Amey, A., Attanucci, J., & Mishalani, R. (2011). Real-time ridesharing: Opportunities and challenges in using mobile phone technology to improve rideshare services. *Transportation Research Record: Journal of the Transportation Research Board, 2217*(1), 103–110.

Arentze, T. A., Hofman, F., Joh, C. H., & Timmermans, H. J. P. (1999). The development of ALBATROSS: Some key issues. In W. Brilon, F. Huber, M. Schreckenberg, & H. Wallentowitz (Eds.), *Traffic and Mobility* (pp. 57–72). Berlin: Springer.

Arentze, T. A., & Timmermans, H. J. P. (2004). ALBATROSS—a learning-based transportation oriented simulation system. *Transportation Research Part B: Methodological, 38*(7), 613–633.

Balmer, M., Meister, K., Rieser, M., Nagel, K., & Axhausen, K. W. (2008). Agent-based simulation of travel demand: Structure and computational performance of MatSIM-T. In *Second TRB Conference on Innovations in Travel Modeling*.

Banks, J., Carson, J. S., II, Nelson, B. L., & Nicol, D. M. (2005). *Discrete-Event System Simulation* (4th ed.). Englewood Cliffs: Prentice-Hall.

Bellemans, T., Kochan, B., Janssens, D., Wets, G., Arentze, T. A., & Timmermans, H. J. P. (2010). Implementation framework and development trajectory of FEATHERS activity-based simulation platform. *Transportation Research Record, 2175*(1), 111–119.

Bowman, J. L., & Ben-Akiva, M. E. (2000). Activity-based disaggregate travel demand model system with activity schedules. *Transportation Research Part A: Policy and Practice, 35*, 1–28.

Brereton, F., Bullock, C., Clinch, J. P., & Scott, M. (2011). Rural change and individual well-being: The case of Ireland and rural quality of life. *European Urban and Regional Studies, 18*(2), 203–227.

Bundesinstitut für Bau-, Stadt- und Raumforschung. (2015). *Laufende Stadtbeobachtung – Raumabgrenzungen: Stadt- und Gemeindetypen in Deutschland. [Ongoing city observation – spatial demarcations: Types of cities and communities in Germany.]*. Retrieved November 18, 2020 from https://www.bbsr.bund.de/BBSR/DE/forschung/raumbeobachtung/Raumabgrenzungen/deutschland/gemeinden/StadtGemeindetyp/StadtGemeindetyp.html

Cascetta, E. (2009). *Transportation Systems Analysis* (2nd ed.). Berlin: Springer.

Chan, N. D., & Shaheen, S. A. (2012). Ridesharing in North America: Past, present, and future. *Transport Reviews, 32*(1), 93–112.

Dählmann, K., Samland, U., & Sauer, J. (2019). Developing fuzzy inference systems from qualitative interviews for travel mode choice in an agent-based mobility simulation. In C. Benzmüller, & H. Stuckenschmidt (Eds.) *KI 2019: Advances in Artificial Intelligence* (pp. 146–153). Berlin: Springer.

Dählmann, K., & Sauer, J. (2018). A hybrid fuzzy controller for human-like decision making in modal choice situations. In H.-J. Bungartz, D. Kranzlmüller, V. Weinberg, J. Weismüller, & V. Wohlgemuth (Eds.), *Adjunct Proceedings of the 32nd EnviroInfo Conference* (pp. 281–286).

Dählmann, K., & Sauer, J. (2019). Towards an integrated agent and environment architecture for simulation of human decision making and behavior. In: J. Marx Gómez, A. Solsbach, T. Klenke, V. & Wohlgemuth (Eds.), *Smart Cities/Smart Regions – Technische, wirtschaftliche und gesellschaftliche Innovationen* (pp. 241–255). Springer Vieweg.

Deakin, E., Trapenberg Frick, K., & Shively, K. M. (2010). Markets for dynamic Ridesharing? Case of Berkeley, California. *Transportation Research Record: Journal of the Transportation Research Board, 2187*, 131–137.

Follmer, R., & Gruschwitz, D. (2019). *Mobilität in Deutschland - MiD Kurzreport. Studie von infas, DLR, IVT und infas 360 im Auftrag des Bundesministers für Verkehr und digitale Infrastruktur (FE-Nr. 70.904/15)*. Bonn, Berlin. Retrieved November 4, 2020 from http://www.mobilitaet-in-deutschland.de/pdf/infas_Mobilitaet_in_Deutschland_2017_Kurzreport.pdf

Furuhata, M., Dessouky, M., Ordóñez, F., Brunet, M.-E., Wang, X., & Koenig, S. (2013). Ridesharing: The state-of-the-art and future directions. *Transportation Research Part B, 57*, 28–46.

Hamari, J., Sjöklint, M., & Ukkonen, A. (2016). The sharing economy: Why people participate in collaborative consumption. *Journal of the Association for Information Science and Technology, 67*(9), 2047–2059.

Heinrichs, M., Krajzewicz, D., Cyganski, R., & von Schmidt, A. (2016). Disaggregated car fleets in microscope travel demand modelling. *Procedia Computer Science, 83*, 155–162.

Heinrichs, M., Krajzewicz, D., Cyganski, R., & von Schmidt, A. (2017). Introduction of car sharing into existing car fleets in microscopic travel demand modelling. *Personal and Ubiquitous Computing, 21*, 1055–1065.

Holz-Rau, C. (2009). Mobilität und Erreichbarkeit – (Infra)Strukturen umgestalten? [Mobility and Accessibility – Transforming (Infra)Structures?]. *Informationen zur Raumentwicklung* Heft 12/2009 (pp. 797–804)

Hu, L., & Bentler, P. M. (1999). Cutoff criteria for fit indexes in covariance structure analysis: Conventional criteria versus new alternatives. *Structural Equation Modeling: A Multidisciplinary Journal, 6*(1), 1–55.

Jahns, M., & Woisetschläger, D. M. (2017). *Wesermarsch-Umfrage – Ergebnisse der Online-Umfrage in der Region Wesermarsch im Rahmen des Projektes NEMo "Nachhaltige Erfüllung von Mobilitätsbedürfnissen im ländlichen Raum" [Wesermarsch survey – Results of the online survey in the Wesermarsch region as part of the NEMo project "Sustainable fulfilment of mobility needs in rural areas".].* Retrieved November 4, 2020 from https://nemo.informatik.uni-oldenburg.de/blog/wp-content/uploads/2017/08/2017-08-10_Auswertung_Wesermarschumfrage_kurz.pdf

Janssens, D., Wets, G., Brijs, T., Vanhoof, K., Arentze, T. A., & Timmermans, H. J. P. (2004). Improving performance of multiagent rule-based model for activity pattern decisions with Bayesian networks. *Transportation Research Record, 1894*, 75–83.

Janssens, D., Wets, G., Brijs, T., Vanhoof, K., Arentze, T. A., & Timmermans, H. J. P. (2006). Integrating Bayesian networks and decision trees in a sequential rule-based transportation model. *European Journal of Operational Research, 175*(1), 16–34.

Janzen, M., & Axhausen, K. W. (2018). Decision making in an agent-based simulation of long-distance travel demand. *Procedia Computer Science, 130*, 830–835.

Lamberton, C. P., & Rose, R. L. (2012). When is ours better than mine? A framework for understanding and altering participation in commercial sharing systems. *Journal of Marketing, 76*, 109–125.

Maretzke, S. (2016). Demografischer Wandel im ländlichen Raum. So vielfältig wie der Raum, so verschieden die Entwicklung. [Demographic change in rural areas. Development is as diverse as these areas itself.]. *Informationen zur Raumentwicklung* Heft 2/2016 (pp. 169–187)

Märki, F., Charypar, D., & Axhausen, K. W. (2014). Agent-based model for continuous activity planning with an open planning horizon. *Transportation, 41*, 905–922.

Meurer, J., Stein, M., Randall, D., Rohde, M., & Wulf, V. (2014). Social dependency and mobile autonomy—supporting older adults' mobility with ridesharing ICT. In *CHI 2014 Proceedings of the SIGCHI Conference on Human Factors in Computing Systems* (pp. 1923–1932).

Muthén, L. K., & Muthén, B. O. (2012). *Mplus User's Guide.* Retrieved November 4, 2020 from www.statmodel.com

Ortúzar, J. D. D., & Willumsen, L. G. (2011). *Modelling Transport* (4th ed.). London: Wiley.

Pieper, N., Jahns, M., & Woisetschläger, D. M. (2017). 'Getting the hitchhiking ball rolling on rural areas'—drivers and barriers of peer-to-peer ridesharing usage intention. In: B. Otjacques, P. Hitzelberger, S. Naumann, V. Wohlgemuth (Eds.), *From Science to Society—the Bridge Provided by Environmental Informatics* (pp. 267–274). Aachen: Shaker Verlag.

Riesner, A. (2014). Bedeutung und Förderung von Mobilität in ländlichen Räumen. [Importance and promotion of mobility in rural areas.] *Zeitschrift für Geodäsie, Geoinformation und Landmanagement (zfv)* 139 (pp. 41–49).

Roorda, M. J., Miller, E. J., & Nurul Habib, K. M. (2006). Assessing transportation policy using an activity based microsimulation model of travel demand. In *33rd Annual Conference of the Canadian Society for Civil Engineering 2005: Gateway To Excellence* (pp. 3518–3527).

Stachowiak, H. (1973). *Allgemeine Modelltheorie [General Model Theory]*. Wien: Springer.

Steinrück, B., & Küpper, P. (2010). Mobilität in ländlichen Räumen unter besonderer Berücksichtigung bedarfsgesteuerter Bedienformen des ÖPNV. [Mobility in rural areas with special consideration of demand-driven forms of public transport]. *Arbeitsberichte aus dem vTI-Agrarökonomie* Heft 02/2010, Johann Heinrich von Thünen-Institut, Braunschweig. Retrieved November 4, 2020 from https://literatur.thuenen.de/digbib_extern/bitv/dk043302.pdf.

Sugeno, M. (1985). *Industrial applications of fuzzy control*. Amsterdam: Elsevier.

Train, K. E. (2003). *Discrete choice methods with simulation*. Cambridge: Cambridge University Press.

Umweltbundesamt (Eds.) (2009). *Feinstaubbelastung in Deutschland [Fine dust pollution in Germany]*. Retrieved November 4, 2020 from https://www.umweltbundesamt.de/sites/default/files/medien/publikation/long/3565.pdf

Wiernik, B. M., Ones, D. S., & Dilchert, S. (2013). Age and environmental sustainability: A meta-analysis. *Journal of Managerial Psychology, 28*(7/8), 826–856.

Winkel, R. (2008). Öffentliche Infrastrukturversorgung im Planungsparadigmenwandel [Public infrastructure supply in the change of planning paradigm]. *Informationen zur Raumentwicklung* Heft 1/2.2008 (pp. 41–47)

Wooldridge, M. (2009). *An introduction to multiagent systems*. London: Wiley.

Wooldridge, M. (2013). Intelligent Agents. In G. Weiss (Ed.), *Multiagent Systems* (pp. 3–50). Cambridge: MIT Press.

Part III
Business Models and Applications

Using an Imovative Approach for the Structural Support of Business Idea Generation

Ali Akyol and Jantje Halberstadt

Abstract One of the biggest challenges in lives of citizens in rural areas is the lack of mobility services. Citizens in rural areas are dependent on their own car to drive to work or to reach their daily accomplishments. To enhance the mobility in rural areas, new mobility services and new sustainable business models are needed. In this article we, therefore, introduce a process model that supports a structured generation of business ideas by integrating imitational and innovational aspects into a so-called imovational approach. We applied this model to the context of project NEMo and show how to derive new and sustainable ideas for mobility services.

Keywords Business model generation · Imovative mobility services · Carpooling

1 Introduction

Generating innovative and sustainable business ideas is considered a crucial precondition for developing successful business models and a key source of competitive advantage (Eppler et al. 2011; Mitchell and Coles 2003, 2004). At the same time, it is one of the most challenging tasks, as it involves the complex interplay of a variety of factors, such as the appropriate integration of knowledge and experiences in different fields, awareness of challenges as a basis for business opportunities, team cooperation, and creativity (Chesbrough 2006; Briggs et al. 2003; Garfield et al. 2001; Fay et al. 2006). Although some business ideas might seem to simply magically appear to entrepreneurs in a lucky moment, most successes are, at least to some point, the result of a searching process. Thus, more studies are focusing on the factors influencing entrepreneurial opportunity recognition as well as if and how successful idea generation processes can be adapted (Zahra et al. 2005; George et al. 2016). Several approaches have already been suggested in the academic literature

A. Akyol (✉) · J. Halberstadt
University of Vechta, Vechta, Germany
e-mail: ali.akyol@uni-vechta.de; jantje.halberstadt@uni-vechta.de

© The Author(s), under exclusive license to Springer Nature Switzerland AG 2021   81
J. Marx Gómez et al. (eds.), *Progress in Sustainable Mobility Research*,
Progress in IS, https://doi.org/10.1007/978-3-030-70841-2_5

as well as in the start-up and/or management consulting areas (Bereznoy 2018; Karimi et al. 2016; Bocken et al. 2015; Hawkins 1999; Gordijn and Akkermans 2001). However, most of the existing work focuses on creating innovation without strategically including imitation. Undoubtedly, when restricting the term to the stealing of product or service innovations, the imitation of an idea commonly has a negative connotation (Jacobs et al. 2001). Nonetheless, having a closer look at successful businesses can offer inspiration during the idea generation process. The wheel must not be repeatedly reinvented. Existing successful approaches can be further developed or transferred to other settings, for example, other markets with specific requirements. This should hold specifically true in the field of sustainability entrepreneurship, where the core aim is not to maximize profits but to generate ecological and/or social impact through entrepreneurial activities (Kraus et al. 2017; Spiegler and Halberstadt 2018). Thus, sustainability entrepreneurs themselves must have an interest in spreading successful solutions. This is why we suggest a process integrating imitational and innovational aspects into a so-called imovational approach in the early idea generation phase and not only in the business model development, where the analysis of possible competitors comes into play (Osterwalder et al. 2011). Underlining that using a methodical process cannot guarantee success, we will show that it can offer reasonable support for generating business ideas, especially under given circumstances. Underlining that using a methodical process cannot guarantee success, we will show that it can offer reasonable support for generating business ideas, especially under given circumstances as we find them in projects like in the NEMo[1] context.

In the following, we introduce our business idea generation process based on the relevant specifics of project NEMo and environment. We start with a brief summary of the initial situation, followed by the introduction of the three main steps we use for business idea generation. For each step, we explain the general procedure and then focus on providing examples of how we applied it in the project. The article ends with a discussion including guidelines for the next steps as well as the possibilities of strategically including citizens in the process. In addition to sharing the insights from project NEMo in this anthology, we would also like to motivate others to use and evaluate the suggested model in additional settings.

2   Developing Business Ideas Using a Three-Step Approach

In the following, we will introduce the structural approach that assisted us when generating business ideas. Subsequently, we show how we applied it to project NEMo.

---

[1] https://nemo-mobilitaet.de.

2.1 Step 1: State of the Art: Situation Analysis

To capture the entrepreneurial potential of a certain situation, it can be helpful to systematically analyze the current conditions. We divide our analysis into six sections that will be described below.

Main Actors/Stakeholders As we start from a project perspective with a given team and several stakeholders involved, we firstly ask: "Who is involved?" Starting with the founder (team) or the core team of project members mainly involved in the idea generation process, various information is collected, for example, on the number and characteristics of the people being identified as the core team as well as a brief analysis of their relevant strengths and weaknesses. In addition, interconnections, as well as frequent interactions, are identified. In the next step, other stakeholders possibly influencing the idea or future businesses are selected, who can complement the process or act as possible (future) partners. Being aware of the people involved is specifically important for three reasons. First, it is necessary to delineate common goals. Second, having information on the team and stakeholders allows identifying available resources that can be used for future business (development processes). Third, it ensures that actual and future roles can be defined from the beginning, which avoids problems in the workflow.

Common Goal Next, the core team must agree on its main targets. Is there a certain topic of interest? Is the planned entrepreneurial activity meant to solve a societal problem or to focus on maximizing profit (sustainability entrepreneurship or business entrepreneurship)? Are you developing ideas for yourself or for others (consultant/supportive entrepreneur, first-step entrepreneur, or managing entrepreneur)? What are the overall motivations underlying the desire to become an entrepreneur? What are the expectations of third parties asking you to develop business ideas? Based on this information, common goals should be derived, leading to a core vision.

Available Resources Based on the team and stakeholder analysis, the available resources can be allocated to support a certain direction of idea development as well as the idea and future business itself. The available resources include material resources, such as available space or production factors, as well as immaterial resources, such as patents, time, networks, or knowledge.

Environment/Setting After the structured analysis of the people involved, the goal, and the available resources, the current environment must be examined. A variety of environmental factors might influence the idea development as well as the future business. Therefore, a careful analysis of these factors helps recognizing business opportunities. This includes obtaining detailed information, for example, on (1) the country and/or region; (2) the respective legal conditions regarding the common goal or possible business activities in general; (3) the economic surroundings; (4) social conditions, such as societal norms and values; (5) geographical and logistical circumstances; (6) digital supplies like access to proper WiFi; and, (7) other supportive or challenging factors. Based on this information, one can draw a picture of all the specific characteristics and requirements of the current situation.

Problem Analysis/Customer Needs   Finally, certain problems that can be addressed with entrepreneurial activity can be identified based on the information collected so far. It includes delineating potential customer needs to address with business solutions. Although our experience shows that the ideas collected at this stage are often substantially reworked in the following process, they can be seen as the first step toward the final concrete business idea. However, this is a crucial point where, depending on the idea direction, it might be helpful to return to the setting again and conduct an additional analysis of a certain area of interest.

2.2   Step 2: Imitation

In the next step, we systematically analyze matching markets and identify business cases with imitative potential that might either function as role models that inspire the creative process in general or deliver approaches that can be applied to the current situation.

Definition of Relevant Markets   Based on analysis of the situation, markets or market branches can be identified that might deliver solutions for the problems or customer needs defined in step 1. If sufficient approaches already exist, one can investigate why these still do not solve the identified problem or why customers do not adopt them. These approaches might have the potential to be improved in some way. However, they may also lead to the realization that the defined problem or customer need might have to be reworked, which means returning to step 1. More likely, similar markets might have business cases that can be applied to the current situation or international research might lead to ideas that have not yet been applied in a national or regional setting. Nonetheless, in this step, one or several markets with imitative potential must be defined, which can be global as well as niche markets.

Selection of Suitable Business Cases   To analyze the product and/or service in more depth, suitable business cases have to be selected from the market(s) being defined. It is recommended that a list of selection criteria is prepared to support the selection procedure. These criteria can be derived from the conditions determined in step 1 since those that best fit one's own goals obviously have greater imitative potential. As an additional criterion, the most successful businesses might be selected. With regard to the variety of success measures and the related discussion of advantages and disadvantages (Sandau et al. 2018), we recommend a pragmatic approach that includes information that is easily available. Since it is a preselective step in a practice-oriented research process, it is also sufficient to include non-academic literature, for example, global player or market leader lists, or online statistics and traffic data, when matching empirical data is not available. In addition to the success criterion, it is important to select cases with as much information as possible.

Analysis of Selected Cases   The selected cases have to be analyzed. This analysis focuses on both the designed product/service and the underlying revenue and business models. For this step, a variety of academic and non-academic literature, tools, and techniques in the area of competitor analysis can be used (Bergen and Peteraf 2002; Hatzijordanou et al. 2019; Griffiths et al. 2019). Some of the most mentioned points, however, are (1) product/service analysis (including marketing strategy, e.g., pricing and distribution as well as production factors), (2) target customer analysis (including unique value-added and competitive advantage), (3) revenue model (including direct as well as indirect income approaches), (4) support structure (including private and professional networks as well as strategic partnerships), and (5) finances (including cost structures as well as investments, funding, etc.).

Evaluation of Results   After collecting relevant information on the selected cases through a structured analysis, the results have to be carefully evaluated. On the one hand, the positive aspects should be identified to underline the direct imitative potential (best-practice cases). On the other hand, negative aspects, such as experiences shared on what went wrong or information on challenges faced, can also be useful so as to avoid the same or similar mistakes, or even to derive an improved and further developed idea from lessons learned and current challenges.

Selection of Possible Role Model Solution(s)   Based on the results, role model solutions and respective information must be selected from the data with regard to the common goal defined in step 1, the related problems to be solved, and/or the future target group. The questions to be asked here are as follows: *How can an identified product, service, or approach be used to solve your problems? In which products or services would your future customers be interested? What can you learn from a specific business or revenue model? Are there any good market entry and/or marketing strategies that can be used? Did you find interesting partnerships or networks that can be useful in your situation? Can an approach be fruitfully combined with others?*

2.3   Step 3: Innovation

In the last step, the results of steps 1 and 2 are to be used to create innovative ideas. The innovation phase starts with two parallel steps because ideas based on the selected role-model businesses can be generated based on two different perspectives both closely related to creativity. Their purpose is to further develop existing approaches and/or develop new solutions based on the knowledge generated in the previous steps.

Creative Adaption to Current Settings   One way of generating new ideas is reworking existing business models. By selecting certain role-model solutions and systematically tailoring them to the problem at hand and/or the identified customer needs, a new product, service, or business approach emerges. Innovation might be inspired by considering certain environmental specifics, such as legal or geographical requirements, as well as specific customer needs. However, this is a combination of imitation and innovation, so we speak of an imovative procedure in this case.

Creative Development of New Solutions   Another way of generating new ideas is by being inspired by role models. Having knowledge of a variety of entrepreneurial approaches related to certain aims can lead to a different perspective when applying creative methods for business idea generation. Parallel to further developing existing business ideas, we also suggest generating new ideas based on the information that has been collected. Although we can refer to various creative methods (Luther 2020) that can be used here, the key element is that when information on relevant or related business cases was provided beforehand, it allowed us to use different parts of our minds. Therefore, one should let the cases inspire him or her.

Creation of Value-added for Future Customers   When coming up with a new business idea—no matter if generated during an inspirational or imovative process—it is always important to tailor a product/service toward customers' needs. Even the brightest innovation is worthless if no one is willing to use the resulting product or service. Studies show that even if a new product or service is objectively a better solution, people might not adopt it due to, for example, a lack of trust or habituation leading to lock-in effects, where people restrict themselves to something they are used to (Barnes et al. 2004; Stack et al. 2016). Thus, we propose constantly paying attention to the customer's, users', and, in case of sustainability entrepreneurship, beneficiaries' perspective. At this stage, when defining concrete entrepreneurial ideas for the first time, it is essential to double-check their relevance for and fit to future consumers. There are, again, various options in the area of market research that can support this phase, for example, conducting interviews or experiments and market tests, market sensing, or co-creation approaches (Dahan et al. 2010; Prahalad and Ramaswamy 2004; Wilson and Laskey 2003; Youn and Vogel 2017; Hancock and Longbottom 2016). Early development of prototypes, which can be shown to potential customers, however, is strongly recommended. Integrate future users as soon and as intensively as possible and do not abandon them while further developing an idea.

Business Model Development   After finding an interesting and suitable business idea, one should develop it further into a full business model. Although several components of a business model have already played a role in the idea generation process, they have not been completely considered and defined yet. The business model canvas suggested by Osterwalder et al. (2011) has been shown to be a useful framework for building and reworking a business model (Lima and Baudier 2017; Blank 2013; Franco-Santos 2016). Although this structure was initially developed for profit-oriented entrepreneurial activity, it can be easily adopted in other settings, such as socially and/or ecologically focused businesses, where different priorities have to be considered and where different target groups (such as beneficiaries and customers) must be addressed (Qastharin 2016).

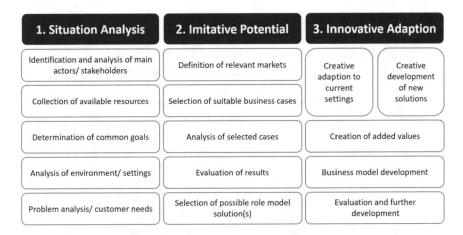

Fig. 1 Imovative idea generation process

Implementation, Evaluation, and Further Development   Finally, the products or services can be brought to the market. Although the focus in this framework is on idea generation, we included the business model development and the implementation so as to capture the entire process. In addition, we follow the lean start-up approach (Ries 2011; Eisenmann et al. 2012), underlining that it is important to avoid endless loops of trying to perfect a business model. Some entrepreneurs with great ideas spend months or even years reworking their product or business model before bringing it to the market and lose valuable time. Thus, we propose implementing the idea as soon as possible, integrating customers as soon as possible, and testing the product according to validated learning. This can be referred to as the so-called build–measure–learn loop, where start-up activity is described as turning ideas into products, measuring how the target group reacts and then learning whether to pivot or persevere (Eisenmann et al. 2012; Bosch et al. 2013; Trimi and Berbegal-Mirabent 2012).

Figure 1 summarizes the developed process.

3   Applying the Approach to the NEMo Context

This section is divided into three parts. In the first part, a situation analysis is carried out. This is followed by the section on identifying imitation potential and the section of applying the results of the analysis to innovative business ideas.

3.1   Situation Analysis

As part of the NEMo team, the working group at the University of Vechta focuses on the development of sustainable business ideas for the project region of Wesermarsch and Oldenburg. Both business models that directly influence mobility, such as car sharing or advances in transport systems, and those with indirect implications for mobility, such as task- or product-sharing in merging communities, are worth considering. However, the main focus is on infrastructure and mobility services. Due to the prominent information and communication technology (ICT) expertise of the NEMo team, we were to specifically focus on innovative ways of improving mobility in rural areas using current technological progress. The activities in project NEMo are, thus, centered around a mobility platform that can include and combine a variety of entrepreneurial solutions. The core team assigned to the development of the business was the team at the University of Vechta together with colleagues from the University of Oldenburg. In addition, researchers from additional disciplines were involved, for example, experts in law and sociology. The core team consisted of two to five people whereas the entire NEMo team included nine professors and 10 junior researchers with a variety of characteristics and competencies. As the majority of team members were from the IT field, we centered our activities on developing a community platform with various solutions, with direct as well as indirect effects, for transport and mobility in rural areas, as explained in the introduction. Therefore, the working group on business development interacted with various teams with expertise in different areas of ICT. In addition, the working groups on "law," "service management," and "social theory" also assisted with their specific competencies. Finally, we worked closely together with stakeholders from politics, companies, and involved citizens. Currently, mobility is one of the basic needs of citizens. Due to demographic changes and the inadequate infrastructure in rural areas, this need often remains unmet in these areas (ADAC 2019). Citizens in rural areas are dependent on their cars. If a person in this group does not own a car due to health or financial reasons, he or she will become dependent. The mobility innovation concepts to be developed should, therefore, counteract the dependence associated with driving one's own car and creating alternatives. As NEMo stands for "sustainable fulfillment of mobility needs in rural areas," the common goal was to develop business ideas that contribute to improving mobility in rural areas in a sustainable way. This means that economic, ecological, and social factors had to be simultaneously taken into account with regard to the transport-related solutions. In our case, the analysis of the concrete setting concentrated on the model regions "Wesermarsch" and the "district of Oldenburg". In the context of project NEMo, the analysis of the setting and certain regional areas was conducted with a specific focus on discovering weaknesses in existing mobility and potentials for improving mobility. The setting analysis considered multidimensional information, with five clusters being specifically relevant: area, population and population density, public

Table 1 Total area, population, and population density

City/region	Total area km^2	Number of inhabitants	Population density (inhabitants per km^2)
City of Oldenburg	102.99	163,830	1509.74
Rural area of Oldenburg	1063.00	127,000	119.47
District of Wesermarsch	822.01	89,239	108.56

transport, car usage, distribution and reachability of points of interest,[2] and citizen needs. In the following, we summarize the core findings.

3.1.1 Total Area, Population, and Population Density

The district of Wesermarsch has a total area of 822.01 km^2 and a population of 89,239. This corresponds to a population density of 108.56 inhabitants per square meter (Landesamt für Statistik Niedersachsen 2017). In addition, the rural region of Oldenburg is also part of the model government although the city of Oldenburg is not included. The administrative district of Oldenburg consists of 15 municipalities and a total area of 1.063 km^2. A total of 127,000 inhabitants live in its 15 municipalities and the population density is 119.47 inhabitants per square meter (Landkreis Oldenburg 2016). The city of Oldenburg has a total area of 102.99 km^2 and a population of 163,830 with a population density of 1509.74 inhabitants per square meter.

As shown in Table 1, the population density in the rural regions, the rural area of Oldenburg, and the district of Wesermarsch are significantly lower than that of the city of Oldenburg.

3.1.2 Public Transport Connections

Public transport can be defined as the transport of persons by vehicles traveling on the road, rail, and waterway networks (Peters 2005). As there is no ship traffic in the model region, this is not considered in the analysis. In the municipality of Wesermarsch, public transport operations are covered by VBN (Verkehrsverbund Bremen/Niedersachsen) and VWB (Verkehrsbetrieb Wesermarsch GmbH). Although Wesermarsch consists of nine municipalities, only four municipalities (Berne, Brake, Elsfleth, and Nordenham) are served every hour by VBN's regional train RS4 (NordWestBahn 2020). In addition, there are ten bus lines, six of which are not served during school hours. The partner company of VBN, VBW, operates sixteen bus lines, nine of which also do not operate during school hours. The minimum time between two departures is 30 minutes whereas most bus stops are

---

[2]We will use grocery stores as example points of interest in Sect. 3.1.4.

required to provide service every 60 min. During school hours, service is provided by 26 bus lines operated by VBN and VWG. During school holidays, however, service is only provided by 11 bus lines.

In the city of Oldenburg, public transport is clearly better developed. VBN covers public transport with four regional trains and one IC (intercity). Within Oldenburg, there are two stops for the trains. The first one is the main station, and the second is the station in Wechloy Oldenburg. There are 18 bus lines in Oldenburg, offered by VBN, and run from the Oldenburg central station to the districts of Ammerland, Oldenburg, and Wesermarsch (VBN 2020). The station in Oldenburg Wechloy, which has been in operation since December 2014, enables students to reach Oldenburg University more quickly (Eilers 2014). In addition to VBN, public transport is also offered by VWG (Verkehr und Wasser GmbH). In Oldenburg, more than 18 lines cover 750 stops in a period of 15–60 min (VWG 2020). Because some stops are served by more than one line, the waiting time at some stops is reduced to considerably less than 15 min. Lappan in Oldenburg is the central bus stop, which is served by all 18 bus lines. This ensures that passengers can change buses at Lappan to travel in all directions.

3.1.3   Car Usage

The first to be analyzed is the city of Oldenburg, where 163,830 inhabitants lived in 2015, 84.5% of whom are over 18. In total, this is about 138,436 persons who are potentially entitled to own a passenger car. The Next step is to remove 97% of the inhabitants older than 65 years (21%). The result is to calculate from 163,830 all citizens in legal age plus the 3 % of citizens older than 65 years. The results are from 163,830 citizens 105,064 could have a driving license (Statista 2020).

At that time, 94,640 cars were registered, excluding commercial cars, mobile homes, and ambulances (Landesamt für Statistik Niedersachsen 2020a). Thus, it is calculated that approx. 90 vehicles are registered per 100 inhabitants. Since not every person in a household needs their own vehicle, it can be generally stated that most households own at least one car.

In the district of Oldenburg, where the population density was lower, about 127,000 inhabitants lived in 2015. The proportion of people who reached the age of 18 was 83.6% (106,172) (Landesamt für Statistik Niedersachsen 2020a). The same calculation brings the following results. The results are from 127,000 citizens 80302 could have a driving license.

In the same year, 96,938 cars were registered in the district of Oldenburg (Landesamt für Statistik Niedersachsen 2020b). As a result, there are approx. 121 registered vehicles per 100 inhabitants.

In the district Wesermarsch, lived in the year 2015 about 89,239 inhabitants, of which the share of persons who were of age was 83.6% (Landesamt für Statistik Niedersachsen 2020a,b). With 62,577 vehicles registered in 2015, around 83 vehicles were registered per 100 inhabitants in the Wesermarsch district. The

Table 2 Overview of registered vehicles per 100 inhabitants

City/region	Total area km^2	Total inh.	Inh. legal age	3% of >65 y.o.	Legal age and 3% of >65 y.o.	Reg. Cars	Cars per 100 inh.
Oldenburg	102,9	163,830	138,436	1032	105,064	94,640	90
District of Oldenburg	1.06300	127,000	106,172	800	80,302	96,938	121
Wesermarsch County	822,01	89,239	74,604	562	56,426	62,577	111

calculations show that more than 111 cars are registered per 100 inhabitants. Table 2 summarizes these numbers.

3.1.4 Distribution and Reachability of Points of Interest: The Case of Grocery Stores

One way to achieve the project's goal of improved mobility is to improve the accessibility of the local supply of products and services. Thus, we analyzed various places that people frequently visit in our model region. These points of interest were connected to health care (doctors, pharmacies, and hospitals), childcare and education (kindergartens, schools, and universities), work (main companies and industrial areas), and daily care (shops and supermarkets). Here, the important information we gathered was on the distribution of the respective points of interest and their accessibility. To ensure an accessible local supply of products and services, the distance from a citizen's place of residence to a point of interest should not exceed 500–1000 m as the crow flies or approximately 10 min by car (Burgdorf et al. 2014). As an example, we briefly introduce our analysis of grocery stores. In the district of Wesermarsch, there are approximately 50 grocery stores (LEG), of which approximately half are located in the larger towns (Berne, Burhave, Jaderberg, and Rodekirchen). Only one-third of grocery stores are suitable for purchasing basic supplies; the other two thirds are kiosks, bakeries, butcher shops, or farm shops (IGES 2017). As only a few citizens live in the immediate vicinity of a grocery store, it becomes clear that most households are dependent on their car. This means that basic services can only be reached by bicycle, car, or bus.

3.1.5 Citizen Needs

To include the inhabitants' perspective at an early stage, we also included the survey on mobility requirements in the model region. This helped us better understand the setting from a future customer perspective. Based on the setting analysis, we were able to identify areas of focus that require entrepreneurial solutions with regard to mobility optimization. We compiled the following list of requirements for our business solutions:

- The business ideas should sustainably meet the mobility needs of citizens in rural areas.
- Mobility must be tailored to citizens from rural areas and people in the model region.
- The mobility concepts to be developed should be sustainable.
- The concepts to be developed should be financially self-sustaining in the long term.
- The mobility concepts should strengthen the community and form networks.
- Business models could include incentive systems, for example, citizens being rewarded with bonus points when showing environmentally conscious behavior.
- The ideas can provide citizens with the opportunity to become mobility providers themselves.
- The concepts to be developed should support the self-organization of citizens for their mobility.
- The business ideas should be based on, but are not reduced to, ICT.

3.2 Identifying Imitational Potential

In the next phase, we started by agreeing on the most relevant markets and then divided the model region into two different areas. First, we concentrated on services in markets that directly contribute to mobility, for example, by offering services that use the existing cars or combine public with private transport. Second, we also looked at selected markets with indirect contributions to mobility; in other words, those offering services reducing the need for transport and logistics by, for example, allowing the sharing of goods or services or supporting a sense of community. See Table 3 for the selected markets.

Next, the markets with a focus on certain business cases were analyzed. We used the most popular and most successful cases (based on a mixed-sources approach including online statistics) and added cases with specific relevance to the model region. As an example, we present the market and case analysis in the area of carpooling. Defining carpooling as an arrangement between people to make a joint

Table 3 Overview of registered vehicles per 100 inhabitants

No.	Active business models (direct effects)	No.	Passive business models (indirect effects)
1	Carpooling offer (also for events and concerts)	5	Supermarket delivery service
2	Group pick-up service	6	Babysitting vs. shopping
3	Supermarket pick-up service	7	Community cooking
4	Company carpooling	8	Supermarket tracking

journey in a single vehicle, the following are the most prominent providers in Germany: Besserfahren.de, Blablacar.de, Fahrgemeinschaften.de, Mitfahren.de, and Pendlerportal.de.

3.2.1   Analysis of the Carpooling Market

This market analysis is based on the process model of Theobald (2016), which consists of six steps (Theobald 2016). The first step is the consolidation of the market to be considered. In addition, the different segments of the market are analyzed. Here, carpooling opportunities and carpooling agencies in these segments are analyzed. In the research we conducted for this market analysis, we followed the Weinl method (Weinl 2013). In the second step of the analysis, the question position is defined. In this case, the question is which mobility service providers exist in the market. In the third and fourth steps, a qualitative and quantitative market profile of the providers is created. The facts to be considered are the assessment of the market dynamics, and in step four, the identification of possible barriers, as well as technology trends and market trends. In the fifth step, the analysis is evaluated. The last step describes how to save the data.

Table 4 provides an overview of the carpool providers and mobility centers "Blablacar",[3] "Fahrgemeinschaft",[4] "Die Hüruper Mitfahrbänke",[5] "Besser-mitfahren",[6] "MIFAZ – Deine Mitfahrzentrale",[7] "matchridergo",[8] "mitfahren",[9] "troodle",[10] and "twogo".[11] In addition, the overview also shows the characteristics of each provider. Thus, the providers are analyzed according to different criteria to identify their distinguishing features.

By conducting the market analysis, we were able to identify the advantages as well as disadvantages of the respective markets. As shown in Table 4, we also identified certain specifics that might have significant influences on success. That led us to ask questions such as the following: Can we offer an approved version? Can we offer a better price? Are there any shortcomings that we can overcome? Are there any customers who have not yet been sufficiently considered? With regard to carpooling, we found that privately organized carpooling in general mainly occurs on certain occasions, such as when people drive together to school, to a specific event, or to sports. This is often discussed spontaneously and in person in a familial

---

[3]https://www.blablacar.de.

[4]https://www.fahrgemeinschaft.de.

[5]https://www.bobenop.de/projekte/mitfahrbank.

[6]https://www.bessermitfahren.de.

[7]https://www.mifaz.de.

[8]https://www.matchridergo.de.

[9]https://www.mitfahren.de.

[10]https://troodle.me.

[11]https://www.twogo.com.

Table 4 Overview of market analysis: mobility providers and mobility centers sources. BB ('Blablacar'), FG ('Fahrgemeinschaft'), DHM ('Die Hüruper Mitfahrbänke'), BMF ('Bessermitfahren'), MZ ('MIFAZ—Deine Mitfahrzentrale'), MR ('matchridergo'), MFP ('mitfahren.de'), T ('troodle.me') and , TG ('twogo.com')

Criteria/provider	Description	BB	FG	DHM	BMF	MZ	MR	MFP	T	TG
Target group	What is the driver's goal? C: commuting, SJ: single journey	SJ	C/SJ	SJ	C/SJ	C	C	C/SJ	SJ	C
Range	What is the range of this service?	City	City	Rural	City/Rural	City/Rural	City/Rural	City	City/Rural	City/Rural
User	How many users (estimate) does the platform have?	5.5m	1.5m	Unknown	1.1m	50K 3.5K	Unknown	5	7K	
Registration	Is registration necessary to use the platform?	Yes	Yes	No	No	No	Yes	Yes	Yes	Yes
Costs(€)	What is the average cost of the platform? Are there extra costs?	0.05/Yes	0.05/No	o.n.o./No	o.n.o./No	0.05/No	0.15/No	Driver/No	0.03	Driver/Yes
Journeys	How many journeys per annum are offered on the platform (estimate)?	2.6 m	1.3 m	Unknown	1.5 m	100 K	12 driver	4.5 m	Unknown	Unknown
Communication	How do the driver and fellow passengers communicate? T: Telephone/SMS, E: E-Mail, A: platform app, P: personal	T/A	T/E	P	T/E	T/E	A	T	A	A

Standpoint	Does the platform use the standpoint of the user? Does the platform track the user?	No/No	Yes/No	No/No	No/No	Yes/No	Yes/Yes	No/No	Unknown	Yes/No
Application	Does the platform have an app and is it possible to use the platform on one's mobile phone?	Yes	Yes	No	No	No	Yes	No	In development	Yes
Specifics	Does the platform have specific characteristics?	22 Countries	No fee	Anonymity/ use as needed	Autonomy	–	Timetables	Inclusion of bus and rail service	Hitchhiking	No fee for business

or friend circle, so a platform is not necessarily used in this case. However, a potential market may exist in a variety of contexts where people do not yet take advantage of others who are driving a similar direction, as they might not know each other or do not have sufficient information on others' mobility. The analyzed platforms, however, often do not offer short-distance carpools, for example, driving to sports, the supermarket, or the pharmacy. The portals mainly offer longer-distance routes, for example, from Oldenburg to Berlin. Thus, one option can be to broaden the service to short-distance trips and to focus on motivating people to use the service for arranging short-distance carpooling. At a later point, this analysis also helped to develop the revenue model and possible prices. However, based on the information we gathered in this step, we were able to select role-model solutions from all the selected markets.

3.3 Applying the Analysis Results to Innovative Business Ideas

Business models can be developed with different approaches. The term "business models" can have different definition (Schallmo 2013). In the creative part, we held different workshop sessions using various creativity techniques and worked in groups so that in the end, we had several creative loops, with some of them even occurring during the subsequent step, namely, the business model development process. We mainly worked with the core team; however, in some sessions, we also integrated colleagues from project NEMo from the other disciplines, colleagues from totally different projects, and citizens from the model region. Thus, the creative development parts were conducted in intra- and interdisciplinary groups. As a first step, we mainly focused on those initial approaches that directly focus on mobility. Most of the approaches—and even the role-model cases—were designed for urban areas. After further considering the details and business models, it became clear that they were only apt for a larger city environment. Car sharing, for example, only makes sense when there is a critical mass of people using the cars so that people are able to pick up a vehicle within an accessible radius. Nonetheless, we determined that carpooling and taxi services are suitable when they are adapted to rural regions in a creative way. Taking into account the requirements identified by the survey and the citizens frequently integrated into the process, we recognized the general idea and further developed our ideas to address challenges such as security issues when hitchhiking, reliability concerning availability, and comfort (Jahns et al. 2017). In addition, we used the existing infrastructure and integrated it as a feature in our carpooling solutions. One option was to use bus stations as pick-up points that can be equipped with digital information boards that provide information about possible rides complementing regular public transport. Another opportunity was seen in using organized buses, for example, for seniors, being offered by some villages in our model region or by companies. We also integrated a feature that allows the setup of a collective transport (when a critical mass is reached). In one of the workshops, we critically discussed the potential of someone

Table 5 Overview of potential imovative business models

	Direct influence on mobility	Indirect influence on mobility
Selected markets	• Car Sharing (even for concerts and events) • Carpooling • Delivery Services • Taxis (especially prosumer models) • Station Connections	• Neighborhood Communities • Product Sharing Portals • Service Sharing Portals • Neighborhood Restaurants • Bonus-point shops

asking others to fetch or bring something for him or her, for example, when they go shopping, instead of going to the shop himself or herself. This can save time and transport; however, it also implies some difficulties. For example, people must be willing to take the extra time to shop for third parties and the person "placing the order" has to provide detailed information and trust that the delivery will take place. Considering that we identified that many people regularly drive the same or similar routes (to work, school, sports, etc.) without knowing it, we conducted a workshop on how we could use this fact. People need to have the opportunity to exchange information on their regular routes, which do not necessarily have to be daily trips but can also include weekly appointments or other trips. However, data security when people exchange information, and transport security when they arrange joint rides are important points. Among others, these aspects were taken into account when integrating a feature into the app, which connects people driving from or to similar areas, such as industrial parks for work or school, and allows shared driving. In addition to those solutions that directly focus on mobility, we also designed approaches that might have indirect effects on mobility. This is the case when people, for example, share products or services. This can reduce additional needs for driving and, at the same time, may have positive effects on community development in rural areas. Table 5 shows some examples used in the imovative process. In addition, community innovations were addressed, especially in citizen workshops.[12]

While working on a variety of solutions, we identified one additional limitation in the existing solutions. Until recently, there was no way of skillfully combining different means of transport. One could drive, take the bus, share a vehicle, and so on. Thus, we decided to (1) integrate several alternatives in our solution and (2) also added a feature that offers advice on the optimum combination by using an algorithm that can include flexible information on traffic and availability of mobility services, as well as personal preferences. This makes it possible that the fastest or most preferred way to reach a certain place might be taking a ride to the next station, then taking a bus and switching to another ride or walking.

---

[12]The selected solutions with indirect effects will be integrated and tested in the app in a step-by-step approach, while integrating the active business models first.

To prepare the business models, business model canvases were used since they were easy to adapt to the different needs and allowed us to integrate various target and stakeholder groups (BMWi 2020a,b; Hausmann and Heinze 2016). As underlined in our approach, focusing on potential user needs is of specific importance. Thus, we followed the lean entrepreneurship approach and created test versions as soon as possible, to evaluate them in our model region. We additionally integrated citizens in (mobility) workshops and prototyping events and conducted additional interviews. This process of testing and further development is still ongoing. The whole group aims to remain continuously involved in the implementation of the different features and to analyze usage behavior for the community app. It can be shown that easy handling, trust in the supplier, the technical solution, and the community collaboratively using the app can improve mobility—this holds specifically true when the users are at the same time the ones providing the services (prosumers).

4   Conclusion and Next Steps

In this article, we introduced an innovative approach that can assist in identifying and implementing sustainable business models. The approach was designed within the context of project NEMo; however, it can be adapted to other situations. Thus, we would like to motivate others to use and evaluate the suggested approach. With frequent application, it can be further developed and assist in identifying a broad range of ideas and in developing and implementing successful sustainable business models in different areas.

Our own evaluation has already shown that it is a helpful tool within the context of project NEMo. We identified and discussed a large number of possible business ideas, developed in imovative ways, as they are based on existing businesses, as well as in purely innovative ways. Since we were not able to further develop all ideas and implement all the identified business models in our model region, we had to carefully select the most promising ones. As described above, we finally decided to build an integrated approach that focuses on offering a variety of mobility solutions that can also be combined. An algorithm allows the calculation of individual optimum routes and means of transport. The app also allows for the integration of features with indirect effects on improved mobility in rural areas, such as community building and sharing opportunities.

One of the most important experiences during this project was the constant integration of experts from different disciplines and of citizens in the model region. The experts from various fields ensured that the business model development would be viewed from different perspectives and that the legal conditions and technical possibilities, for example, would be kept in mind. Integrating citizens was essential as they are the future consumers or even prosumers, when they are part of the mobility service production (Akyol et al. 2018; Sandau et al. 2018). Both groups were found to be specifically relevant for the idea generation as well as the business model generation. However, for future activities, we suggest that the group of stakeholders being integrated into the process should be broadened. Being aware of possible cacophonic effects when integrating too many groups of interest, we urge the early integration of (potential) entrepreneurs when applying the approach in a research context, as we did in project NEMo. As a next step, we, therefore, propose integrating institutions offering entrepreneurial support, such as business incubators or start-up centers.

This publication is also a first step towards distributing our results. Our mobility solution for rural areas was created to be applied to additional regions in our model region. The app or parts of the app should be transferred to various contexts. In a practical context, we can assist in adapting the solution to regional specifics. In a research context, we can support follow-up projects that focus on analyzing and fostering entrepreneurial opportunity recognition and business model development, as well as projects identifying and implementing innovative and imovative sustainable entrepreneurial solutions.

References

ADAC e.V. (2019). *Verkehr & Mobilität: Standpunkte, Statistiken und Studien*. Retrieved November 26, 2020 from https://www.adac.de/_mmm/pdf/fi_mobilit%C3%A4tsicherung_l%C3%A4ndlicher_raum_0216_257264.pdf

Akyol, A., Halberstadt, J., Hebig, K., Jan, D. K., Jelschen, A. W., Sandau, A., et al. (2017). Flexible software support of imovated mobility business models. In *Proceedings of the 31st EnviroInfo Conference*. Luxembourg.

Barnes, W., Gartland, M., & Stack, M. (2004). Old habits die hard: path dependency and behavioral lock-in. *Journal of Economic Issues, 38*(2), 371–377.

Bereznoy, A. (2018). Innovative business models in the strategic adaptation of multinationals to emerging economy environment. higher school of economics research *SSRN Electronic Journal*, Paper No. WP BRP, 85.

Bergen, M., & Peteraf, M. A. (2002). Competitor identification and competitor analysis: a broad?based managerial approach. *Managerial and decision economics, 23*(4–5), 157–169.

Blank, S. (2013), Why the lean start-up changes everything. *Harvard Business Review, 91*(5), 63–72.

BMWi. (2020 a). Business Model Canvas. Retrieved November 20, from https://www.existenzgruender.de/DE/Gruendung-vorbereiten/Businessplan/Business-Model-Canvas/inhalt.html

BMWi. (2020 b). Business Model Canvas. Retrieved November 20, from https://www.existenzgruender.de/SharedDocs/Downloads/DE/Checklisten-Uebersichten/Businessplan/16_Business-modell-Canvas.pdf?__blob=publicationFile

Bocken, N. M. P., Rana, P., & Short, S. W. (2015). Value mapping for sustainable business thinking. *Journal of Industrial and Production Engineering, 32*(1), 67–81.

Bosch, J., Olsson, H. H., Björk, J., & Ljungblad, J. (2013). The early stage software startup development model: A framework for operationalizing lean principles in software startups. In *International Conference on Lean Enterprise Software and Systems* (pp. 1–15). Berlin: Springer.

Briggs, R., van De Vreede, G.-J., & Nunamaker, J. (2003). Collaboration engineering with thinklets to pursue sustained success with group support systems. *Journal of Management Information Systems, 19*(4), 31–64.

Burgdorf, M., Krischausky, G., & Müller-Kleißler, R. (2014). Berechnung und Visualisierung von Indikatoren zur Nahversorgung. In J. Strobl, T. Blaschke, G. Griesebner & B. Zagel (Eds.), *Angewandte Geoinformatik 2014* (pp. 590–597).

Chesbrough, H (2006). *Open Business Models: How to Thrive in the New Innovation Landscape.* Boston, MA: Harvard Business School Press.

Dahan, N. M., Doh, J. P., Oetzel, J., & Yaziji, M. (2010). Corporate-NGO collaboration: Co-creating new business models for developing markets. *Long Range Planning, 43*(2–3), 326–342.

Eilers, K. (2014). Pendler können zehn Minuten länger schlafen. Retrieved November 20, from https://www.kreiszeitung.de/lokales/oldenburg/oldenburg-ort703376/neue-bahn-haltestelle-oldenburg-wechloy-soll-nahverkehr-entlasten-3999543.html

Eisenmann, T. R., Ries, E., & Dillard, S. (2012). Hypothesis-driven entrepreneurship: The lean startup. In *Harvard Business School Entrepreneurial Management Case* (pp. 812–095).

Eppler, M. J., Hoffmann, F., & Bresciani, S. (2011). New business models through collaborative idea generation. *International Journal of Innovation Management, 15*(6), 1323–1341.

Fay, D., Borrill, C., Amir, Z., Haward, R., & West, M. A. (2006). Getting the most out of multidisciplinary teams: A multi-sample study of team innovation in health care. *Journal of Occupational and Organizational Psychology, 79*(4), 553–567. https://scholar.google.de/scholar?hl=de&as_sdt=0%2C5&q=Getting+the+most+out+of+615+multidisciplinary+teams%3A+A+multi-sample+study+of+team+innovation+in+health+care&btnG=

Franco-Santos, M. (2016). Designing better performance measurement systems in universities using the business model canvas. In *5th World Conference on Production and Operations.* Havana, Cuba.

Garfield, M., Taylor, N., Dennis, A, Satzinger, J. (2001). Research report: Modifying paradigms—individual differences, creativity techniques, and exposure to ideas in group idea generation. *Information Systems Research, 12*(3), 322–333.

George, N. M., Parida, V., Lahti, T., & Wincent, J. (2016). A systematic literature review of entrepreneurial opportunity recognition: Insights on influencing factors. *International Entrepreneurship and Management Journal, 12*(2), 309–350.

Gordijn, J., & Akkermans, H. (2001). Designing and evaluating e-business models. *IEEE intelligent Systems, 4*, 11–17.

Griffiths, M., Fenton, A., & Fletcher, G. (2019). *4.1 Competitor analysis. Strategic digital transformation: A results-driven approach.* London: Taylor & Francis

Hatzijordanou, N., Bohn, N., & Terzidis, O. (2019). A systematic literature review on competitor analysis: Status quo and start-up specifics. *Management Review Quarterly, 69*, 415–458.

Hausmann, A., & Heinze, A. (Hrsg.). (2016). *Cultural Entrepreneurship—Gründen in der Kultur- und Kreativwirtschaft* (1st ed.). Wiesbaden: Springer VS.

Jacobs, L., Samli, A. C., & Jedlik, T. (2001). The nightmare of international product piracy: exploring defensive strategies. *Industrial Marketing Management, 30*(6), 499–509.   https://www.sciencedirect.com/science/article/pii/S0019850199001054?casa_token=I0g2FX2xbroAAAAA:9VWIi8PTXz5kGwysEvTG62baXe9TPIrZfzs5zG25o6uV_9Nn1FVJ6ypwqT--Vfqm6upXvpYaREw

Jahns, M., Samland, U., Woisetschläger, D., & Henkel, A. (2017). *Zwischenbericht: Anforderungserhebung: Zwischenbericht (Stand: 02/2017) im Rahmen des Projektes NEMo – Nachhaltige Erfüllung von Mobilitätsbedürfnissen im ländlichen Raum.* Retrieved November 20, 2020 from https://www.nemo-mobilitaet.de/blog/wp-content/uploads/2018/04/NEMo-Anforderungserhebung_Jahns_Samland_Update_v2.pdf

Hawkins, B. (1999). *How to generate great ideas (creating success).* London: Kogan Page.

IGES. (2017). BMVI-Modellvorhaben "Versorgung & Mobilität" Modellregion Land-kreis Wesermarsch. Retrieved November 20, from https://landkreis-wesermarsch.de/uploads/files/praesentation_iges_zwischenergebnisse_bmvi_movo_vermob.pdf

Karimi, S., Biemans, H. J., Lans, T., Aazami, M., & Mulder, M. (2016). Fostering students' competence in identifying business opportunities in entrepreneurship education. *Innovations in Education and Teaching International, 53*(2), 215–229.

Kraus, S., Niemand, T., Halberstadt, J., Shaw, E., & Syrjä, P. (2017). Social entrepreneurship orientation: Development of a measurement scale. *International Journal of Entrepreneurial Behavior & Research, 23*(6), 977–997.

Landesamt für Statistik Niedersachsen. (2017). *LSN-Online – Regionaldatenbank.* Retrieved November 20,2020 from http://www1.nls.niedersachsen.de/statistik/html/default.asp

Landesamt für Statistik Niedersachsen. (2020 a). Retrieved November 20, from http://www.lnvg. de/interaktive-karte-streckennetz/?no_cache=1

Landesamt für Statistik Niedersachsen. (2020 b). Retrieved November 20, from https://www. statistik.niedersachsen.de/startseite/themen/verkehr/verkehrsstatistiken-in-niedersachsen-tabellen-strassenverkehr-175181.html

Landkreis Oldenburg. (2016). *Sehenswürdigkeiten, Wirtschaft, Freizeit.* Retrieved November 20, 2020 from https://www.dein-niedersachsen.de/regionen/landkreis-oldenburg

Landkreis Wesermarsch. (2017). *Bevölkerung und Katasterflächen.* Retrieved November 20, 2020 from: http://www.landkreis-wesermarsch.de/unser-landkreis/zahlen--daten--fakten/ bevoelkerung.php

Lima, M., & Baudier, P. (2017). Business model canvas acceptance among French entrepreneurship students: Principles for enhancing innovation artefacts in business education. *Journal of Innovation Economics Management, 2,* 159–183.

Hancock, C., & Longbottom, D. (2016). Market sensing using images and emotional scaling. In D. Longbottom, & A. Lawson (Eds.) *Alternative market research methods: market sensing.* London: Taylor & Francis.

Luther, M. (2020). *Das große Handbuch der Kreativitätsmethoden: Wie Sie in vier Schritten mit Pfiff und Methode Ihre Problemlösungskompetenz entwickeln und zum Ideen-Profi werden.* managerSeminare Verlags GmbH.

Mitchell, D., & Coles, C. (2003). The ultimate competitive advantage of continuing business model innovation. *Journal of Business Strategy, 24*(5), 15–24.

Mitchell, D., & Coles, C. (2004). Business model innovation breakthrough moves. *Journal of Business Strategy, 25*(1), 16–26.

NordWestBahn. (2020). RS 4 Streckenverlauf. Retrieved November 20, from https://www. nordwestbahn.de/de/regio-s-bahn/unsere-region/streckennetz/linie/rs-4

Osterwalder, A., Pigneur, Y., Oliveira, M. A. Y., & Ferreira, J. J. P. (2011). Business model generation: A handbook for visionaries, game changers and challengers. *African Journal of Business Management, 5*(7), 22–30.

Peters H. (2005). *Gesamt- und regionalwirtschaftliche Beschäftigungswirkungen des öffentlichen Personennahverkehrs am Beispiel des Raums Köln: theoretische Grundlagen und empirische Abschätzungen.* Kölner Wissenschaftsverlag.

Prahalad, C. K., & Ramaswamy, V. (2004). Co-creation experiences: The next practice in value creation. *Journal of Interactive Marketing, 18*(3), 5–14.

Qastharin, A. R. (2016). Business model canvas for social enterprise. *Journal of Business and Economiscs, 7*(4), 627–637.

Ries, E. (2011). *The lean startup: How today's entrepreneurs use continuous innovation to create radically successful businesses.* Crown Books.

Sandau, A., Dietrich, B., Akyol, A., Wagner vom Berg, B., & Gómez, J. M. (2018). Steigerung der Sensibilität für nachhaltige Mobilität durch die mobile Reiseapplikation Guyde. In: *Tagungsband Multikonferenz Wirtschaftsinformatik 2018* (pp. 1137–1148).

Schallmo, D. R. A. (2013). *S. 22f: Geschäftsmodelle erfolgreich entwickeln und im-plementieren. Mit Aufgaben und Kontrollfragen.* Springer-Verlag, Berlin.

Spiegler, A. B., & Halberstadt, J. (2018). SHEstainability: How relationship networks influence the idea generation in opportunity recognition process by female social entrepreneurs. *International Journal of Entrepreneurial Venturing, 10*(2), 202–235.

Stack, M., Gartland, M., & Keane, T. (2016). Path dependency, behavioral lock-in and the international market for beer. In: *Brewing, beer and pubs* (pp. 54–73). London: Palgrave Macmillan.

Statista. (2020). *Bestand an Pkw-Fahrerlaubnissen (Klasse B) in Deutschland am 1. Januar 2020 nach Altersgruppen und Geschlecht*. Retrieved November 20, 2020 from https://de.statista.com/statistik/daten/studie/263168/umfrage/fahrerlaubnisse-der-klasse-b-in-deutschland-nach-altersgruppen

Theobald, E. (2016). *Vorgehensweise bei der strategischen Marktanalyse. Paper, Hochschule Pforzheim*. Retrieved November 20, 2020 from https://www.management-monitor.de/de/infothek/White_Paper_Marktanalyse.pdf?m=1519297736.19.07.2018

Trimi, S., & Berbegal-Mirabent, J. (2012). Business model innovation in entrepreneurship. *International Entrepreneurship and Management Journal, 8*(4), 449–465.

VBN. (2020). *Verkehrsangebot*. Retrieved November 20, 2020 from https://www.vbn.de/mobilitaet/verkehrsangebot

VWG Oldenburg. (2020). *Liniennetzplan Oldenburg*. Retrieved November 20, 2020 from https://www.vwg.de/documents/vwg_liniennetzplan_tagnetz_2020.pdf

Weinl, K. (2013). *Erfolgreich recherchieren – Informatik*. Berlin: Walter de Gruyter.

Wilson, A., & Laskey, N. (2003). Internet based marketing research: A serious alternative to traditional research methods? *Marketing Intelligence & Planning, 21*(2), 79–84.

Youn, S., & Vogel, T. (2017). Market research, consumer insight, and creativity. In: *Proceedings of the 2017 Conference of the American Academy of Advertising* (pp. 1–3).

Zahra, S. A., Korri, J. S., & Yu, J. (2005). Cognition and international entrepreneurship: Implications for research on international opportunity recognition and exploitation. *International Business Review, 14*(2), 129–146.

Mobility in Rural Areas as it Relates to the Agricultural and Food Industries and People Employed in Them

Doris Schröder

Abstract This article from Landesinitiative Ernährungswirtschaft (LI Food) aims to provide an introduction to the LI Food initiative and discusses the importance and structure of the food industry. The agricultural and food industries face a number of challenges directly or indirectly related to rural mobility. Here we will discuss some of these, with the aim of outlining the potential for developing sustainable mobility concepts.

Keywords Food industry · Rural areas · Logistics · Distribution · Mobility · Consumers

1 Landesinitiative Ernährungswirtschaft in Lower Saxony: LI Food

LI Food brings together expertise and experience across all sectors of the food industry in all of Lower Saxony. The renewed extension to LI Food's mandate commenced on January 1, 2010. Since July 1999, LI Food has been jointly organised by The University of Vechta and DIL, Deutsches Institut für Lebensmitteltechnik e.V. in various guises at the former Kompetenzzentrum Ernährungswirtschaft (food industry centre of expertise). The current phase of the project runs from 2019 to 2021.

LI Food aims to be a cross-sector, technology-agnostic expert network with a strong focus on the market and real-world applications. Its objective is to mobilise and unlock innovation potential in Lower Saxony. The focus is on innovation-

D. Schröder (✉)
Landesinitiative Ernährungswirtschaft LI Food, University of Vechta, Vechta, Germany
e-mail: doris.schroeder@uni-vechta.de

© The Author(s), under exclusive license to Springer Nature Switzerland AG 2021
J. Marx Gómez et al. (eds.), *Progress in Sustainable Mobility Research*,
Progress in IS, https://doi.org/10.1007/978-3-030-70841-2_6

103

oriented, environmentally and socially sustainable growth (LI Food 2019a). LI Food's core tasks consist of:

- networking
- initiating and supporting innovation projects
- establishing and maintaining partnerships
- public relations
- supporting our sponsor (Lower Saxony Ministry of Business, Employment, Transport and Digitalisation)

The food industry is Lower Saxony's second largest industry after the automotive industry (Lower Saxony Ministry of Food, Agriculture, Consumer Protection and Regional Development 2010). In contrast to the automotive industry, the food industry is highly heterogeneous in structure—this important sector of the economy is built around a large number of small and medium-sized enterprises. Strong price pressures mean that smaller companies in particular invest well under 1% of their turnover in research and development. By actively bringing together businesses, the research community, politicians and society, LI Food aims to support the food industry in meeting challenges in five specific areas, using a range of different measures. The key to successfully developing the food industry in Lower Saxony lies in targeted innovation (LI Food 2019b). Over the next few years, LI Food will be focusing on the following specific areas:

Healthy Eating   The importance of healthy eating is not limited to nutrition-related illnesses. Social and political pressures mean that this is becoming an increasingly important issue for the food industry. Consumers are increasingly adopting a more critical approach to food and its effects on health and well-being. There is a trend towards alternative diets, with vegetarian and vegan diets in particular becoming increasingly popular. Against this backdrop, in future we plan to focus more closely on issues such as poor eating habits and much-discussed regulatory efforts (for example, measures aimed at reducing fat, salt and sugar in foods), and to explore these issues together with food businesses in Lower Saxony (LI Food 2019b).

Entrepreneurship   Our efforts in terms of entrepreneurship are primarily focused on developing innovative products, technologies, services and business models. Making existing products more sustainable and healthy, for example, can expand the potential market for the product. Entrepreneurs are people who initiate and sponsor innovation. Encouraging a spirit of entrepreneurship not only leads to the generation of great ideas, it also ensures that these ideas are put into practice in the market. By collaborating with various business incubators, LI Food ensures excellent networking between a range of stakeholders at all stages of the supply chain. A further objective is to encourage developments from within companies ('intrapreneurship') in order to ensure that companies are well positioned to undertake future development (LI Food 2019b).

Digitalisation   The Lower Saxony food industry produces high quality food and is in a position to continuously improve this food. Consolidating expertise from the food and IT industries within our network should enable new technologies such as blockchain and big data to provide greater transparency in food production. Digital technologies can improve food safety by improving traceability within the supply chain. LI Food would like to work with food businesses in this area with the aim of developing practical solutions (LI Food 2019b).

Sustainability   There are many aspects to sustainability in the food industry, ranging from efficient use of resources and future protein sources to environmental footprints and nutritional issues. We will be organising projects and events concerned with issues such as utilisation of side-streams and alternative protein sources. Environmental, social and economic sustainability in food production is often a key determinant of food attractiveness, is increasingly one of the key drivers of innovation and is ultimately one of the key factors driving consumer buying decisions (LI Food 2019b).

Food Technology   The food industry in Germany and especially in Lower Saxony already produces very high quality products. Legal requirements, retailer specifications and consumer expectations help ensure a high level of quality and safety. Research is continually delivering new approaches and technologies to further improve the quality and sustainability of food industry processes. LI Food has set itself the goal of promoting the implementation of these research results within the food industry, with the aim of enhancing the industry's innovation potential (LI Food 2019b).

Social Acceptance   The food industry's central role in food production means that it has a large effect on economic development and the employment market in the state of Lower Saxony (European Union 2018). With upstream and downstream industries—agribusiness—many supply chains are tightly integrated right from the field or animal shed to the plate. Small and medium-sized businesses are the mainstay of the industry (Lower Saxony Ministry of Food, Agriculture, Consumer Protection and Regional Development, 2010 pp. 3 and 7). Consequently, innovation and the use of new technologies are essential for future viability. Because small and medium-sized businesses often lack in-house research and development capabilities, there is a need to support the industry in transforming itself into a socially, environmentally and economically sustainable, socially accepted system of food production.

LI Food is supporting businesses with the challenges imposed by increasing competition within the industry and rising consumer expectations, and—through its academic and business network—is helping to give impetus to efforts to maintain competitiveness. There is strong pressure on the industry from society for more transparency in food production. Resulting measures are implemented by means of legal statutes or via voluntary agreements, for example with food retailers (Lower Saxony Ministry of Food, Agriculture, Consumer Protection and Regional Development 2010, p. 24ff.). LI Food aims to contribute to this debate, highlight existing information sources to improve transparency, highlight the relationships between individual issues, provide a broader perspective on these issues and so contribute to greater social acceptance.

In the 20 years it has been active, LI Food has established an extensive agricultural and food industry network from scratch. This network brings together major players in the Lower Saxony food industry at all points in the supply chain. In addition to businesses, it includes researchers, administrators, politicians, the finance sector, education, industry associations, business development organisations and others.

2 The Agricultural and Food Industries in Lower Saxony and their Significance

Below, we describe the state of upstream and downstream sectors and regional strengths in food and agricultural production within Lower Saxony. Economically, the food industry is considered part of the manufacturing sector (the secondary sector). The associated agricultural sector is part of the primary production sector (the primary sector). Both sectors are more important in Northern Germany (Mecklenburg-Western Pomerania, Schleswig-Holstein and Lower Saxony) than in other regions of Germany, as land use for agriculture in these regions is higher than the national average. In terms of manufacturing, food businesses (e.g. dairies, mills, bread, meat and sausage factories) are again highly significant. The agricultural and food industries in Lower Saxony are of huge economic significance and also provide jobs in rural areas (Windhorst and Grabkowsky 2007).

2.1 Regional Strengths

The importance of the primary sector—specifically highly productive agriculture—and food businesses in the secondary sector, which process the agricultural products within Lower Saxony's food industry, can be explained by the available potential in Lower Saxony. Within Lower Saxony, it is possible to distinguish three rural regions with particular production strengths (Windhorst and Grabkowsky 2007).

The coastal and other grassland areas in the northeast of the Weser-Ems region are dominated by the dairy industry. East Friesland's nutrient-rich, marshy soils are often not suitable for arable use due to their high groundwater levels. Consequently this area is home to animal feed growers specialising in beef and dairy farming.

In the southern part of the Weser-Ems region, by contrast, there is a significant amount of intensive animal farming and livestock production (Windhorst and Grabkowsky 2007). The food industry in the Oldenburger Münsterland region (around Cloppenburg and Vechta) in particular is characterised by unusually tight integration between producers of agricultural raw materials and upstream and downstream manufacturers. Farmers produce raw materials which are processed locally by a highly efficient processing industry (abattoirs, dairies, etc.). This secures additional jobs in these businesses and generates income (Windhorst and Grabkowsky 2007). Upstream industries (machinery producers, the animal feed industry, etc.) and numerous service providers (transport businesses, livestock building cleaning companies, etc.) are also closely integrated with producers or processors of agricultural products (Niedersächsisches Ministerium für Ernährung, Landwirtschaft, Verbraucherschutz und Landesentwicklung 2010).

There is also a significant amount of sugar beet and wheat cultivation in the Hildesheimer Börde fruit-growing region and around Hanover and Göttingen. Arable farming in these high-yielding soils is focused on sugar beet cultivation, which is the highest yielding of all crops. Sugar beet cultivation also benefits from excellent downstream processing infrastructure locally, which ensures short transport distances, fast, low-cost processing and a reliable market for the product (Windhorst and Grabkowsky 2007).

Regional anomalies in Lower Saxony are found in the Lüneburg Heath and the surrounding geest, where potato cultivation has become increasingly established. This region is characterised by sandy soils, associated with a lack of water, permitting only moderate yields. A large number of mixed farms have been established here, some of which use direct marketing to sell their products. Potato cultivation makes up a large part of agricultural production in this region, to the extent that every second potato in German is now grown in Lower Saxony. In addition, the potato processing industry is also a major player in this region. As a raw material, potatoes form the basis for a number of quality products, such as refined starch products and potato protein, which are manufactured and processed by local businesses (Windhorst and Grabkowsky 2007).

2.2 Agriculture and Food Businesses

In Lower Saxony, producer regions and agricultural businesses are close to major sales channels (Lower Saxony Ministry of Food, Agriculture, Consumer Protection and Regional Development 2019, p. 4). In addition to meat processing, milk processing in Lower Saxony is also of major importance, as around one fifth of all milk in Germany is produced and processed in Lower Saxony (Lower Saxony Ministry of Food, Agriculture, Consumer Protection and Regional Development 2019, p. 9). Agricultural products are processed by the food industry and artisan producers, producing highly diverse supply chains which play a major role in shaping the rural environment (Lower Saxony Ministry of Food, Agriculture and Consumer Protection 2019, p. 11).

It is clear from a description of the differing available potential in different regions of Lower Saxony that there is no such thing as a 'typical' rural area in Lower Saxony. As described above, the Lower Saxony countryside is characterised by highly varied settlement structures, locations, access to major economic zones and environmental and ecological conditions. There are also in some cases marked differences in economic structures, as well as economic growth and demographic trends (NIW 2003). The goal should therefore be to exploit and expand available potential in order to secure long-term jobs and to enhance development in rural areas. Mobility is an important factor for achieving this goal.

3 Areas Where Food Industry Businesses have Scope for Mobility-Related Optimisation

In the above discussion, we have emphasised the importance of the food industry. Because many businesses, especially manufacturers, are located in rural areas, they too are affected by the challenges posed by the lack of mobility concepts and poor infrastructure connections forming the subject of this volume. There are already concepts for logistics and distribution of food from rural areas (Martikainen et al. 2014; Rogoff 2014). Of particular note is that efficient logistics help businesses to realise direct cost savings (Xu et al. 2015; Jack et al. 2010). There nonetheless remains much unused potential in this area. The mobility of people in rural areas is not a key topic of interest either for research or in practice. There is, for example, a dearth of innovative concepts for employees and their journeys to work. Improving the supply of food to people in rural areas is also seen as an area where the food industry is in a position to make a direct contribution. The view is that this is an area where there is a significant overlap between the work of LI Food and project NEMo.[1] Below, we explore in brief these two areas with a view to identifying potential areas for future collaboration.

4 Skill Shortages and Challenges

The local environment within which agricultural and food industry businesses operate plays a significant role in the shortage of skilled workers. Mose and Nischwitz (2009), for example, note that the skills shortage is particularly acute in rural areas characterised by ageing and shrinking populations (Mose and Nischwitz 2009). In northeast Lower Saxony, businesses are increasingly blaming mobility issues for skills shortages, as staff have to commute long distances to work (NIW 2012, p. 9). This frequently means that individual employees are driving to work alone—with adverse effects for their wallets and the environment.

One option for improving this situation is shared mobility through schemes such as carpooling. Local businesses, for example, could join together and make use of the functions provided by the NEMo app. This could both eliminate any safety

---

[1]https://nemo-mobilitaet.de.

concerns and optimise routes. In addition to staff with a driving license and their own car, there are also a significant number of trainees, who, at the start of their training, are generally too young to drive, do not have a driving license or car and have difficulties in starting a traineeship at businesses that are not accessible by public transport. Here again, the NEMo app could offer businesses an important tool for organising internal carpooling with older staff or between trainees, perhaps also for getting to and from courses at vocational training colleges. The app also offers the ability to arrange ad hoc car-sharing, additionally providing a sustainability boost for businesses.

Other options, such as mobility services provided directly by the company, could also be integrated into the NEMo solution. Wernsing Feinkost GmbH in Essen (Oldenburg) is a shining example of best practice in this area. It has organised a special bus to pick up trainees and bring them into work. The company launched this service in response to the situation described above (Wernsing Feinkost GmbH 2020).

Public transport is not sufficiently well structured to enable workers in rural areas to travel to work by bus or train. At best, there may be carpools for staff who drive to work from the same town or village. In the case of shift work, or for people working on different shifts or in different departments within a company, even that may not always be possible. Projects like this can make companies in rural areas more attractive and boost employer branding. Use of social media helps to raise the profile of and awareness of such services among young people.

It is not just staff who benefit from such services. By reducing climate-damaging CO_2 emissions, optimising routes and sharing transport also help to protect the environment. Carpooling also fosters communication and interaction between people in rural areas and between colleagues who might otherwise never meet. Both ultimately have a positive effect on a company's image and on social acceptance of the food industry.

5 Consumers and Mobility

Above, we gave an overview of food production in the various regions of Lower Saxony and explored employee mobility. Following on from this, it is also clear that consumers who buy this food also need to get to food stores. In rural areas in particular, availability of food is often not remotely comparable to that in urban areas. Although online ordering is now viewed as a genuine alternative, developing innovative supply concepts for rural areas that are tailored to demand and take account of mobility-related challenges remains a desirable objective.

Being able to go shopping on foot, by bike or cargo bike, or using public transport encourages climate-friendly behaviour. The volume of shopping and distance to the nearest supermarket often represent a significant obstacle, however.

Enabling collection and delivery services—both for food and for other everyday items—to be organised by neighbours or workmates is another potential area of use for the NEMo app. This would be especially useful for older people who do not have their own car. A shopping group of this kind could be a useful alternative, which could also help to strengthen community ties in villages as well as offering environmental benefits. In addition, food and other retailers in villages could team up to consolidate consumer traffic by, for example, providing regular buses to pick up and return home customers from the surrounding area. Currently, this kind of service is particularly popular with older customers who do not drive (Roehrig 2017). It could, however, also be opened up to other groups. Solutions like this would be easy to integrate into the NEMo app and would extend the range of mobility options available. The app could also help with route optimisation for such services. It might also be possible to consolidate orders from local producers via the app and organise either collection from a single location or delivery. Similar schemes already exist in Sweden. Examples: HelloFresh delivery service, Qool Collect collection points in Munich, Mein Marktstand shopping service in Oldenburg, Einkaufsservice Göttingen shopping service in Göttingen.

6 Outlook

From the above it is clear that there are strong links between the food industry in all its various guises and mobility. Food industry businesses are generally located in rural areas and are forced to confront the challenges posed by a lack of infrastructure. Products and employees have to be transported. The food industry also plays a major role in supplying people living in the countryside.

In developing sustainable mobility concepts for rural areas, it is therefore important to think about specific challenges in the rural context, but also to utilise the potential offered by collaboration with food industry stakeholders. In this context, LI Food is therefore planning to continue to work with the NEMo team after completion of the project. A range of stakeholders from the business world should be involved in leveraging the innovation potential outlined here to create added value for the people and the economy in rural areas by optimising mobility.

References

European Union. (2018). *Leistungsbeschreibung – Fachlicher Teil (Teil B)*. Ausschreibung Landesinitiative Ernährungswirtschaft, AZ: 0036-DLG/2018-03.26.

Jack, E. P., Powers, T. L., & Skinner, L. (2010). Reverse logistics capabilities: Antecedents and cost savings. *International Journal of Physical Distribution & Logistics Management, 40*(3), 238–246.

LI Food. (2019a). *Internetauftritt der LI Ernährungswirtschaft*. Retrieved December 9, 2020 from https://www.li-food.de

LI Food. (2019b). *Landesinitiative Ernährungswirtschaft. Flyer zur Projektvorstellung* (pp. 1–2). Quakenbrück.

Martikainen, A., Niemi, P., & Pekkanen, P. (2014). Developing a service offering for a logistical service provider—case of local food supply chain. *International Journal of Production Economics, 157*, 318–326.

Mose, I., & Nischwitz, G. (2009). Anforderungen an eine regionale Entwicklungspolitik für strukturschwache ländliche Räume Hannover. *E-Paper der ARL* Nr. 7.

Niedersächsisches Ministerium für Ernährung, Landwirtschaft, Verbraucherschutz und Landesentwicklung. (2010). *Die Ernährungswirtschaft in Niedersachsen*. Hannover.

Niedersächsisches Ministerium für Ernährung, Landwirtschaft und Verbraucherschutz. (2019). *Die Ernährungswirtschaft in Niedersachsen*. Hannover.

NIW. (2012). *Regionalmonitoring Niedersachsen – Regionalreport 2012*. Retrieved December 9, 2020 from https://www.mb.niedersachsen.de/download/89316/Regionalreport_2012.pdf

Roehrig, C. (2017). Vom Senioren- zum Bürgerbus: ehrenamtlich betriebene Fahrdienste anerkanntes ÖPNV-Angebot oder Lückenfüller?, *Nahverkehr* 35(1+2) (pp. 6–12)

Rogoff, J. (2014). *Improving systems of distribution and logistics for regional food hubs*. The Central Appalachian Network and the Department of Urban Studies and Planning, Massachusetts Institute of Technology. Cambridge, MA, USA.

Wernsing Feinkost GmbH. (2020). *Für ein gutes Miteinander*. Retrieved December 12, 2020 from https://www.wernsing.de/nachhaltigkeit/fuer-ein-gutes-miteinander/

Windhorst, H.-W., & Grabkowsky, B. (2007). *Die Bedeutung der Ernährungswirtschaft in Niedersachsen*.

Xu, S. X., Cheng, M., & Huang, G. Q. (2015). Efficient intermodal transportation auctions for B2B e-commerce logistics with transaction costs. *Transportation Research Part B: Methodological, 80*, 322–337.

Part IV
Technical Requirements
and Implementations

A Sustainable Software Architecture for Mobility Platforms

Phillip Bühring, Dilshod Kuryazov, Alexander Sandau, and Andreas Winter

Abstract Project NEMo aims at providing new mobility means to facilitate sustainable fulfillment of mobility needs in rural areas. In order to meet the core objectives of project NEMo, the envisioned mobility platforms must be sustainable itself by providing flexibility in co-evolution with changing and novel mobility needs, services, and business models. Thus, in order to be technically sustainable, the architectural provision behind a mobility platform has to be flexible and adaptable. SENSEI and DORI provide architectural support to enable sustainability on software engineering level. They are applied to project NEMo in order to achieve the aforementioned goals to create, extend and adapt a NEMo inter-modal mobility scenario. SENSEI provides flexibility, adaptability and long-term sustainability by utilizing model-driven, service-oriented and component-based concepts to provide flexible orchestration of NEMo's functionality. The users of a mobility platform further need support for interacting with the mobility platform. To this end, the DORI approach is applied to design user interactions in project NEMo. DORI intends to provide flexible interaction modeling support for designing state-based interactivity models to describe the overall interaction by GUI states and transitions between these states. It defines abstract GUI widgets and their underlying implementations, separately. This contribution summarizes the sustainable architecture of project NEMo and shows the extensibility and adaptability of the NEMo mobility platform.

Keywords Mobility platform · Reusable mobility services · Sustainable software architecture · Separation of concerns · Interaction modeling

P. Bühring · A. Sandau · A. Winter (✉)
Carl von Ossietzky University of Oldenburg, Oldenburg, Germany
e-mail: phillip.buehring@uol.de; alexander.sandau@uol.de; winter@se.uol.de

D. Kuryazov
Urgench Branch of Tashkent University of Information Technologies Named After Muhammad al-Khwarizmi, Urgench, Uzbekistan
e-mail: kuryazov@se.uol.de

© The Author(s), under exclusive license to Springer Nature Switzerland AG 2021
J. Marx Gómez et al. (eds.), *Progress in Sustainable Mobility Research*,
Progress in IS, https://doi.org/10.1007/978-3-030-70841-2_7

1 Introduction

The interdisciplinary research project NEMo[1] (Jelschen et al. 2016) aims at the sustainable fulfillment of mobility needs in rural areas considering social, demographic, accessibility, legal, economic, and ecological conditions and objectives. It intends to facilitate the provision of *smart mobility services* based on social self-organization. Project NEMo develops novel business models (Akyol et al. 2017) that increase utilization of public and private transport, while reducing the overall stream of vehicles on the streets (Kuryazov et al. 2019). In smarter cities, which also include rural areas, information and communication technologies (ICT) are viewed as the key enabler to support these objectives implementing a mobility platform that is accessible through various devices and media. This contribution strictly focuses on designing a flexible and adaptable, i.e., a *sustainable software architecture* to provide appropriate ICT support.

Like any software system, the NEMo mobility platform needs to evolve to remain up to date with new or modified requirements, e.g., new business models, mobility services, and their implementations. Continuously adapting the mobility platform leads to more complex and less maintainable software systems (Lehman 1996). Due to the innovative nature of project NEMo, a sustainable software architecture plays an essential role in simple and fast development, integration and maintenance of new mobility services (Jelschen et al. 2016). Even during the course of the project, developing the NEMo system required various revisions and adaptations.

The application domain of smart mobility services also requires highly flexible software support. The NEMo mobility platform should be able to support all kinds of mobility needs and scenarios, modes of transportation, and business models. According to (Combemale et al. 2016), the evolution of the NEMo mobility platform has to facilitate the recombination of existing mobility services to provide enhanced services, as well as completely new, unanticipated usage scenarios.

Finally, with the overall objective of project NEMo aiming at sustainability, it is only appropriate to strive for it in terms of software design. A rigid, monolithic software system would lead to high maintenance costs, and ultimately to its phaseout, close down, and forced replacement (Rajlich and Bennett 2000). To be sustainable, the NEMo mobility platform must make architectural provisions for sustainability, flexibility, and adaptability (Kateule and Winter 2018). In this way, a smart system can be continuously adapted and made smarter and smarter.

A major use case, that is expected to play an essential role for the NEMo mobility platform, is inter-modal routing, combining the different modes of transportation, e.g., walk, bike, bus, train, carpooling, etc. The existing infrastructure and functionality of the ICT Platform and Services (ICTS) project (Wagner vom Berg 2015) is already able to support the use case of inter-modal routing to a large extent. On the top of this platform, the ICT Services project builds another software system to

---

[1] https://nemo-mobilitaet.de.

combine its basic software services and offer value-added services to support the designated business processes. These mobility services are reused in developing the sustainable prototypical NEMo mobility platform in Sect. 3.

1.1 Challenges

Due to the fast development of early prototypes of ICTS to enable applied research on rural mobility at early stages, the existing infrastructure was designed and developed without a particular focus on flexibility, sustainability, and adaptability. In order to achieve sustainable development and maintenance of the mobility platform, project NEMo addresses to several challenges considering sustainability, innovation, and evolution:

- The software architecture of the mobility platform has to be developed focusing on flexibility, adaptability, extensibility, and long-term sustainability.
- The existing functionality of the existing mobility platforms has to be easily reused, enhanced, and modified.
- The realization of the mobility platform has to focus on consistent separation of functionality (services) and implementation (components), following the principle of *separation of concerns* (Dijkstra 1982).
- Development of novel, flexible user interfaces has to be automated so that changes and new user requirements can easily be adapted in user interactions of the mobility platforms.

These challenges are considered as the main engineering and technical-conceptual challenges that can be resolved by the novel software engineering trends, which are addressed in this contribution.

1.2 Objectives

In order to solve the scientific challenges described in Sect. 1.1, this section describes several objectives that are addressed throughout this contribution. The sustainability objectives of project NEMo, from a software engineering point of view, are manifold:

Sustainable Software Architecture First of all, there is a need for a flexible, adaptable, and extensible software architecture that incorporates the existing functionality, but highlights flexibility, adaptability, and long-term sustainability. A sustainable software architecture serves as a common blueprint in reusing existing features of mobility platforms and developing and adapting new features.

Reusable Mobility Services In case of existing mobility platforms, the existing functionality of the mobility platforms should be enhanced, modified, and reused.

Future changes (i.e., extensions, optimization, and corrections) based on the research findings within project NEMo have to be adaptable and reusable.

Separation of Concerns   Sustainable software architecture and reusable mobility services should support novel business models, model-driven and service-oriented mobility services and component-based functionality enabling consistent separation of functionality (services) and implementation (components). This allows for eased maintenance of business models, mobility services, and components.

Interaction Modeling   As long as users interact with mobility platforms by using various user interfaces and media devices, there is a need for a model-driven, flexible interaction modeling feature by separation of user interaction and user interface designs. Utilization of interaction modeling provides developing user interaction independent from various platforms and devices.

These objectives remain on the central focus throughout this contribution. So far, some prototypical results are achieved by providing the existing mobility platform with the flexible, sustainable, and adaptable software support based on component-based, service-oriented software development and maintenance. This feature supports including the achieved research results in an interdisciplinary research project like NEMo to its software support from a software engineering's perspective.

The remainder of this contribution is outlined as follows: Sect. 2 introduces a reference architecture for sustainable mobility platform development. The same section describes the central concepts of the SENSEI and DORI approaches. Section 3 sketches the application of SENSEI and DORI approaches to the NEMo mobility platform based on the reference architecture using an example. Section 4 defines several user requirements that have to be adapted in the running NEMo mobility platform example throughout this contribution. Section 5 presents the complete solution combining all requirements defined in Sect. 4. Section 6 explains the core results and contributions of this research and draws conclusions about sustainable architecture and SENSEI in project NEMo.

2 Conceptual Idea

This section sketches the theoretical foundations of the engineering technologies used in development of the NEMo mobility platform. These foundations consist of a sustainable reference architecture (explained in Sect. 2.1), an introduction of the SENSEI (Sect. 2.2) and DORI approach (Sect. 2.3). A sustainable reference architecture helps to develop an evolvable mobility platform for providing mobility services.

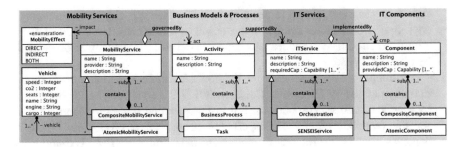

Fig. 1 Four-layer NEMo taxonomy for mobility platform (Akyol et al. 2017)

2.1 Sustainable Reference Architecture for Mobility Platforms

One of the main objectives in project NEMo is the development and application of a sustainable reference software architecture. Figure 1 depicts the four-layer NEMo taxonomy (Akyol et al. 2017). This taxonomy serves as a common blueprint and foundation in developing the sustainable NEMo mobility platform. The taxonomy provides clear separation of concerns by distinguishing between the *mobility services, business models, information-technology-(IT)-services, and IT-components.*

As the NEMo taxonomy depicted in Fig. 1 enables separation of concerns, mobility platforms developed based on this taxonomy can achieve higher level of sustainability, adaptability, and flexibility. Each level of the taxonomy can be sustained separately, independent from the rest. It allows for eased adaptation of changes in user requirements, business models, IT-services, and IT-components.

Mobility Services   In general, the mobility platform offers mobility services by means of transportation (vehicle) and offered by providers. A mobility service can also be comprised of more fine-grained mobility services which is referred to as a composite mobility service. This is due to the inter-modal nature of mobility services. Any mobility service can be performed directly by transporting people, indirectly by transporting things, or both by transporting people and things at once. Each mobility service may be associated with several *business models* and *processes.*

Business Models and Processes   In the second column, the taxonomy describes business models and processes that might be related to many mobility services. The business models and processes consist of activities performed by the users and providers of the mobility platform. The activities can further be defined as tasks that the users should perform before, while, and/or after using the mobility service. The activities are supported by *IT-services.*

IT-Services   An IT-service defines a piece of functionality. It adds appropriate functionality to the activities focusing on human behavior (Jelschen 2015). An IT-service is a description of what a software component should do. In case of the mobility platform, each mobility service is provided by several IT-services, e.g., each inter-model mobility service combines several IT-services supporting the transportation mode. In the same vein, each IT-service provides a functionality, e.g., finding the nearest stations to an origin or destination, finding sub-routes with different transport modes, etc. These IT-services are usually implemented by *IT-components*.

IT-Components   IT-components are the concrete implementations of the functionality defined by IT-services (Jelschen 2015). A service can be implemented by several combined components. For instance, a find route service might use several components for each transportation means, e.g., bus, walk, etc. Figure 2 depicts a sustainable reference architecture based on the NEMo taxonomy in Fig. 1. In this architecture, the mobility services on the top level are described by business models and processes in the second level. These business models are then defined as IT-services, whereas each activity (i.e., functionality) is defined as one abstract service in a service catalog. In the same vein, these services are implemented by IT-components enabling reuse and sustainability of IT-services and IT-components.

Each level of the architecture in Fig. 2 can be sustained separately, independent from the rest of the taxonomy. It allows for eased adaptation of changes in user requirements, business models, IT-services, and IT-components.

This sustainable reference architecture in Fig. 2 is utilized in Sect. 3.1 to develop a concrete mobility platform. As there is a need for technical support for realizing this reference architecture, the SENSEI approach explained in Sect. 2.2 is utilized as realization technology.

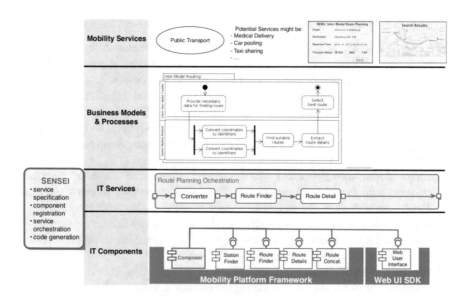

Fig. 2 Sustainable reference architecture for mobility platforms (Jelschen 2015)

2.2   SENSEI Approach

The sustainable reference architecture explained in Sect. 2.1 serves as a common blueprint for model-driven (Kleppe et al. 2003), service-oriented, and component-based development and maintenance of the mobility platforms (Breivold and Larsson 2007). This section explains the SENSEI approach making the sustainable reference architecture as the central architectural provisions for developing model-driven, service-oriented and component-based mobility platform. Eventually, the SENSEI approach serves as main technical grounds for realizing sustainable reference architecture depicted in Fig. 2.

SENSEI (Software EvolutioN SErvice Integration) (Jelschen 2015, 2020) provides service-oriented software design facilities (service orchestration) on an abstraction level close to the application domain of mobility needs. Strictly separated from this layer, concrete implementations of these services are realized in component-based terms. An automated mapping from services to components bridges the gap between service-oriented specification and component-based realization.

SENSEI provides a toolchain-building support framework providing flexibility, reusability, and productivity. It combines service-oriented, component-based, and model-driven techniques to automatically map high-level, process models (*service orchestrations*) onto reusable and interoperable components possessing the required capabilities and generate code that combines and coordinates them in the required manner (Jelschen 2015). Using the SENSEI framework, applications are built sustainably by combining (and reusing) components providing clearly specified functionality (services). For this purpose, services are kept in a *service catalog*. A *component registry* maps this functionality to potential implementing components (*Service-Component-Matching*). Based on *orchestrations of the services*, suitable components are automatically linked to the desired application by the *SENSEI generator*. SENSEI consists of the following core concepts which can easily be mapped to the four levels of the reference architecture in Fig. 2.

Service Catalog   A service catalog serves as a central repository containing service definitions that are described in a standardized way. The mobility services are defined in the SENSEI service catalog. All services defined in the service catalog have names and descriptions, along with input and output parameters, and associated data types. The implementations (*IT-components* in the reference architecture) of these services usually provide traveling information for various imaginable modes of transport, and the users of the service might only need a subset of them. At the same time, the service catalog would become extremely cluttered if a service were to be defined for every possible variant. SENSEI solves this issue by introducing *capabilities* to describe service variants concisely. Services define capability classes to represent aspects that can vary independently. This service catalog is utilized to collect mobility services in project NEMo.

Component Registry   The component registry establishes relations between services defined in the service catalog and *IT-components* that provide the functionality. Services are implemented by components offered by various providers. Each entry in the component registry refers to a component and lists one or more services it implements. With each service, the provided capabilities are specified in the same way as required capabilities for *orchestrations*. Existing mobility services, provided by the NEMo mobility platform, are wrapped for SENSEI compatibility and interpreted as implementations behind mobility services in orchestrations.

Service-Component-Matching   Considering *required* capabilities of orchestrated services, *provided* capabilities of registered components, as well as constraints resulting, e.g., from data type compatibility concerns, a suitable composition of components will be searched for to realize the orchestrations.

Service Orchestrations   Service orchestrations (e.g., depicted in Figs. 5 and 8) allow to instantiate and combine abstract services from the service catalog to create more complex functionality, using a process-oriented, graphical modeling language. In order to fulfill business models and processes (in the reference architecture), IT-services are orchestrated using one or many IT-services from the service catalog. For instance, different, single IT-services provide different routing services by different transport modes and capabilities, whereas they are orchestrated to provide the complete inter-modal routing scenarios for developing a mobility platform in project NEMo.

Application Generation   To conclude the process, the SENSEI orchestration model is mapped to a particular target platform providing a runtime environment, e.g., WSO2,[2] the middleware used by the ICT Platform project. This step is performed by a model-driven code generator. It results in a fully auto-generated component that depends on the components found in the previous step to perform the work specified by the orchestrated services. The result is an executable software application, ready to be deployed, e.g., to the WSO2 application server. After all, the deployed application can be called by different means of media such as mobile, web, desktop, and other frontend clients.

Based on the sustainable reference architecture depicted in Fig. 2, the SENSEI approach is applied to the concrete NEMo mobility applications in Sect. 3.

2.3   DORI Approach

The mobility platform is bound to offer a wider range of functionality (e.g., route planning, carpooling, etc.), and is supposed to be used in an everyday context by people with limited technical proficiency, which creates a need for *user interaction*. The SENSEI orchestrations are based on the input-process-output principle, and

---

[2]https://wso2.com.

thus not capable of interacting with the user at runtime. Thus, there is a need for another, complementary approach to enable users to interact with the mobility platform and utilize its services in their daily routing planning activities.

In order to provide such flexible, model-driven means for the development of *user interactions* with the mobility platform, the students' project group DORI (Do Your Own Reactive Interface[3]) has developed a concept and tool support for modeling user interactions through the use of the DORI Domain Specific Language, which was based on UML state charts and the IFML (Interaction Flow Modeling Language) (Brambilla and Fraternali 2014). *Interaction diagrams* representing the interactive behavior of applications are executed by a dedicated interpreter. Following the SENSEI structure given in Sect. 2.2, abstract behavior is represented in the *abstract widget catalog*. Its *platform-specific* implementation is provided by the concrete widget *catalog*.

Abstract Widget Catalog   This contains abstract Widgets and Functions. Abstract Widgets serve as "blueprints" for the actual interaction states (called Abstract Widget Instance (AWI)), defining the set of data fields in their possession, as well as the events which they may react to. Conceptually, they are similar to SENSEI services. They may also contain Sockets, enabling composition or parallel processing, albeit only on instance level. The second kind of abstract elements, Abstract Functions, define a return type and a set of parameters.

Widget Catalog   The concrete catalog consists of a list of concrete widgets for each of the pre-defined abstract widgets. While abstract widgets merely describe a signature, their concrete counterparts contain implementation-dependent information. Concrete Widgets contain a path to the implementation of the UI element which is supposed to represent it and Concrete Functions a path to the implementation of their logic (e.g., a REST endpoint). Their roles are similar to those of SENSEI components.

Platform Catalog   This catalog contains a list of platforms. In the context of DORI, a platform is a set of elements whose implementations target a common platform. This allows interpreters targeting different platforms to choose the appropriate concrete implementations from the catalog before executing a model. So far, there are two interpreters available; one based on Java Server Faces to enable desktop applications and the other one supporting the android platform.

Interaction Diagram   The flow of user interactions through states (AWIs) and transitions is described by interaction diagrams. The states are instantiated from the pre-defined abstract widgets; transitions may be supplemented with guards and Parameter Binding Groups (see Fig. 4). The Parameter Binding Groups (1) define which events may trigger their host-transition, (2) which (abstract) functions are to be called once its host-transition fires, and (3) how data is transferred between the involved variables. Since the interaction diagrams themselves are based on abstract elements, they may be realized on different

---

[3] https://uol.de/se?pg-dori.

platforms, which makes this approach quite useful for multi-platform or multi-device applications, as it would be the case for the NEMo mobility platform. DORI is applied to development of the NEMo application in Sect. 3.

3   NEMo Application

The sustainable reference architecture for the mobility platform in Sect. 2.2 is used as blueprint for model-driven, service-oriented, and component-based development and maintenance of the NEMo mobility platform. As the proof of the concept, this section applies the SENSEI and DORI approaches to the NEMo mobility platform. This section depicts a simplified scenario of the mobility platform. Section 4 defines several additional user requirements (i.e., change requests) raising a need for changing, adapting, and sustaining the existing mobility platform. According to these user requirements, Sect. 5 describes what changes and adaptations are required in the user interface, orchestration, and interaction model in order to adapt these requirements to the mobility platform. It is shown that using the SENSEI/DORI approach results in a technical sustainable software evolution.

The inter-modal routing finds routes to connect a point of origin and a destination (*Brake* and *Vechta* in this example). Combining different modes of transport, e.g., walking, riding a bike, taking a bus or train, driving a private car, or joining a carpool, makes this inter-modal routing.

Figure 3 depicts the user interface of this simple inter-modal routing use case representing two different states of user interaction with the mobility platform. In the first window, origin and destination of a route, and time of departure are entered for searching possible routes between these places.

Once the *Add Tour* button is clicked (left side of Fig. 3), all possible routes, regardless of the transport mode, are calculated and added to the list of routes visible on the dashboard (right side of Fig. 3). Upon selection of a route, it is drawn on the

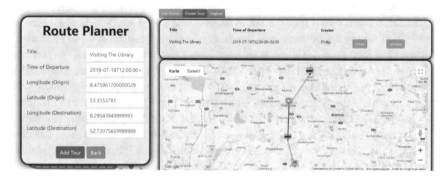

Fig. 3   Mobility service UI. (Mapdata ©2019 GeoBasis-DE/BKG (©2009), Google)

map below the list. In this example, the user interface is based on Java Server Faces, using a slightly modified dialect to access the data of the DORI interaction states from the .xhtml sources describing their corresponding UI counterparts.

3.1 Interaction Model

The DORI Interaction Diagram behind this example makes use of seven abstract widget instanced (AWI) in total (see Fig. 3), although only four of them are of immediate interest for the use case. The *Dashboard-AWI* (centermost in Fig. 4) serves as a hub for the application. Depending on the incoming events it allows for switching to other widgets (e.g., *Login, Profile*, and *RouteFinder*). It also grants access to a list of pre-calculated routes (or tours). A map is used to depict the selected route. For this purpose, both *RouteList-* and *RouteMap* widgets are nested within the *Dashboard* through the use of sockets. The *RouteList* widget possesses three data fields: a list of route-objects, an ID determining which of the routes is to be removed once the event *removeRoute* is received, and finally the navigation data of the route which supposed to be sent to the *RouteMap* widget for depiction once the user triggered the *showRoute* event. The *RouteMap* widget itself does nothing but contains a field to store the route data received by the *RouteList* widget. Via the *gotoRouteFinder* event on the *Dashboard*, a user can switch to the *RouteFinder* widget, which is coupled to the route planning dialog as shown in Fig. 3. The *RouteFinder* widget allows a user to define new routes to be added to the Dashboard's *RouteList*, and possesses one data field for each of the input fields visible in the form of Fig. 3. The event *findRoute* starts the process meant to calculate routes, afterwards stores the calculated routes within the user's list, and finally returns to the *Dashboard*. This is done with the help of two subsequent transitions with a pseudo-state between them: the first transition calls the function meant to calculate the new routes (navigational) data, ultimately referencing to a WSO2 service, which in turn executes the SENSEI orchestration (Fig. 5) used in this example. Necessary parameters are prepared beforehand using *Parameter Bindings* (longitude, latitude, etc.). *Parameter Binding* is also used to store the resulting route data within the intermediate pseudo-state.

3.2 IT-Services

According to the sample mobility scenario explained above, the following IT-services are needed:

Converter As shown in Fig. 3, origin and destination locations are initially given by coordinates. But all locations and routes are processed by their identifiers

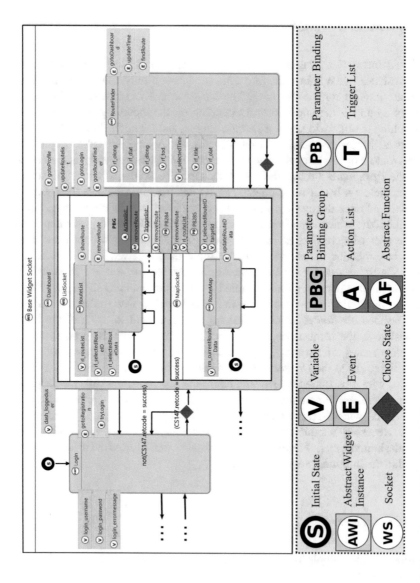

Fig. 4 Simplified interaction model for calculating inter-modal routes

within the already existing implementation. Thus, a converter service is needed to convert coordinates to identifiers of these locations.

Route Finder   This service is utilized for finding all possible routes between origin and destination. It finds all routes by combining different transport modes.

Route Details   In the existing ICT mobility platform, mobility services return the subset of route data, i.e., the identifiers of locations connecting sub-routes. Detailed information including stops (i.e., coordinates, names, etc.) between the given two locations is then extracted by this additional service.

These three services are defined in the SENSEI service catalog. All services defined in the service catalog have names and descriptions, along with input and output parameters, and associated data types, also modeled in the catalog as data structures. These pre-defined services are implemented by IT-components already existing in the previous ICT-implementation (Wagner vom Berg et al. 2010). Within the generation step, these components are linked to manifest the SENSEI orchestration.

3.3   IT-Components

IT-components are the concrete implementations of the functionality defined by IT-services. As long as some mobility functionalities are already developed as the outcome of the Electric Mobility Showcase program (Wagner vom Berg et al. 2010), these existing functionalities of ICT are invoked as components in the context of project NEMo. Existing mobility services provided by the ICTS are wrapped for SENSEI compatibility and interpreted as implementations behind mobility services in the SENSEI orchestrations. These components are published as REST Web services and made available to reuse in the framework of the NEMo mobility platform.

Various route planning algorithms are used in project NEMo. For instance, new route planning services come with their own planer algorithms in the form of further IT-components. To include those, a service implementation can firstly be embedded behind its sole routing service, which has to be combined with a global one. This allows for early adaptation of the new mobility services in an unoptimized way. Later, the routing services can be implemented in a global routing component to provide an optimized routing in Sect. 5.

3.4   Service Orchestrations

In order to fulfill this particular mobility services, IT-services defined above are orchestrated selecting from the service catalog. Figure 5 depicts a SENSEI orchestration model for the initially simple mobility platform above. Services are instantiated from the catalog by selecting the required capabilities. In the

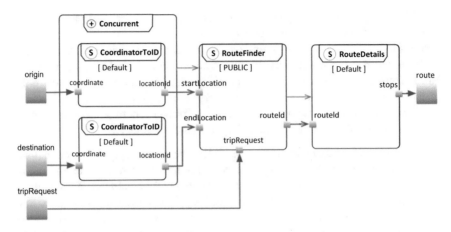

Fig. 5 Service orchestration before changes

orchestrations, the invocation order of services defined by the control flows (gray arrows) and the flow of data among these services is defined by the data flows (green arrows) connecting the inputs and outputs (green boxes) of the services. Services are marked with an encircled "S" ahead their names. The input parameters of the overall orchestration are defined by bigger green boxes, e.g., three boxes on the most left side of Fig. 5 with names *origin, destination*, and *tripRequest*, and one green box named *route* on the most right side.

The orchestration consists of applying two instances of the service *Coordinator-ToID*. As the origin and destination locations of the searched route are given in the form of the coordinates, these services convert the coordinates to identifiers. Then, the converted identifiers are sent to the *RouteFinder* service as *startLocation* and *endLocation*, whereas it also receives the third parameter *tripRequest*. The latter consists of the time of departure and the modes of transportation. In this case, the *RouteFinder* service provides the capability *PUBLIC*, meaning the service searches for all possible combination of transport modes including bus, train, walk, bike, etc. After finding an optimal route, the route finder service sends its identifier to the *RouteDetails* service, where further details about the found route are extracted. Eventually, the result of this orchestration is displayed in the second user interface depicted in Fig. 3.

4 User Stories (Change Requests)

Section 3 has explained a simplified mobility service example. This mobility service is the subject to various changes such as extensions, improvements, and optimization because of evolving user requirements over time. In this sense, the mobility platform must be sustainable, easy to adapt, and flexible to meet new and changed user requirements. In order to demonstrate *sustainability of the reference architecture* and associated technical support explained in Sect. 2, this section introduces several user requirements (i.e., change requests) for the mobility platform explained in Sect. 3.

Text-based Location Information While route planning, the user wants to be able to give the names of the origin and destination locations instead of their geographic coordinates.

Points of Interest The users want to spend their spare time (waiting time between the changes of transport modes) meaningfully. For instance, if a traveler should change transport from train to train, from train to bus, or vice versa, there might be waiting time more than 1 h. Then, travelers like to travel to *points of interest (PoI)*, i.e., coffee shops, restaurants, ATMs, museums, gardens, fast food chains, etc. Thus, they want to see recommended points of their interest on the map in the second UI of the mobility platform.

Biking The user wants to travel any subsection of a given route by bike if that subsection is less than 5 km. For example, if there are subsections of the given route which is less than 5 km and using bus, all of such subsections should be replaced by the *bike* transport mode. Suppose, in these cases rental bikes are available as a new mobility service. Travelers use these rental bikes instead of any other transport means.

These user requirements are defined as extensions, optimization, and improvements for the simple mobility platform. They must be adapted in the existing mobility platform. The following sections explain what to do in the user interface, service orchestration, and interaction model of the mobility platform in order to extend the simple initial NEMo mobility platform. The compete graphical descriptions for all adaptations are given in Sect. 5.

4.1   Text-Based Location Information

This section depicts what changes have to be made to change location coordinates to location names.

User Interface On the first graphical user interface, four input fields *(Longitude (Origin), Latitude (Origin), Longitude (Destination), Latitude (Destination))* are removed from the user interface. New input fields *(Origin and Destination)* are added in order to allow the user to specify origin and destination locations by their names instead of their geo-coordinates. The *RouteList* is also extended by the columns *Origin* and *Destination*. The changes made to the graphical user interface are reflected in Fig. 6.

Interaction Model Analogously, the *RouteFinder* widget's data fields for *longitude* and *latitude* are removed and two new ones, *origin* and *destination*, are added. The same changes are also reflected in the parameter sets of the abstract functions *calculateRoute* and *addRoute*, as well as in the parameter bindings. The

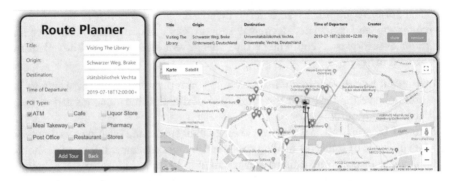

Fig. 6 UI after changes. Mapdata ©2019 GeoBasis-DE/BKG (©2009), Google

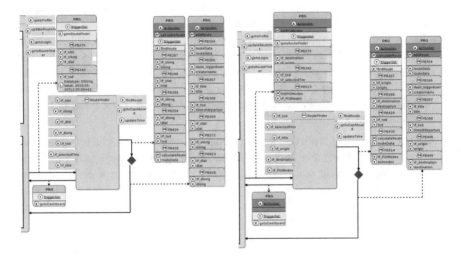

Fig. 7 Interaction model before (left) and after (right) the changes

last change is to actualize the (one) parameter binding used to initialize the data fields of *RouteFinder* with default values just before it becomes the active state by adding the origin and destination fields as targets. The changes related to the first user story are depicted in Fig. 7.

Orchestration   In order to support textual location names, a new IT-service called *Geocoder* is entered to the service catalog and its implementation is registered in the component registry. In this case, the implementation of the *Geocoder* service invokes a ready-to-use geocoding service of Google Inc. This service provides conversion of location names to location coordinates. The rest of the process remains unchanged. These changes are depicted in the left part of Fig. 8.

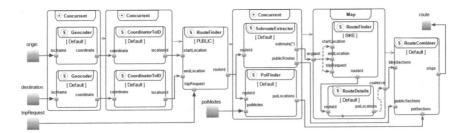

Fig. 8 Service orchestration after changes

4.2   Points of Interest

This section explains what changes have to be made on the UI, orchestration, and interaction model in order to add support for bridging waiting time.

User Interface   The NEMo mobility platform supports bridging waiting time by finding the points of interest (e.g., ATMs, coffee shops, etc.), if a traveler has to wait more than 1 h while changing the means of transportation. In order to adapt this user story, several types of point of interest are added to the graphical user interface, so that the user can choose where she/he wants to visit during that spare time. The changes made on the graphic user interface can be seen in Fig. 6. Here, the user can tick different types of PoIs, he is interested in.

Interaction Model   A new data field stores the list of types of PoI which a user wants to spend spare time and thus to be included in the resulting route data. A new Parameter Binding prepares the parameter accordingly. Due to the types of data fields (List of Strings) and the current technical limitations of the DORI-Editor, a new Function *initPOIModes* is used to initialize the (empty) list when transitioning from the *Dashboard* to the *RouteFinder* widget. The changes related to the second user story are depicted in Fig. 7.

Orchestration   The chosen types of PoI are then given to the overall orchestration as *poiModes*. To find the PoI locations, a new service called *PoIFinder* is added to the service catalog. This service receives the route identifier and the PoI types as input and returns the PoI locations. This service is instantiated on the service orchestration to find point of interest locations based on the user request. This service can be invoked together with the *SubrouteExtractor* service in parallel which is explained below. This parallel invocation of services helps to improve the runtime performance of the overall orchestration. The changes in the service orchestration are displayed in Fig. 8.

4.3   Biking

This section presents the changes made in the user interface, interaction model, and service orchestration in order to fulfill adding biking as a new mobility service for short distances.

User Interface   *Bike* transport mode has to be used to travel sub-routes less than 5 km. This does not request changing the graphical user interface and only requires adapting the orchestration.

Interaction Model   In the same vein neither the user interface nor the signature of the WSO2 endpoint is modified to adapt this request. No changes have to be made to the DORI interaction model, as well.

Orchestration   The orchestration has to be extended with several changes to add the additional mobility service. A new service called *SubrouteExtractor* extends the service catalog. This service receives a route identifier and extracts all subsections within that route which are less than 5 km. These subsections are then processed to a loop as a map, where the route finder service is invoked for each with the *bike* transport mode. There, the route finder service has to be associated with the capability *BIKE*. In the same loop in the orchestration in Fig. 8 the route details are also extracted for each subsection. After finding all sub-routes that can be traveled by bike, these results are sent to the *RouteCombiner* service to combine all *bike sections, public sections*, and *point of interest locations*. Finally, the result is assigned to the variable *route* and returned to the second graphical user interface (Fig. 6) of the mobility scenario. These changes are depicted in Fig. 8.

5   Complete Solution

This section presents the complete extension of the mobility platform explained in Sect. 3 combining all extensions depicted in Sect. 4.

User Interface after Changes   Figure 6 depicts the screenshot of the extended graphical user interface of the mobility scenario. The graphical user interface displays two states; the left window to search routes and the right window to show results.

The routes may be searched based on the names of their respective origin and destination location, which initially required input of their geo-coordinates. Additionally, the route planner user interface provides a list of PoI Types in order to enable travelers to visit their favorite points of interest, if they are expecting longer waiting time. In the search results, the map depicts several indicators to show points of interest based on the PoI requests of travelers. Finally, there is no change in both graphic interfaces to provide biking for short distances.

Interaction Model   Figure 7 shows the relevant parts of the interaction diagram in its original state (left) and the final version (right) incorporating all the necessary changes to fulfill the three change requests.

The changes are not very complex. Adding location names requires the deletion (or transformation) of some simple elements (four variables of the *RouteFinder*, the four parameters for each of the functions *calculateRoute* and *addRoute* and the eight bindings used to prepare their parameters) and subsequent addition of further elements (inserting the fields for origin and destination across widget, functions and bindings). Adding *PoIs* is handled by adding one function for initializing the list of PoI types, as well as adding the list itself to the *RouteFinder* widget, the *calculateRoute* function (as a parameter) and finally a new Parameter Binding in order to transfer it from the widget to the function itself. Adding the bike mobility service does not require any changes to the interaction model.

IT-Services   To adapt the user stories, several new IT-services are added to the SENSEI service catalog. These services are: *Geocoder* which converts location names to location coordinates, *SubrouteExtractor* which finds sub-routes less than 5 km, and extension of the *RouteFinder* service with the *BIKE* capability, and *PoIFinder* which finds the points of interest for the given types and on the given route. As long as different services deliver different outputs, these results are combined by the *RouteCombiner* service, eventually.

IT-Components   The implementations of these IT-services are provided by the IT-components registered in the SENSEI component registry. For providing the implementations of the newly defined IT-services, the component registry is also extended with respective components. A new component for the *Geocoder* service is added to the component registry, whereas it invokes the *geocode* service of Google API. A new component for the *SubrouteExtractor* service is locally implemented, and a new component implementing the existing *RouteFinder* service is extended which invokes the route finder service of ICTS with the *BIKE* transport mode. The latter requires to add a new capability to the *RouteFinder* service.

Service Orchestrations   All IT-services in the service catalog are defined as abstract services. These abstract services are then instantiated as concrete services whenever they are utilized in the orchestration model. Figure 8 shows the service orchestration model for the mobility scenario, which takes into account all change requests.

The orchestration is extended by the new services *Geocoder, SubrouteExtractor, PoIFinder, RouteCombiner*, and *RouteFinder* with new capability to adapt the aforementioned change requests. The two instances of the *Geocoder* service, two instances of the *CoordinatorToID* service, *SubrouteFinder* and *PoIFinder* are placed in the *concurrency* container to accomplish higher runtime performance of the overall orchestration. As the *SubrouteExtractor* service instance returns the map of sub-routes, this value is processed in the map to find the *bike* routes for each subsection by the *RouteFinder* service (with *bike* capability) and their details by the *RouteDetails* service. Finally, all *bike sections, public sections,* and *PoI sections* are combined into a single result *route* by the *RouteCombiner* service instance. These changes and extensions are made in the orchestration model without affecting the underlying implementations and any other artifacts. This allows for sustainable evolution of the mobility platform. Modeling service orchestrations allows to remain abstract from technical implementation and does not require programming skills or expert knowledge of the diverse technologies used by components.

6 Evaluation and Contributions

This section evaluates the objectives on sustainable software development and evolution, validates the reference architecture, and discusses the application of SENSEI and DORI in the context of the NEMo mobility platform.

The NEMo mobility platform is subject to software evolution and has to remain up to date with new or modified mobility requirements, e.g., new business models, mobility services, and implementations. Continually adapting the mobility platform leads to more complex and less maintainable software systems. Due to the innovative nature of project NEMo, a sustainable and adaptable software architecture plays an essential role in providing simple and fast development, integration and maintenance of new features, i.e., sustainable software development.

The reference architecture explained in Sect. 2.1 serves as architectural provisions for developing the NEMo-like mobility platforms focusing on sustainability, flexibility, and adaptability. The architectural provision covers the major use case; inter-modal routing combining the different modes of transportation, e.g., walk, bike, bus, train, carpooling, etc. The ICT mobility infrastructure, which was developed in advance to project NEMo, is already able to support the use case of inter-modal routing. However, it has not been designed with a focus on software sustainability, which makes it hard to evolve.

Sustainability objectives defined in Sect. 1.2 are entirely achieved by the reference architecture (Sect. 2.1), and the application of the SENSEI (Sect. 2.2) and the DORI approach (Sect. 2.3).

Sustainable Mobility Platform by Sustainable Reference Architecture
A flexible, adaptable and extensible reference software architecture serves as a common underlying blueprint for developing mobility platforms highlighting flexibility, adaptability, and long-term sustainability. This architecture provides clear extension points for services and components to enable software adaptations easily.

Reusability   The existing mobility services and their implementations (components) can be reused, enhanced and modified, and future changes (i.e., extensions, optimization, and corrections) based on the research findings within project NEMo can be incorporated within the mobility platform without much technical knowledge and effort.

Separation of Concerns   The sustainable reference architecture and its associated technical support (SENSEI and DORI) provides consistent separation of novel business models, model-driven, service-oriented mobility services, and component-based functionality enabling separation of functionality (services) and implementation (components).

Interaction Modeling   It provides a model-driven, flexible interaction modeling feature for separation of user interaction and user interface designs.

This contribution has demonstrated the application of the SENSEI and DORI approaches to develop a sustainable and flexible mobility platform based on the sustainable reference architecture in the framework of project NEMo. The clear separation of concerns, i.e., services and components in SENSEI, allows to specify application behavior on a non-technical level, close to the application domain. Service orchestrations are comparatively easy to adapt or extend, and the corresponding software application can be re-generated, allowing for fast turnarounds, and resulting in a high degree of flexibility. The use of SENSEI reduces the effort required to develop and maintain the mobility platform, particularly when sustainability raises.

The only prerequisite of applying the proposed approach is the provision of basic functionality, as in the case of project NEMo, already available in the form of components provided by the existing ICT Platform. The component-based structure supported by SENSEI promotes building up the catalog of both services and components, so that over time existing functionality can be readily reused, adapted, extended or new ones can be added. Both aspects potentially increase productivity and serve as the basis for sustainable mobility platforms.

References

Akyol, A., Halberstadt, J., Hebig, K., Kuryazov, D., Jelschen, J., Winter, A., et al. (2017). Flexible software support of innovated mobility business models. In *Adjunct Proceedings of the 31st EnviroInfo Conference* (pp. 27–34). Luxembourg, Shaker Verlag.

Akyol, A, Halberstadt, J., Hebig, K., Jelschen, J., Winter, A., Sandau, A., et al. (2017). Flexible software support for mobility services. In M. Eibl, & M. Gaedke (Eds.), *Informatik 2017* (pp. 2027–2038). Bonn: Gesellschaft für Informatik.

Brambilla, M., & Fraternali, P. (2014). *Interaction flow modeling language: Model-driven UI engineering of web and mobile apps with IFML*. Morgan Kaufmann.

Breivold, H. P., & Larsson, M. (2007). Component-based and service-oriented software engineering: Key concepts and principles. In *EUROMICRO 2007—Proceedings of the 33rd EUROMICRO Conference on Software Engineering and Advanced Applications* (pp. 13–20).

Combemale, B., Cheng, B. H., Moreira, A., Bruel, J.-M., &, Gray, J. (2016). Modeling for sustainability. In *2016 IEEE/ACM 8th International Workshop on Modeling in Software Engineering (MiSE)* (pp. 62–66)

Dijkstra, E. W. (1982). On the role of scientific thought. In: E. W. Dijkstra (Ed.), *Selected Writings on Computing: A Personal Perspective* (pp. 60–66). New York: Springer.

Jelschen, J., Küpker, C., Sandau, A., Wagner vom Berg, B., Marx Gómez, J., &, Winter, A. (2016). Towards a sustainable software architecture for the NEMo mobility platform. In *Adjunct Proceedings of the 30th EnviroInfo Conference* (pp 41–47).

Jelschen, J. (2015). Service-oriented toolchains for software evolution. In *2015 IEEE Ninth International Symposium on the Maintenance and Evolution of Service-Oriented and Cloud-Based Environments (MESOCA)* (pp 51–58).

Jelschen, J. (2020). *Software Evolution Services, A Framework for the Integration and Development of Flexible and Reusable Toolchains.* Dissertation, University of Oldenburg to appear.

Kateule, R., &, Winter, A. (2018). Architectural design of sensor based environmental information systems for maintainability. In H.-K. Arndt, J. Marx Gómez, V. Wohlgemuth, S. Lehmann, & R. Pleshkanovska. (Eds.) *Nachhaltige Betriebliche Umweltinformationssysteme: Konferenzband zu den 9. BUIS-Tagen* (pp. 87–96). Wiesbaden: Springer Fachmedien Wiesbaden.

Kleppe, A., Warmer, J., &, Bast, W. (2003). *MDA explained: The model driven architecture: Practice and promise.* Reading: Addison-Wesley Professional.

Kuryazov, D., Winter, A., &, Sandau, A. (2019). Sustainable software architecture for NEMo mobility platform. In *Smart Cities/Smart Regions – Technische, wirtschaftliche und gesellschaftliche Innovationen* (pp. 229–239). Springer Fachmedien Wiesbaden.

Lehman, M. M. (1996). Laws of software evolution revisited. In *Software Process Technology* (pp. 108–124). Berlin: Springer.

Rajlich, V. T., & Bennett, K. H. (2000). A staged model for the software life cycle. *Computer, 33*(7), 66–71.

Wagner vom Berg, B. (2015). *Konzeption eines Sustainability Customer Relationship Managements (SusCRM) für Anbieter nachhaltiger Mobilität.* Shaker Verlag.

Wagner vom Berg, B., Köster, F., Marx Gómez, J. (2010) Elektromobilität: Zukunft oder Gegenwart? – Förderung der Elektromobilität durch innovative infrastruktur- und Geschäftsmodelle. In Schermann, M. (Ed.), *MKWI 2010 Working Conference on Automotive Services* (pp.111–124). Norderstedt: Books on demand GmbH.

Mobility Platforms as a Key Element for Sustainable Mobility

Alexander Sandau, Johannes Schering, Ali Amin Rezaei, Cedrik Theesen, and Jorge Marx Gómez

Abstract Transport causes negative impacts on people and the environment. Since the traffic volume will tend to increase rather than decrease, appropriate solutions are strongly needed. On the one hand, an efficient transport system that guarantees the smooth exchange of goods and services is a prerequisite for economic development and a central location factor. On the other hand, mobility is a basic need for individuals because it is a cornerstone of personal freedom and ensures prosperity and enables social participation. The formation of carpools can contribute to reducing the negative economic, social, and ecological effects. However, in rural areas the approach faces special challenges due to the mostly sparsely populated area. Information and communication technologies can provide important assistance in organizing carpools. The presented approach delivers a suitable system for introducing carpools as an attractive and sustainable supplementary alternative in rural areas.

Keywords Sustainable mobility · Mobility platform · Demographic change · Rural areas · carpooling

1 Introduction

Mobility is an essential aspect of a modern society and an efficient economy. On the one hand, an efficient transport system that guarantees the frictionless exchange of goods and services is a prerequisite for economic development and a central location factor. On the other hand, mobility is a basic need for the individual because it is a cornerstone of personal freedom. In most cases, participation in working and social life presupposes being mobile. Mobility therefore ensures prosperity and enables social participation (Knie et al. 2016, BMUB 2016).

A. Sandau (✉) · J. Schering · A. Amin Rezaei · C. Theesen · J. Marx Gómez
Carl von Ossietzky University of Oldenburg, Oldenburg, Germany
e-mail: alexander.sandau@uol.de; johannes.schering@uol.de; ali.amin.rezaei@uol.de; cedrik.theesen@uol.de; jorge.marx.gomez@uol.de

© The Author(s), under exclusive license to Springer Nature Switzerland AG 2021
J. Marx Gómez et al. (eds.), *Progress in Sustainable Mobility Research*,
Progress in IS, https://doi.org/10.1007/978-3-030-70841-2_8

Mobility in its current form or the transport sector in general is not sustainable and stands in a tension between economic, social, and ecological interests. The benefits for society and the economy are offset by negative effects on people and environment. In 2015, the transport sector was responsible for around 18% of Germany's greenhouse gas emissions (UBA 2019). Efficiency gains are offset by a steady increase in transport volume. Therefore, the transport sector in Germany accounts for almost 30% of the national energy consumption (BMUB 2016). In addition, there are negative effects on the environment and quality of life, for instance, pollutant or noise emissions (Brenck et al. 2016). Great efforts are needed to achieve the national climate protection targets and to make the transport system independent of fossil fuels by 2050 and thus largely climate neutral. The traffic forecast for 2030 clearly shows the urgent need for action: by 2030 freight traffic will increase by 38% and passenger traffic by 13% (BMVI 2014).

An important lever to achieve a more sustainable mobility is to change the behavior of individual road users. A look at the modal split in passenger transport shows that in Germany and most EU countries motorized individual transport accounts for more than 80% of the total traffic. The remaining 20% is accounted for the environmentally compatible means of transport (e.g., bus, train, bicycle, footpaths) (Canzler and Knie 2016). Therefore, appropriate incentives are needed to make individual mobility behavior more sustainable to decrease the climate impact. These include the promotion of non-motorized transport, local public transport, and intermodal and multimodal means of transport, as addressed by measures of mobility management (Flämig et al. 2017).

Steadily increasing vehicle costs (maintenance, fuel, tolls, parking space management) would have to increase interest in carpooling. It is therefore necessary to create framework conditions that make it as easy as possible for interested parties to maintain a carpool. Modern carpooling platforms could contribute to solving this problem. But financing them is difficult, as one central motivation in carpooling relies on saving money. Implementing user charges as a source of financing is contrary to that motivation (Fürst and Leander 2014).

1.1 Problem Situation

Especially the commuter traffic, the distance traveled by employees between home and work has been steadily increasing in Germany for years. While 53% of all employees commuted in 2000, this figure had risen to 60% by 2015. In the same period, the average length of the one-way trips to work increased significantly from 14.6 to 16.8 km (BBSR 2017). Expressed in passenger-kilometers, commuter traffic accounts for a ~20% of the total traffic volume with an annual amount of ~280 billion kilometers. This means that the share has almost doubled in the last 40 years (BMVI 2017). Motorized private transport accounts for a particularly high proportion of the commuter traffic. When it comes to "work" as a reason of transport, employees use the car as a means of transport on around 65% of all trips.

This shows that only slightly more than one-third is accounted by environmentally friendly means of transport (e.g., bus, train, bicycle). The motorized private transport even accounts for 86% of all business trips (Pütz 2015). In addition to the negative environmental effects, there are also considerable individual negative health effects. A permanently increased stress level due to long periods in rush-hour traffic is only one of the consequences. Stress also occurs because occupational or private expectations cannot be met. Relatively frequent complaint complexes in this context are headaches, exhaustion, and fatigue or aching limbs.

The reasons for the increasing commuter traffic are manifold. For instance, the flexibilization and specialization of work means that employees can no longer find a job at every place of residence that matches their qualifications and personal aspirations. This results in a kind of mobility constraint in order to achieve jobs (Pütz 2015). The increased volume of commuting traffic can also be attributed to the fact that the number of employees in Germany has risen sharply in recent years. Also, tax incentives play a key role: the depreciation of trips to and from the workplace, which is intended to relieve the economic burden on employees, rewards longer trip to workplaces, and generates traffic (Bratzel 2008). A further observation concerns the decreasing proportion of the so-called inland commuters whose place of residence and workplace are within the same municipality. This circumstance is a consequence of the increasing spatial and functional separation of living and working places (Einig and Pütz 2017).

1.2 Objective

The aim of this contribution is to show how information and communication technologies (ICT) can be used to sensitize road users to sustainable mobility and to influence individual mobility behavior accordingly. A focus lies on mobility supply in rural areas, as the pressure to act is particularly greater here, for example, due to demographic developments, greater distances, and thinner local transport networks. At first related work will be examined and central criteria for a platform for sustainable mobility will be derived. Afterwards, the conceptual system will be presented and the mobile application *Fahrkreis* will be introduced. The article concludes with a conclusion and recommendations.

2 Related Work

Ongoing urbanization and demographic change will have a major long-term impact on our society and thus also on transport and mobility. Rural areas are affected by the consequences of demographic change heavily: Due to the migration of young people to structurally strong regions and cities as well as low birth rates, the population in many rural regions has been declining steadily for decades. This has resulted in a significant aging of the population: the proportion of senior citizens is above average in many rural regions (BMEL 2016; Plazinić et al., 2018). These developments pose special challenges for ensuring the mobility of the affected citizens in the long term. As the population shrinks, the demand for goods and services declines accordingly. Consequently, institutions of social infrastructure, supply, and culture close or migrate to urban areas. As a result, the population of rural areas must overcome greater distances in order to be able to use these facilities (IGES and ADAC 2016). Furthermore, rural areas suffer by a lack of effectiveness (Antonowicz 2017) and the inadequacy of the public transport (Milbourne et al., 2014). Reflected in the low utilization of public transport and scarcity of bus frequency (Barreto et al. 2018), which turns out to be very cost-inefficient (Gogola et al. 2018); and inadequate to the real demand of passengers, which can also be especially affected by "erosion" of the transport services supply from the viewpoint of the variety of the destinations and its frequency (Budčjovice 2017).

The impact is complex, as the decline in population does not automatically lead to a decline in traffic. In contrast, the changed age structure or new mobility patterns influence the demand for mobility. It is therefore becoming increasingly necessary to pay attention to aspects such as user-friendliness, accessibility, and age-appropriate mobility chains (BMI 2011). In this context, various solutions have emerged in recent decades to ensure sufficient mobility for the population (BMVI 2016). A distinction can be made between approaches that are organized by the public sector or by private commitment (civil society and business). On the part of the public sector, solutions have emerged in the following areas: Reorganization and optimization of public transport services, flexible forms of public transport, combination of passenger and freight transport and linking mobility options. In the context of private commitment, examples include take-away services, sharing models, private-sector initiatives such as pick-up and drop-off services and mobility services based on public commitment (e.g., citizen buses) (IGES and ADAC 2016).

The basis for lasting success of a carpooling platform lies in reaching a critical mass of users. A low density of participants leads to the fact that mediation requests are not or only unsatisfactorily answered. Especially in the start-up phase, the associated loss of credibility poses a problem for platform operators (Agatz et al. 2011). Two approaches are pursued to facilitate the achievement of critical mass. On the one hand, the networking of individual carpool platforms is encouraged in order to create a comprehensive offer (Chan and Shaheen 2011). On the other hand, the deeper integration of carpools into the mobility supply of regions across modes of transport is being pursued (Vaughn et al. 1999). However, operating a carpooling platform does not offer many opportunities to generate revenue. Currently, platform operators apply one or more of the four models described below (Amey et al. 2011):

1. Free mediation; revenue via sale of advertising on the platform
2. Withholding of a transaction fee in case of accounting via the platform
3. Development and operation of carpool solutions for companies or institutions
4. Development and operation of carpool solutions on behalf of state administrative institutions

In addition to these approaches, various mobility applications have been established on the market driven by the advancing digitalization and the associated spread of smartphones, some of these are also related to sustainability issues. Daimler's "moovel" app offers users access to mobility by combining services such as carsharing and pooling, public transport, taxi services and rental bicycles and so on. Users can search and pay for connections through one mobile application. The fact that "moovel" informs the user of existing mobility capacities increases capacity utilization and is less harmful to the environment compared to using one's own car.

The digitalization enables completely new approaches to mobility and simplifies travel planning. As an everyday companion and multifunctional device, the smartphone plays a key role in this context using time- and location-independent access to multimodal mobility. The effects of an aging society and the needs of older people need to be taken into account: In the medium term, there will be still a need for parallel classic access to mobility services (e.g., via timetables), but the use of smartphones will also be a matter of course for the growing generations of seniors in old age (IGES and ADAC 2016; Limbourg 2015).

How a travel information system can succeed in providing users with access to comprehensive mobility services (multimodal mobility information and planning, travel assistance, and formation of carpools) on the one hand and in sensitizing them to sustainability issues on the other is shown in the following sections on the basis of the mobility platform *Fahrkreis* which was developed during project NEMo.[1]

3 Mobility Platform for Sustainable Mobility

To promote sustainable mobility, it is crucial to change society's mobility behavior by influencing the individual. It is fundamental for the success, to become aware of the motives and explanatory theories of behavior regarding the choices of means of transport. In science, the mobility behavior of individuals, especially motives for using private cars, is a much-discussed topic. Especially the following two theories shaping the scientific discussion. The theory of planned behavior been used successfully to explain a wide range of conscious behavioral decisions. It describes the formation of a behavioral intention, which in turn is influenced by the three parameters attitude, subjective norm and perceived behavioral control. The theory comprises rational choice models which, as the basis for decisions between alternative courses of action, proceed strictly after weighting costs and benefits. Available individual resources will be considered as well. Although theory cannot exist as the sole explanatory model for traffic behavior, it is an important supplement to attitudinally oriented explanatory approaches.

In the analysis of Neoh et al. (2017), the circumstances, attitudes, and demographics are the three main elements that can affect the use of carpooling. In

---

[1] https://nemo-mobilitaet.de.

Table 1 Impact factors on traffic behavior

Impact factor	Description
Monetary	• Especially car users show strong resistance to cost-related measures for the formation of carpools • Most frequently cited motive (Farrokhikhiavi et al. 2011)
Environmental	• One of the major motives for carpooling • There are often differences between the expressed intention to behave and the demonstrated behavior
Behavior	• Central influencing factor • Poor public transport connections encourage willingness to participate (overlap with time factor)
Convenience	• Fundamentally strong influence on mobility behavior (Seebauer 2011) • Aspect of subjective comfort is more in favor of participation • Aspect of time flexibility counteracts participation in carpools (Agatz et al. 2011; Amey et al. 2011)
Time	• Widely recognized as an influencing factor, but evaluation problematic • Overlap with factor behavioral offer in relation to carpooling
Security	• Not the actual safety is relevant, but the subjective perception of safety; distorted risk perception (Amey et al. 2011) • Has a negative effect on the willingness to form carpools
Knowledge	• Not a motive but a prerequisite. However, motives can be caused by knowledge (Seebauer 2011) • Relevant for carpooling is knowledge of transport services and their impact (Farrokhikhiavi et al. 2011; Chan and Shaheen 2011)
Habitual	• Represents a barrier for the decision on new action alternatives (Bamberg et al. 2003) • Has a behavior-stabilizing effect after a decision to change has been taken

that study internal (demographic and judgmental factors) and external (third-party interventions and situational factors) influential factors are considered. It turned out that socio-demographic factors, such as age, gender, and income, do not have a significant effect on carpooling (Neoh et al. 2017). According to that analysis women were slightly more likely to carpool than men. The study also revealed that judgmental factors which also called psychological factors are more important than demographic factors in decision making for using carpooling. However, attitudes and norms tend to have the biggest influence on likelihood to use carpooling services (Olsson et al. 2019). Table 1 shows the most important factors influencing the perception of means of transport.

3.1 Influencing Impacts Factors on the Choice of Transport Modes

Influencing the choice of the mean of transport can be implemented through mobility management measures. A central component is the provision of information. In the context of today's information systems, mobility platforms already comprehensively provide this function.

The *Fahrkreis* Travel Information System (TIS) is a system for multimodal travel planning and assistance for customers. The objective is to enable customers to travel with special consideration of individual mobility needs and possibilities as well as sustainability efforts. The objective is to develop and support sustainable, and innovative mobility services as well as business models for rural areas. The focus is on generating social benefits that directly benefit citizens and indirectly benefit the environment.

On the provider side, the system is fully integrated into an operative and analytical Customer Relationship Management (CRM) environment (Wagner vom Berg 2015). Communication and interaction between customer and the system is guaranteed by the mobile travel planning and assistance application *Fahrkreis*.

In order to be able to address the largest possible user group and to ensure the highest degree of dissemination, the platform must achieve a high degree of awareness in the application area. The key findings of our empirical study in the application area reveals the devastating result on the question of the knowledge of existing carpool platforms. As of considerable importance, the communication channels through the platform must be made known for targeting users. The most suitable marketing approach are word of mouth, mail by work council, mail by the employer (with information brochure), which have in common that there is a familiar link in the form of a person or an organization between the potential users of the platform. All other information channels that directly address the user have been classified as less suitable. Social network platforms such as Facebook or Twitter seem to be suitable for addressing younger users; after all, each "like" is also a kind of word of mouth.

To implement a successful marketing campaign for a multimodal mobility platform it is helpful to address factors that make potential users think about carpooling. Unsurprisingly, the idea of joining a carpool is being considered primarily for cost reasons. This could also explain why people on higher incomes tend to be less willing to do so. With the two reasons for refusal ranked first (unpunctuality, unreliability) it is noticeable that these could be avoided relatively easily by choosing a suitable carpool partner by the system. The third ranked reason (loss of flexibility) and the fourth ranked reason (dependency on others) are, however, inseparably linked to carpooling. The problem is that the trip from work to home is much more irregular than the trip to work. A platform that can support the formation of dynamic carpools could successfully counteract this tendency. Especially when errands are done after work and for people with family and children, carpooling is rather unattractive as it makes daily planning even more complex. The more fixed the working hours are, the more suitable it is to ride along. Shift work is better than flextime, as the start and end times usually coincide exactly. But the status of an employee can also hinder the formation of driving communities. For example, a cleaner may have reservations about going with the CEO, or managers may not be willing to take people with them.

3.2   Current State of Research

Carpooling refers to the situation where two or more individuals travel in the same car to reduce the number of single-occupancy vehicles on the road (Neoh et al. 2017). It allows individuals to have the flexibility and speed of private cars, but with reduced costs and an ecological footprint for travelers and the society (Furuhata et al. 2013). In addition, carpooling requires little public investment since the infrastructure already exists (Garrison et al. 2011).

First, it is necessary to clarify the difference between common terminologies in this domain. The term carpooling became popular in the 1970s as a behavioral response to the oil crisis. In recent years with rising of the technologies which led to the development of more sophisticated mobile apps; made carpooling planning and management more accessible to greater number of the population and thus the carpooling services is now on double digit growth (Amirkiaee et al., 2018). Another element which led to growth in carpooling in a bigger picture refers to promoting of sharing economy in society by rising services such Airbnb or Uber. Besides that, increasing in environmental concerns of the societies is another factor led to growth of the carpooling services (Olsson et al. 2019).

Most of researches in the domain of carpooling referred to the transportation in and between urban areas and were less focused to the rural areas. Reviewing the literature related to rural areas revealed some common research questions that tried to be answered by multiple researches in the domain. As an example, Joseph (2018) exposed the following research questions: Is carpooling feasible in rural regions; is there a reasonable demand for carpooling services in rural areas? What segments of the population are interested in carpooling services? What are the different factors that are facilitating and/or inhibiting the growth of carpooling services in rural communities? How carpooling can affect the environment? How carpooling can affect social exclusions in rural areas?

As reflected in the literature, based on social, economic, and environmental dimensions, it is recognized that the successful economic transport service and sustainable mobility system needs to properly address the following points: recognize the adverse effects of motorized transport on the environment; determine the level of social exclusion of those who do not own a private car; rising costs and lack of conventional fuels for the transportation sector; demographic changes (Gogola et al. 2018) and elderly people access to facilities and services, especially to health centers (Plazinić et al., 2018).

Thus, the implementation of sustainable, context-oriented, and integrated public transport systems (Gogola et al. 2018) improves quality of life, playing an important role in the development of sparsely populated regions and in their human resources competitiveness level (Budčjovice 2017), in order to mitigate transport deprivation and social exclusion (Plazinić, 2018). Moreover, carpooling services in rural areas offer a potential for the creation of new markets. Carpooling platforms can be used to create richer data about travel demand patterns and dynamics, which allows the creation of the new sales channels, access unexploited customer demand and to simplify the user payment methods (Mulley et al. 2018). One of the main recognized barrier factors against promoting carpooling in rural areas is the inaccessibility. This involves on the one hand Lack or weak coverage of mobile data which can be addressed by providing alternative interfaces (e.g., hotline) to the platform (Joseph 2018). On the other hand, illiterate and disabled people that can be addressed by supportive technology (Kalogirou, 2018).

4 Mobile Application as Travel Guide

As rural areas indicating, there is a changing demographic situation compared to urban areas. In particular, the average age is significantly higher, which is one reason for a reduced affinity for technology in this region. An important factor in this context is user-friendliness, which is usually the result of a compromise between the desire to provide users with a wide range of useful functions and the desire to keep the platform as easy to use as possible.

The objective of the mobile application is to act as a constant companion in the daily planning and satisfaction of a user's mobility needs. The application will intervene as an intelligent (proactive) assistance and design the individual mobility as efficiently as possible. The focus is always on optimal usability and intelligent information selection. The main features are demonstrated on the mobile application *Fahrkreis*. For a comprehensive mobility app, the following eight key factors are crucial.

Multimodal Mobility   Integration of various means of transport as local public transport, railways, sharing services, taxis or carsharing service, kickscooters providers and therefore covers the most common mobility offers in order to provide the best possible service for residents and visitors.

No Fees   Does not charge higher prices for mobility services than the original apps. Discounts such as the Bahncard are retained in the app.

Door-to-Door Planning   Shows the route as well as the routes to and from the stops to the respective destination (first and last mile is considered).

Realtime   Provides real-time data available on the market for the corresponding means of transport and/or live maps on which the journey can be tracked. Also it provides live information about connections, the route to the next means of transport, disruptions, etc.

Added-Value Services   Offers a pool of additional information, such as places of interest, petrol stations, e-charging stations, car parks or Park+Ride sites.

Customization   Users can define their preferences, for example: fastest, cheapest, barrier-free, transfer-free connection, preferred, environmentally friendly means of transport or individual walking speed.

Authentication, Authorization, and Accounting   Users only need to register once (single sign-on) in order to use all mobility services, including those of third-party providers (Authentication), as well as book and reserve all desired means of transport directly (Authorization). Directly and transparent payment trough the app with a clear overview of the expenses (Accounting).

Data Security Fulfills the valid data protection requirements according to General Data Protection Regulation (GDPR) such as: Information on the processing of personal data and persons responsible; information on purpose, legal basis, recipients of personal data and duration of data processing; and finally, information on user rights such as information, restriction of processing or deletion of data.

The uncertainty of potential users regarding the legal framework must be taken seriously and the need for information met. This requires appropriate knowledge of the operators and their employees in specific legal matters.

4.1 Carpooling as Key Element

The developed TIS is a system for multimodal travel planning and assistance for customers to enable travel with special consideration of individual mobility needs and possibilities as well as sustainability efforts. The aim of this system is to develop sustainable and innovative mobility services and business models for rural areas. The main objective is to generate social benefits that directly benefit citizens and indirectly benefit the environment.

A main function of the TIS is the organization of carpools and their integration in the local mobility offer. This is intended to make unused mobility capacities or free spaces in cars usable and to transform citizens into mobility providers. A central component is the integration of an automated matchmaking algorithm. Matchmaking refers to bringing together the driver and passenger. Within the research project, matchmaking without user interaction is performed by an algorithm and proposed as a mobility result, also as part of a multimodal route. By integrating carpools into multimodal travel chains, mobility supply gaps in rural areas can be covered. Project NEMo distinguishes itself from other existing solutions in Germany such as Blablacar or Fahrgemeinschaft.de by this integration. The algorithm used was originally developed by the company SmartWay for inner-city logistics and is also capable of exchanging individual packages at virtual transfer points between drivers. For the transport of people, the algorithm must be extended and adapted. Based on OpenStreetMap geodata, central locations of utilities and services of general interest were identified and integrated into the system as virtual stops. One important criterion for the selection of virtual stops is the possibility of stopping the vehicles for a short time in order to allow entry and exit. The stops primarily comprise facilities from areas such as transport (bus stops, petrol stations), food (supermarkets), banking and postal services (cash machines) as well as culture and leisure.

Regarding virtual stops, accessibility plays a decisive role. From the citizens' point of view, this generally includes better feeder traffic or safe parking facilities for bicycles at public transport stops (Landkreis Wesermarsch 2017). An improved connection of bus stops increases the attractiveness as a meeting point for carpools, as passengers can reach bus stops better with less effort. This applies to the main traffic routes within a region, where there are numerous bus stops, and which are also heavily frequented by commuters.

To provide added value for users through the carpooling function, a quantitative online survey of 338 participants was conducted to determine central requirements for addressing the demands and needs of users in rural areas (Jahns and Woisetschläger 2017). Pricing plays an important role in the context of carpooling opportunities from the point of view of the target group. Most respondents would like to see either binding pricing (based on public transport tariffs) or a non-binding price proposal as a basis for negotiation. Here, the mobile app provides tangible assistance: Since the individual key figures of the owned car are stored, it is possible to calculate the costs for a carpool individually for each user for the distance covered together. Due to the legal framework, however, only a cost recovery amount is proposed by the system. This ensures that there is no commercial context.

Within the TIS, carpooling opportunities are represented as virtual travel groups. The users determined from the matchmaking algorithm are assigned to a group as soon as they select the carpooling opportunity as an option for the specific mobility requirement. Since mobility is characterized by individual start and destination points, only the segments of the common route are assigned to the travel group. A central challenge in the planning of carpooling opportunities is not only the matching of supply and demand, but also the integration into multimodal chains of routes. In particular, the first and last mile of multimodal journeys with the carpooling mode is complex and complicated. In the planning phase, for instance, interconnected mobility options or accessibility by other modes must be guaranteed. In addition to geographical and mobility restrictions, time restrictions and delays must also be considered. Figure 1 outlines the interaction of the different systems.

Besides the calculation of the individual route for driver and passenger, the system is able to provide closed groups for carpooling associations like schools, companies, or female pooling groups. As one of the broadly discussed results within the citizen workshops, a huge demand for security supporting functions was demanded. Closed groups are managed by a responsible person of an institution or company that invites the customer by mail.

4.2 Data Driven Support in Daily Mobility Planning

Data analysis plays a central role in the successful use of a mobility platform for sustainable mobility. Users of the platform are provided with reports that represent individual mobility behavior. These data and generated reports are especially interesting for third-party recipients. Potential third-party recipients are companies as well as public authorities, e.g., at the municipal level. All companies that would

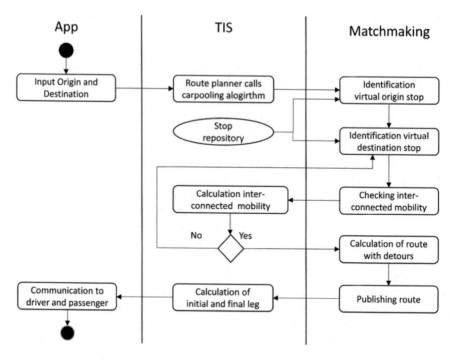

Fig. 1 Interaction of TIS and matchmaking

like to enter the mobility sector (e.g., energy suppliers) or active participants (e.g., car manufacturers and car dealerships) are interested in data on the mobility behavior and preferences of customers. In this context, the data protection of user-related data naturally plays an important role, but even completely anonymous data retains a high information potential for all recipients. Considering these data usage scenarios, different business models and deployment scenarios of the platform are conceivable. For example, the system could be operated as an independent platform for sustainable mobility, with revenues generated through data sales and advertising like those generated by social networks. Furthermore, the platform could also be operated as a regional travel information system in the context of mobility management of cities or public transport modes in order to promote the greater use of sustainable forms of transport. The following pictures show the platform reports in the context of the CRM system.

4.3 Mobility Information

The route search allows the specification of different parameters. Apart from place and time parameters, further information can be provided for the desired route

Fig. 2 Route results with assessment of CO_2 emissions (left) and Trip assistant (right)

calculation, e.g., whether the arrival should take place at a certain time. In addition, a number of passengers can be specified so, for example, in a larger group, the car is no longer taken into account as a means of transport because not all passengers can travel. By individualizing the user profile, a selection can be made for the current route search if several vehicles are specified, so that the calculation of the individual key figures in the dimensions costs and sustainability is carried out correctly.

The system supports a rule-based planning of reoccurring trips, that are also accessible for carpooling users. Furthermore, it is possible to submit mobility demands, that may be filled with carpooling offers. Figure 2 shows the views for the assessment of CO_2 emissions and the trip assistant.

4.4 Travel Assistance

The travel assistant provides an overview of the individual connections and several auxiliary functions on the trip. For instance, the current connection is highlighted by a small green circle. If a partial connection is selected, this section can be displayed in more detail on a map, where it is possible to start the detailed integrated navigation. Also, the user also has the option of evaluating the respective vehicle, connection, and stops on the route section using the feedback button. In addition, the user can manually terminate or cancel an active route. Furthermore, the route can be shared via social networks to attract potential passengers. If a route is successfully completed, the user is assessed according to the sustainability of his chosen mobility option and rewarded accordingly with bonus points. All completed journeys are historicized and made available to the user for later viewing via the app. This gives the user the best possible transparency of his travel behavior. In addition, reviews of the trip can be added later if this has not yet been done.

Fahrkreis, however, should not only provide added value in daily mobility planning and implementation. The mobile application should also be used to influence users in their mobility behavior. The app intends to influence users in their choice of means of transport from the perspective of sustainability (Wagner vom Berg 2015). In this way, users can enter specifications for their desired mobility behavior. The individual dimensions are sustainability, comfort, costs and flexibility.

The support phases differ according to the customer activity: If the customer plans a trip, the user is in the pre-trip planning phase. During this phase, context-sensitive information about the user and his environment is considered. This includes, for example, the individual mobility possibilities, such as the availability of an own car, the current position or the current weather forecast. If the user has added a car to his profile, the car sections are calculated based on the car's key performance indicators (KPIs) in order to achieve a realistic estimation of the environmental impact and costs of this route option.

The active travel phase comprises proactive support during a journey (on-trip). The traveler is supported by an active travel assistance, which, for example, determines the current trip segment based on the current position. At the same time, the travel assistant has the intelligence to compare the traveled trip section with the planned route and to make recommendations for action (Sandau and Stamer 2014). Further assistance functions are integrated within the travel information system, which can provide information about current delays or places of interest (POIs) in the vicinity (for longer transfer times). During the active travel phase, the user has the option of ending or canceling a trip manually. The functionality of a trip interruption is necessary for the correct calculation of the individual travel and emission profile. The manual termination of a trip leads to the successful completion of a trip. This may become necessary if the system does not automatically detect the arrival at the destination, e.g., because the current position was not recognized. To avoid an abuse of the system, manually terminated trips are not rewarded with bonus points.

After a successfully completed route, the user is in the post-trip phase. The user receives a statistical summary of his trip, which is calculated using various KPIs. This includes values for the distance traveled, the costs and the CO_2 emissions caused. More bonus points are awarded for particularly sustainable travel, depending on the mobility options available. The collected bonus points can be exchanged in a digital shop within the app for sustainable mobility related services. Vouchers for test drives with electric vehicles, pedelecs can be redeemed. It is also possible to issue vouchers for sustainable mobility services (e.g., public transport day ticket, carsharing discount). These items or vouchers can be managed centrally by the connected CRM system.

Based on the trips made and the assigned key figures, the TIS provides reporting for the customers. Through the system, the users are able to trace their individual travel behavior and its trend transparently. Different evaluation levels of the mobility behavior can be viewed and set in relation to the average behavior of the platform users. At the same time, the level of individual travel options, the actual travel behavior can be related to the worst and best possible travel options. The integration of reporting and the bonus point shop was implemented using web views. Figure 3 shows the views the trip summary and the bonus point shop.

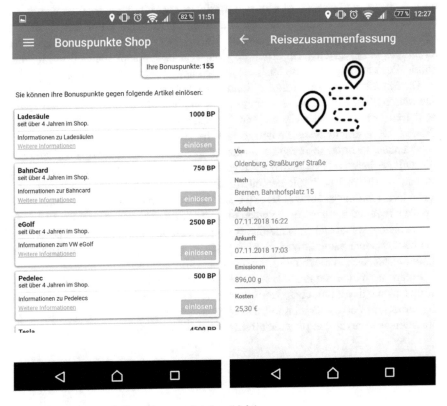

Fig. 3 Trip summary (left) and bonus point shop (right)

4.5   Context Awareness

Notifications are classified by status codes within the push messages and used as a basis for further processing of the information. Notifications can be received in the app at any time. The first group includes messages that can be sent to the *Fahrkreis* app or its users at any time. For example, the travel assistant notifies the user via the reporting system that a new report on mobility behavior is available. This group also includes advertising offers and messages from partner programs. In addition, recommendations for alternative routes or means of transport are proposed to the user as soon as a more intelligent route option is available. The second group comprises messages that are communicated before the start of the journey. This includes the introduction of the personal travel assistant *Fahrkreis* as well as various warning messages as bad weather situations, reminder for recharging or refueling the car, reminder of an imminent departure or traffic jam warnings. The third group includes notifications that may occur during a trip. This includes information about interesting places, upcoming stages of a journey, traffic jam warnings and weather warnings, or public transport disruptions. The fourth group includes notifications after a successfully completed trip. This includes the number of bonus points received and a summary of the traveled trip. All these groups can be supplemented with additional notifications to support future business models and assistance functions.

The *Fahrkreis* app was evaluated in iterative field trials between December 2017 and March 2020 with a successively growing number of users. In a first step, these field trials served to identify technical problems and improve user-friendliness. Citizens were gradually be invited to use the app and provide feedback on their experiences. In order to integrate further planned business models, the *Fahrkreis* app will be iteratively extended by further functionalities. Direct communication between users will be implemented for the next iteration stage. In addition, the travel information system will be extended by further analytical reports, which will enable a regional comparison between the users. Furthermore, several field trials in companies, schools and associations were planned and implemented. The system can be individual parametrized for each institution and their specific demands, like detour distances and much more.

Future activities require research on real-time intelligent matchmaking algorithms as well as the consideration of voluntary mobility services and their digitalization. Also, a comprehensive approach including all actors and mobility providers is necessary to play out all synergies of such a platform.

5   Conclusion and Recommendations

This article explains how a travel application can not only be used to plan mobility but also to sensitize people to sustainable mobility through appropriate functionalities. The survey of potential users has shown that pricing is particularly relevant. This aspect is addressed by corresponding functionalities.

Commuter traffic has a significant negative impact on people and the environment. In view of the tendency for the volume of commuter traffic to increase rather than decrease in the near future, appropriate solutions are needed. The formation of carpools can help to reduce economic, social, and ecological impacts. The formation of carpools in rural areas faces special challenges due to the mostly sparsely populated area. ICT can provide important assistance in organizing carpools in rush-hour traffic. From the authors' point of view, the app presented in this article offers a suitable approach for developing carpools into an attractive alternative in commuter traffic.

With the objective of contributing to a reduction of commuter traffic through the implementation of a mobile application, various challenges were identified. For a successful dissemination of carpooling in the rural area, it must first be known by many citizens in order to generate a critical mass of suppliers and customers. Since the research project NEMo does not provide any funds for large-scale communication measures, cooperation with multipliers is needed to make the offer known. These include, for example, business development institutions, employers, and staff representatives. In order to generate a basic stock of carpools, additional employees could be motivated in cooperation with employers to enter already existing carpools into the mobility platform. From the employers' point of view, there are certainly reasons to reduce or make more sustainable employee transport by promoting carpooling, for example, to reduce the costs of parking space management. These measures can strengthen the image of a company to become more attractive for specialist. Furthermore, from the point of view of the target group, the question must be answered as to why the app should be used at all compared to other mobility applications on the market. To this end, the added value of the application must be highlighted, which consists of the various functions. The app discussed here pursues a comprehensive approach to make mobility more sustainable. In addition to the ride-sharing function, the app offers multimodal mobility information, which can be used to search for various route options. Furthermore, by the end of the project period (July 2019), project NEMo integrated the so-called imovative non-monetary business models that strengthen the community in rural areas and thus also improve the mobility situation of citizens (Sandau et al. 2018). As part of one of these business models, it is planned that drivers will be able to offer both outward and return journeys. This addresses the need of passengers to plan the return journey as well as the outward journey. In addition, the communicative placement of the app offers a lever to attract users. Thus, an app name that is easy to understand and arouses real associations can arouse interest among the target group. At the same time, a regional reference in the app name (for example: "Fahrkreis Wesermarsch") can contribute to a kind of identification.

In addition, carpooling platforms are also open to other mobility-specific topics and their development which can help to reach a critical mass. The most dissatisfying mobility offer in rural areas and the sensitive area of "age mobility" offer starting points for expanding the user potential. The latter, however, would require intensive discussion. Access to potential users would be facilitated if scientific studies were conducted to determine how carpooling platforms could offer solutions to the challenges in the mobility sector.

All in all, mobility platforms are in an extremely dynamic market—with rapid changes and transformations in providers and opportunities. The bottom line is that the many individual providers and suppliers are barely interconnected. As the German government and the European Union frame, Germany is correspondingly far away from the declared goal of "digital connected mobility."

References

Agatz, N. A. H., Erera, A. L., Savelsbergh, M. W. P., & Wang, X. (2011). Dynamic ride sharing: A simulation study in metro Atlanta. *Transportation Research Part B, 45*, 1450–1464.

Amey, A., Attanucci, J., & Mishalani, R. (2011). Real-time ridesharing: Opportunities and challenges in using mobile phone technology to improve rideshare services. *Transportation Research Record: Journal of the Transportation Research Board, 2217*(1), 103–110.

Amirkiaee, S. Y., & Evangelopoulos, N. (2018). Why do people rideshare? An experimental study. *Transportation Research Part F: Traffic Psychology and Behaviour, 55*, 9–24.

Antonowicz, D. (2017). *D.T 2.4.1 Pilot launch report Mazovia*. Interreg Central Europe – RUMOBIL.

Bamberg, S., Ajzen, J., & Schmid P. (2003). Choice of travel mode in the theory of planned behavior: The roles of past behavior, habit and reasoned action. *Basic and Applied Social Psychology, 25*(3), 175–187.

Barreto, L., Amaral, A., & Baltazar, S. (2018). Mobility as a service (MaaS) in rural regions: An overview. In *2018 International Conference on Intelligent Systems (IS)* (pp. 856–860). Piscataway, NJ: IEEE.

Bratzel, S. (2008). Mobilität und Verkehr. In: *Informationen zur politischen Bildung – Umweltpolitik* Nr. 287. Bundeszentrale für politische Bildung.

Brenck, A., Mitusch, K., Winter, M. (2016). Die externen Kosten des Verkehrs. In: O. Schwedes, W. Canzler, & A. Knie (Eds.) *Handbuch Verkehrspolitik* (pp. 401–429). Wiesbaden: Springer Fachmedien.

Budčjovice, Č. (2017). *Macroeconomic effects on development of sparsely populated areas*. Interreg Central Europe.

Bundesministerium des Innern (BMI). (2011). *Demografiebericht. Bericht der Bundesregierung zur demografischen Lage und künftigen Entwicklung des Landes*. Retrieved December 12, 2020 from https://www.demografie-portal.de/DE/Service/Publikationen/2011/demografiebericht-der-bundesregierung.pdf?__blob=publicationFile&v=3

Bundesinstitut für Bau-, Stadt- und Raumforschung (BBSR). (2017). *Immer mehr Menschen pendeln zur Arbeit*. Retrieved March 22, 2018 from http://www.bbsr.bund.de/BBSR/DE/Home/Topthemen/2017-pendeln.html

Bundesministerium für Ernährung und Landwirtschaft (BMEL). (2016). *Bericht der Bundesregierung zur Entwicklung der ländlichen Räume 2016*. Berlin

Bundesministerium für Umwelt, Naturschutz, Bau und Reaktorsicherheit (BMUB). (2016). *Klimaschutzplan 2050. Klimapolitische Grundsätze und Ziele der Bundesregierung*. Berlin.

Bundesministerium für Verkehr und digitale Infrastruktur (BMVI). (2014). *Verkehrsverflechtungsprognose 2030*. Retrieved March 21, 2019 from https://www.bmvi.de/SharedDocs/DE/Anlage/G/verkehrsverflechtungsprognose-2030-schlussbericht-los-3.pdf?__blob=publicationFile

Bundesministerium für Verkehr und digitale Infrastruktur (BMVI). (2016). *Mobilitäts- und Angebotsstrategien in ländlichen Räumen. Planungsleitfaden für Handlungsmöglichkeiten von ÖPNV-Aufgabenträgern und Verkehrsunternehmen unter besonderer Berücksichtigung wirtschaftlicher Aspekte flexibler Bedienungsformen.* Retrieved December 10, 2020 from https://www.bmvi.de/SharedDocs/DE/Publikationen/G/mobilitaets-und-angebotsstrategien-in-laendlichen-raeumen-neu.pdf?__blob=publicationFile

Bundesministerium für Verkehr und digitale Infrastruktur (BMVI). (2017). *Verkehr in Zahlen 2017/2018* 46. Jahrgang. Hamburg: DVV Media Group GmbH.

Canzler, W., & Knie A. (2016). *Die digitale Mobilitätsrevolution. Vom Ende des Verkehrs, wie wir ihn kannten.* München: Oekom Verlag.

Chan, N. D., & Shaheen, S. A. (2011). Ridesharing in North America: Past, present, and future. *Transport Reviews, 32*(1), 93–112.

Einig, K., & Pütz, T. (2017). Regionale Dynamik der Pendlergesellschaft. Entwicklung von Verflechtungsmustern und Pendeldistanzen. *Informationen zur Raumentwicklung* Heft 2/3 (pp. 73–91).

Farrokhikhiavi, R., Schmidt, R., Bruns, A., Horn, D., von der Rohren, S., & Heckert, D. (2011). *Potentiale und Möglichkeiten zur Venetzung intenetgestützter Fahrgemeinschaftsvermittlung für regelmäßige Fahrten (Berufspendler)*, Schlussbericht. Aachen.

Flämig, H., Gertz, C., & Mühlhausen, T. (2017). Personen- und Güterverkehr. In: G. Brasseur, D. Jacob, & S. Schuck-Zöller (Eds.), *Klimawandel in Deutschland. Entwicklung, Folgen, Risiken und Perspektiven* (pp. 215–223). Heidelberg: Springer Spektrum.

Furuhata, M., Dessouky, M., Ordóñez, F., Brunet, M.-E., Wang, X., & Koenig, S. (2013). Ridesharing: The state-of-the-art and future directions. *Transportation Research Part B, 57,* 28–46.

Fürst, E., & Leander, K. (2014). Potential, Möglichkeit und Voraussetzungen für die Errichtung einer Plattform zur Bildung längerfristiger Fahrgemeinschaften. In: H. Proff (Ed.), *Radikale Innovationen in der Mobilität* (pp. 413–426). Berlin: Springer.

Garrison, W. L., Wellar, B., MacKinnon, R., Black, W. R., & Getis, A. (2011). Research commentary: Increasing the flexibility of legacy systems. *International Journal of Applied Geospatial Research, 2,* 39–55.

Gogola, M., Sitanyiová, D., Černický, U., & Veterník, M. (2018). *New demand patterns for public transport due to demographic.* Interreg Central Europe.

IGES Institut, ADAC e.V. (2016). *Mobilität sichert Entwicklung. Herausforderungen für den ländlichen Raum.* Retrieved September 3, 2019 from https://www.adac.de/_mmm/pdf/fi_mobilitaet%20sichert_entwicklung_studie_0316_259064.pdf

Jahns, M., & Woisetschläger, D. (2017). *Wesermarsch-Umfrage: Ergebnisse der Online-Umfrage in der Region Wesermarsch im Rahmen des Projektes NEMo "Nachhaltige Erfüllung von Mobilitätsbedürfnissen im ländlichen Raum".* Retrieved September 22, 2019 from https://www.nemo-mobilitaet.de/blog/wp-content/uploads/2017/08/2017-08-10_Auswertung_Wesermarschumfrage_kurz.pdf.

Joseph, R. (2018). Ride-sharing services: The tumultuous tale of the rural urban divide. In *AMCIS 2018 Proceedings.*

Kalogirou, K., Dimokas, N., Tsami, M., & Kehagias, D. (2018). Smart mobility combining public transport with carpooling: An iOS application paradigm. In *2018 IEEE 20th International Conference on High Performance Computing and Communications; IEEE 16th International Conference on Smart City; IEEE 4th International Conference on Data Science and Systems (HPCC/SmartCity/DSS)* (pp. 1271–1278). Piscataway, NJ: IEEE.

Knie, A., Rammler, S., & Zimmer, W. (2016). Mut zur Zukunft. Der Wandel zur neuen Mobilitätsgesellschaft – Ansätze für einen Politikwechsel. In *Internationales Verkehrswesen, 68*(3), 10–12.

Landkreis Wesermarsch. (2017). *BMVI-Modellvorhaben "Versorgung & Mobilität": Modell-region Landkreis Wesermarsch: Dokumentation Fachwerkstatt Mobilität: "Bus & bessere Verkehrsmittelverbindung".* Retrieved September 22, 2018 from http://www.landkreis-wesermarsch.de/uploads/files/2017-09-11_fachwerkstatt_wesersprinter_dokumentation.pdf

Limbourg, M. (2015). Mobilität im höheren Lebensalter in ländlichen Gebieten: Probleme und Lösungsansätze. In U. Fachinger, & H. Künemund (Eds.) *Gerontologie und ländlicher Raum: Lebensbedingungen, Veränderungsprozesse und Gestaltungsmöglichkeiten* (pp. 77–98). Wiesbaden: Springer Fachmedien.

Milbourne, P., & Kitchen, L. (2014). Rural mobilities: Connecting movement and fixity in rural places. *Journal of Rural Studies, 34*, 326–336.

Mulley, C., Nelson, J. D., & Wright, S. (2018). Community transport meets mobility as a service: On the road to a new a flexible future. *Research in Transportation Economics, 69*, 583–591.

Neoh, J.G., Chipulu, M., & Marshall, A. (2017). What encourages people to carpool? An evaluation of factors with meta-analysis. *Transportation, 44*, 423–447.

Olsson, L. E., Maier, R., & Friman, M. (2019). Why do they ride with others? Meta-analysis of factors influencing travelers to carpool. *Sustainability, 11*(8), 2414.

Plazinić, B. R., & Jović, J. (2018). Mobility and transport potential of elderly in differently accessible rural areas. *Journal of Transport Geography, 68*, 169–180.

Pütz, T. (2015). Verkehrsbild Deutschland – Pendlerströme. Quo navigant? In Bundesinstitut für Bau-, Stadt- und Raumforschung (BBSR) *BBSR-Analysen KOMPAKT.* Bonn.

Sandau, A., Dietrich, B., Akyol, A., & Wagner vom Berg, B. (2018). Steigerung der Sensibilität für nachhaltige Mobilität durch die mobile Reiseapplikation Guyde. In P. Drews, B. Funk, P. Niemeyer, & L. Xie (Eds.), *Tagungsband Multikonferenz Wirtschaftsinformatik 2018* (pp. 1137–1148).

Sandau, A., & Stamer, D. (2014). Telemetric transport mode validation. In *Proceedings of the 28th Conference on Environmental Informatics – EnviroInfo 2014* (pp. 815–820).

Seebauer, S. (2011). *Individuelles Mobilitätsverhalten in Großstädten.* Dissertation. Karl-Franzens-Universität Graz.

Umweltbundesamt (UBA). (2019). *Emissionsquellen.* Retrieved March 21, 2019 from http://www.umweltbundesamt.de/themen/klima-energie/klimaschutz-energiepolitik-in-deutschland/treibhausgas-emissionen/emissionsquellen

Vaughn, K. M., Abdel-Aty, M. A., & Kitamura, R. (1999). A framework for developing a daily activity and multimodal travel planner. *International Transactions in Operational Research, 6*, 107–121.

Wagner vom Berg, B. (2015). *Konzeption eines Sustainability Customer Relationship Management (SusCRM) für Anbieter nachhaltiger Mobilität.* Aachen: Shaker Verlag.

Part V
Legal Considerations and Limitations

The Erasure Obligation Independent of a Request

Johannes Rolfs

Abstract This contribution aims to answer the legal issue of the erasure concept, which is one of several legal aspects that had to be addressed in project NEMo. A fundamental question arises whether the person who is responsible for the NEMo app must erase personal data even if there is no request to erase it. Different legal requirements of the General Data Protection Regulation (GDPR) will be considered in this contribution: Initially, the erasure obligation under Article 17 will be analyzed based on legal interpretation methods, determining whether it actually reveals an erasure obligation, independent on the existence of a request to erase the data. Furthermore, it will be determined whether an erasure obligation—independent if the responsible person is asked to erase it or not—can be deducted from Article 6 and 9 GDPR or Article 5 GDPR. Regarding Article 5 GDPR, it will be examined whether a legal obligation can be derived at all and which consequences would apply. In this context, it will also be checked whether specific reasons/circumstances could prevent erasure. Finally, this contribution examines at what point of time the erasure of personal data must take place and which requirements have to be fulfilled to erase the data in an orderly procedure.

Keywords Erasure concept · Erasure obligation independent of the request · Art. 17 GDPR · Art. 5 GDPR

1 Introduction

In project NEMo,[1] one focus of the legal work is the compliant design of the application. In particular, it must be ensured that personal data is only processed if there is a legal basis for doing so. In addition to the lawful collection of personal

---

[1] https://nemo-mobilitaet.de.

J. Rolfs (✉)
Carl von Ossietzky University of Oldenburg, Oldenburg, Germany
e-mail: johannes.rolfs@uol.de

J. Marx Gómez et al. (eds.), *Progress in Sustainable Mobility Research*,
Progress in IS, https://doi.org/10.1007/978-3-030-70841-2_9

data, it must also be determined when the collected personal data is to be erased. If possible, this must be determined before the database is created or the personal data are collected. A later implementation and technical assurance of the erasure can become a "Herculean task."[2] The requirement that personal data may not be stored indefinitely is based on the principles relating to the processing of personal data. Art. 5 lit. c) GDPR regulates in this respect the obligation to minimize data and in lit. e) the storage limitation of personal data. Furthermore, the controller must determine storage periods for the single categories of personal data; this results from Recital 39 sentence 10 GDPR. Ensuring that the personal data are only stored for limited time is therefore just as important as the lawful collection of personal data. In order to fulfil this legal obligation, it is necessary for the controller to draw up an erasure concept. How the personal data need to be erased cannot be determined in general terms. However, the personal data can be categorized. In order to be able to define a categorization, it must be determined which reasons lead to the erasure of personal data.[3] Furthermore, the question arises as to "when" and "how" the erasure must take place if there is a reason for erasure.

2 Requirements for an Erasure Concept

It is impossible to construct a general design of an erasure concept. It must be designed individually in each case. However, general criteria can serve as a guide. As long as the European Data Protection Board has not expressed its opinion on it, the "Leitlinie Löschkonzept," published as DIN 66398, can be used for this purpose.[4] This guideline was developed with a view on the BDSG-old,[5] so that any deviations with a view on the GDPR must be taken into account.

In order to be able to meet the requirements of the erasure obligations at all, at least the following "erasure information" should be assigned to the personal data at the time of collection: purpose of the data processing, legal basis for processing, information concerning the end of the legal basis for the processing and the retention period.[6] These aspects cannot be determined in general. They depend on the purpose for which the specific personal data or categories of personal data are processed. The large number of possible variants of the processing purposes, in particular with regard to the legitimate interest of the data controller under Art. 6 (1) lit. f) GDPR, mean that a blanket provision is not possible.[7] However, this "erasure

---

[2] *Keppeler/Berning*, ZD 2017, p. 314 (317).

[3] On the difficulties of developing a data protection approach in practice: *Hole*, Datenschutzberater 2019, p. 124f.

[4] *Keppeler/Berning*, ZD 2017, p. 314 (318).

[5] Bundesdatenschutzgesetz.

[6] *Keppeler/Berning*, ZD 2017, p. 314 (318).

[7] *Abel*, PinG 2017, p. 177 (180).

information" can only be utilized meaningfully if it has been determined which aspects substantiate the erasure of the personal data.

A connecting factor could be found in Art. 17 GDPR. The content of this legal provision is controversial due to its structure and systematic position. Some authors state that Art. 17 (1) GDPR is meant to be an erasure obligation for personal data without a request of the data subject when the requirements of Art. 17 (1) GDPR are met.[8] Others see in this provision only a data subject right.[9] This understanding means that personal data may only be erased when the requirements of Art. 17 (1) GDPR are met and the data subject actively requests the erasure. If Art. 17 (1) GDPR would require a data subject request, the question arises whether the controller has an additional obligation to erase the personal data regardless of a request of the data subject. Such an erasure obligation, which is independent of the request, could result from Articles 5, 6, and 9 GDPR. In this case, it would be necessary to examine which reasons would oblige the controller to erase the personal data. These reasons would have to be considered in an erasure concept.

3   Erasure Obligation Under Art. 17 GDPR

The controller could have an erasure obligation if one of the reasons out of Art. 17 (1) GDPR is present and this obligation is independent of a request.

3.1   Content of the "Right to Erasure"

Art. 17 (1) DSGVO states reasons for the erasure of personal data. In lit. a) it is stated that the purpose for which the personal data were collected or otherwise processed is no longer given. Lit. b) regulates the obligation to erase personal data if the data subject has withdrawn his consent and there is no other legal ground for the processing. Lit. c) provides that the personal data must be erased when the data subject objects to the processing pursuant to Art. 21(1) GDPR and there are no overriding legitimate grounds for the processing, or the data subject objects to the processing pursuant to Art. 21 (2) GDPR. Personal data must also be erased

---

[8]*Piltz*, K&R 2016, 629 (632); *Hennemann*, PinG 2016, p. 176 (177); Trentmann, CR 2017, p. 26 (30 f.); *Paal*, in: Paal/Pauly, DSGVO, Art. 17 Rn. 7, 20; *Herbst*, in: Kühling/Buchner, DSGVO/BDSG, Art. 17 Rn. 2; *Peuker*, in: Sydow, DSGVO, Art. 17 Rn. 1; *Leutheusser-Schnarrenberger*, in: Schwartmann/Jaspers/Thüsing/Kugelmann, DS-GVO/BDSG, Art. 17 Rn. 12 *Keppeler/Berning*, ZD 2017, p. 134 (315).

[9]Explicitly: *Abel*, PinG 2017, p. 177 (180); *Kamlah*, in: Plath, DSGVO/BDSG, Art. 17 Rn. 6. Probably also: *Worms*, BeckOK Datenschutzrecht, Art. 17 Rn. 22 ff.; *Fladung*, in: Wybitul, EU-DSGVO, Art. 17 Rn. 2, 4; *Voigt*, in: Taeger/Gabel, DSGVO BDSG, Art. 5 Rn. 37; *Stollhoff*, in: Auernhammer, DSGVO/BDSG, Art. 17 Rn. 6.

immediately if they have been unlawfully processed (lit. d), if the law of the Member State, which the controller is subject to, obligated him to erase the personal data (lit. e) or if the personal data have been collected in relation to an "information society service" referred to in Art. 8 GDPR (lit. f). If one of these reasons for erasure is applicable, the question arises whether the controller must erase the personal data on his own initiative, or if it only requires an erasure activity on the request of the data subject. If the first were the case, the controller would always have to check which personal data are e.g. no longer necessary to achieve the purpose. Thus, Art. 17 GDPR would substantiate an obligation for an ongoing regular check. If, on the other hand, the erasure would only depend on an explicit request of the data subject, it would always be necessary that a request exists in addition to the ground for erasure. Whether a request is necessary will be examined in the next part. If this is the case, it is controversial which requirements the request for erasure[10] must meet and how much time the controller has to delete the personal data. The law mentions "without undue delay."[11]

3.2 Necessity of the "Request" of the Data Subject for Deletion

Since views on Art. 17 (1) GDRP are controversial, this legal provision must be interpreted. This requires a grammatical, systematic, historical, and teleological interpretation of this provision.[12] These interpretation methods do not stand in a hierarchical relationship, rather on an equal footing next to each other.[13]

3.2.1 Grammatical Interpretation

The wording of Art. 17 (1) GDPR is not clear with regard to the question of the necessity of the request for erasure by the data subject.[14] Primarily, as the title of Art. 17 GDPR shows, it includes a right to erasure of the data subject.

This right is supplemented, though, by the insertion: "(. . .) and the controller shall have the obligation (. . .)". This causes discrepancies with regard to the

---

[10]Exemplary for this: *Kamlah*, in: Plath, DSGVO/DBSG, Art. 17 Rn. 5; *Worms*, in: BeckOK Datenschutzrecht, Art. 17 Rn. 22 ff.; *Kamann/Braun*, in: Ehmann/Selmayr, DSGVO, Art. 17 Rn. 19.

[11]Exemplary for this: *Paal*, in: Paal/Pauly, DSGVO, Art. 17 Rn. 7, 20; *Hennemann*, PinG 2016, p. 176 (177).

[12]Applicability of interpretation methods in European law: *Reimer*, Juristische Methodenlehre, Rn. 270 ff.

[13]*Wegener*, in: Calliess/Ruffert, EUV/AEUV, Art. 19 EUV Rn. 13 ff.; *Selmayr/Ehmann*, in: Ehmann/Selmayr, DS-GVO, Einf. Rn. 91.

[14]Other view: *Abel*, PinG 2017, p. 177 (180), who takes the necessity of the request of the data subject from the wording.

regulatory content of Art. 17 (1) GDPR. In literature, the formulation is understood diversely. Partly, Art. 17 (1) GDPR is regarded as a separate and independent obligation of the controller to erase personal data if one of the reasons listed in Art. 17 (1) lit. (a)–(f) GDPR is given.[15] Others see Art. 17 GDPR as an exclusive right of the data subject to request erasure, if one of the cases of Art. 17 (1) lit. a)–f) GDPR is given.[16] According to this view, an independent obligation of the controller does not exist. The necessity of a request would arise if the "right (. . .) to obtain" is understood as a prerequisite for the "shall have the obligation."[17] At the same time, the wording "(. . .) and the controller shall have the obligation (. . .)" can be understood as an independent legal obligation. A look at other language versions does not help as the wording and sentence structure correspond with the English version.

3.2.2 Systematic Interpretation

In order to get closer to the content of the determination, it is necessary to focus on the systematic position of the legal provision. For this purpose, both the entire complex of the legal regulation, in which Art. 17 GDPR is statured, and the structure of the concrete legal provision must be considered.[18]

Art. 17 GDPR is located in Chapter III. As can be seen from the heading, this chapter includes the "rights of the data subject." The rights of access (Art. 15 GDPR), to rectification (Art. 16 GDPR), to restriction of processing (Art. 18 GDPR), to data portability (Art. 20 GDPR), and the right to objection (Art. 21 GDPR) can be found in this chapter. All these provisions have in common that their wording refers to an exclusive right of the data subject. An obligation of the controller is only described in Art. 22 GDPR. But in this provision the obligation is regulated in a separate paragraph. In Art. 17 (1) GDPR, however, an obligation of the controller is also included in the wording, which constitutes a systematic breach. In contrast to Art. 22 GDPR, the obligation is not mentioned in a separate paragraph. This difference in wording of rules in Chapter III can be put forward for and against

---

[15] *Piltz*, K&R 2016, S. 629 (632); *Hennemann*, PinG 2016, p. 176 (177); Trentmann, CR 2017, p. 26 (30 f.); *Paal*, in: Paal/Pauly, DSGVO, Art. 17 Rn. 7, 20; *Peuker*, in: Sydow, DSGVO, Art. 17 Rn. 1; *Leutheusser-Schnarrenberger*, in: Schwartmann/Jaspers/Thüsing/Kugelmann, DS-GVO/BDSG, Art. 17 Rn. 12 *Kappeler/Berning*, ZD 2017, p. 134 (315); *Nolte/Werkmeister*, in: Gola, DS-GVO, Art. 17 Rn. 7. Critical, but probably also so: *Meents/Hinzpeter*, in: Taeger/Gabel, DSGVO BDSG Art. 17 Rn. 81; *Herbst*, in: Kühling/Buchner, DS-GVO/BDSG, Art. 17 Rn. 8 ff.

[16] Explicitly: *Abel*, PinG 2017, p. 177 (180); *Kamlah*, in: Plath, DSGVO/BDSG, Art. 17 Rn. 6. Probably also: *Worms*, BeckOK Datenschutzrecht, Art. 17 Rn. 22 ff.; *Fladung*, in: Wybitul, EU-DSGVO, Art. 17 Rn. 2, 4; *Voigt*, in: Taeger/Gabel, DSGVO BDSG, Art. 5 Rn. 37.; *Stollhoff*, in: Auernhammer, DSGVO/BDSG, Art. 17 Rn. 6; *Kamann/Braun*, in: Ehmann/Selmayr, Datenschutz-Grundverordnung, Art. 17 Rn. 67.

[17] *Hennemann*, PinG 2016, p. 176 (177).

[18] Concerning the basics of systematic interpretation: *Reimer*, Juristische Methodenlehre, Rn. 311 ff.

an erasure obligation without a request from the data subject. The fact that Art. 17 GDPR is settled in Chapter III with the rights of data subjects would suggest that the controller must solely erase the personal data when a request is made. At the same time, it can be argued that the emphasis on the obligation of the controller in Art. 17 (1) GDPR has the consequence that an erasure obligation without a request from the data subject is regulated here.

If the systematics of Art. 17 (1) GDPR is considered with regard to the reasons for erasure in lit. a)–f), the picture is inconsistent. The reasons for erasure in lit. a), b), c), and f) only make sense if a request or at least an active act of the data subject has been made. This becomes particularly clear with regard to lit. (f). If a request was dispensable in this case, children would be de facto excluded from the use of "information society services," which cannot be intended. The personal data of children would have to be erased immediately if the requirements of Art. 17 (1) lit. f) GDPR were met.[19] However, the situation is different with regard to lit. a), d), and e). In these cases, the necessity of a request will be rather less conclusive.[20] With regard to lit. a), reference is made to the fact that the data subject does not necessarily know where personal data relating to him are stored.[21] Whether this argument applies, however, in view of the classification as an independent erasure obligation of the controller can certainly be viewed critically. It is less a legal problem than an actual lack of information with the data subject. However, the purpose of Art. 17 GDPR is not to eliminate information deficits, but refers to the possibility of enforcing the right of erasure. Furthermore, with regard to erasure in the cases of lit. a), d), and e), it is argued that these provisions only make sense when they are irrespective of the request, as otherwise the enforcement of the erasure right would depend on chance.[22] For the enforcement of these erasure rights, it would depend on chance whether the data subject became aware of the fact that the necessity of the processing no longer exists (lit. a), that the processing was unlawful (lit. d) or that the erasure was necessary for other reasons (lit. e).

However, on closer inspection, this initially conclusive thought proves difficult.[23] If the wording and the systematics of Art. 17 (1) GDPR are considered, no indications can be found which would justify that some obligations for erasure must be granted with a request and others without a request. Furthermore, another difficulty arises when the view is directed to Art. 18 GDPR. It shows that the data subject has a right to choose between erasure and limited processing in the cases

---

[19] See also: *Herbst*, in: Kühling/Buchner, DS-GVO/BDSG Art. 17 Rn. 16; *Paal*, in: Paal/Pauly, Art. 17 Rn. 28.

[20] *Herbst*, in: Kühling/Buchner, DS-GVO/BDSG, Art. 17 Rn. 9; *Leutheusser-Schnarrenberger*, in: Schwartmann/Jaspers/Thüsing/Kugelmann, DS-GVO/BDSG, Art. 17 Rn. 44.

[21] *Kodde*, ZD 2013, p. 115 (117).

[22] *Herbst*, in: Kühling/Buchner, DS-GVO/BDSG, Art. 17 Rn. 9; *Kodde*, ZD 2013, p. 115 (117), with regard to the Commission proposal.

[23] *Herbst*, in: Kühling/Buchner, DS-GVO/BDSG, Art. 17 Rn. 9. Similar: *Meents/Hinzpeter*, in: Taeger/Gabel, DSGVO BDSG Art. 17 Rn. 82; *Kamann/Braun*, in: Ehmann/Selmayr, Datenschutz-Grundverordnung, Art. 17 Rn. 67.

named therein. If it is assumed that Art. 17 (1) GDPR, at least in the cases of lit. a), d), and e), establishes an erasure obligation without a request, the data controller must delete the personal data "without undue delay" if these reasons exist. However, if he fulfils this obligation, he makes the right of the data subject under Art. 18 (1) lit. b) and lit. c) GDPR impossible.

The literature attempts to resolve this contradiction by imposing the obligation to inquire from the data subjects which right they want to pursue, in the cases of Art. 18 lit. b) and lit. c) respectively Art. 17 (1) lit. a) and lit. d) GDPR, on the controller.[24]

In this respect, it is argued that the omission to ask the data subject could be both an abuse of rights and would violate the duty of the controller under Art. 12 (2) sentence 1 GDPR.[25] Particularly with regard to Art. 12 (2) sentence 1 GDPR, the question arises as to whether an obligation can be derived from this and whether the controller has to inquire from the data subject whether specific personal data should be erased or only processed to a limited extent. In this respect, it seems quite conceivable that "facilitating the exercise of the rights under Articles 13 to 22 GDPR" only refers to the procedure with which the rights can be exercised.[26] It seems inconclusive to derive a "demand obligation" from this provision. Furthermore, it should be noted that the wording of Art. 18 GDPR does not contain any obligation for the controller to actively ask the data subject, with a view to the specific individual case, about the exercise of his or her right to elect. Furthermore, the "demand obligation" approach proves difficult because the controller processing the personal data does not necessarily have the contact details of the data subject. He would therefore have to collect and process further personal data, even at a later stage, in order to fulfil his intended obligation to act in the interest of the data subject.

If Recital 64 is taken into account in this respect, this consequence seems difficult. Sentence 2 states that the controller may not store personal data solely for purpose of responding to possible requests for information. In this respect, the "demand obligation" is the counterpart to replying to a request for information. The controller would therefore have to store the contact data without having a reason exceeding the possibly necessary enquiry of the data subject. The fact that this is not wanted can also be inferred from the assessment of Art. 11 GDPR. Even with the principle of data minimization from Art. 5 (1) lit. c) GDPR, the storage of

---

[24] *Herbst*, in: Kühling/Buchner, DS-GVO/BDSG, Art. 17 Rn. 10; *Leutheusser-Schnarrenberger*, in: Schwartmann/Jaspers/Thüsing/Kugelmann, DS-GVO/BDSG, Art. 17 Rn. 12 *Däubler*, in: Däubler/Wedde/Weichert/Sommer, EU-Datenschutz-Grundverordnung und BDSG-neu, Art. 17 Rn. 10; *Stollhoff*, in: Auernhammer, DSGVO/BDSG, Art. 17 Rn. 47; *Dix*, in: Simitis/Hornung/Spiecker gen. Dähmann, Datenschutzrecht, Art. 17 Rn. 6.

[25] *Herbst*, in: Kühling/Buchner, DS-GVO/BDSG, Art. 17 Rn. 10. The latter also bringing forward: *Meents/Hinzpeter*, in: Taeger/Gabel, DSGVO BDSG Art. 17 Rn. 82; *Däubler*, in: Däubler/Wedde/Weichert/Sommer, EU-Datenschutz-Grundverordnung und BDSG-neu, Art. 17 Rn. 10.

[26] As well as: *Bäcker*, in: Kühling/Buchner, DS-GVO/BDSG, Art. 12 Rn. 25 f.

contact data for the purpose of fulfilling a possible "demand obligation" would be problematic.

Furthermore, against an erasure obligation of personal data without a request it could be argued that the supposed obligation in Art. 17 (1) GDPR was only included in order to make the obligation in Art. 17 (2) GDPR logical. Accordingly, the controller must inform third parties that he has been requested to erase personal data and all links. From a regulatory point of view, it would be unusual when paragraph 1 only refers to the data subject and paragraph 2 created an obligation for the data controller based on paragraph 1, without paragraph 1 including the data controller in its wording. This would also suggest that the inclusion of the controller's obligation is only of a clarifying nature. In addition, the fact that the data subject bears the burden of presenting and proving the existence of a reason for erasure speaks in favor of an obligation to erase on the basis of a request.[27]

Overall, the systematic interpretation argues against an obligation of the controller to erase personal data without a request.[28]

3.2.3 Historical Interpretation

In addition to the systematic interpretation, the dogmatic classification of a provision has to be carried out with regard to the historical interpretation.[29] In Recitals 65 and 66 of the GDPR the legislator describes the objective which he pursued by introducing the "right to erasure." In these recitals, the legislator describes that the data subject "in particular" should have "a right to have his or her personal data erased and no longer processed." This wording as well as the argumentation of the Recital 65 as a whole suggests that the legislator wanted to create a right for the data subject only. Some authors bring forward the Recital 39 sentence 9 GDPR against this opinion. This recital indicates the necessity of determining a retention period. Recurring to this, it may be argued that an independent erasure obligation of the controller is necessary.[30] Although the substance of this is to be approved, Recital 39 is not helpful in answering the question of whether Art. 17 (1) GDPR provides for an erasure obligation independent of the request. Recital 39 refers to the general requirements that exist with regard to the processing of personal data. Recital 39 does not make any comments with regard to Art. 17 GDPR. Furthermore, it can be pointed out that Art. 17 (7) GDPR-E (COM) contained an obligation for the data controller to ensure that the time limits for erasure or verification of the necessity of

---

[27]Concerning the "Beweis- und Darlegungslast": *Stollhoff*, in: Auernhammer, DSGVO/BDSG, Art. 17 Rn. 42; *Kamann/Braun*, in: Ehmann/Selmayr, DS-GVO, Art. 17 Rn. 19; *Kamlah*, in: Plath, DSGVO/DBSG, Art. 17 Rn. 5. Probably other view.: *Worms*, in BeckOK Datenschutzrecht, Art. 17 Rn. 27.

[28]Same result but without further explanations: *Kamlah*, in: Plath, DSGVO/DBSG, Art. 17 Rn. 5.

[29]Historical interpretation in general: *Reimer*, Juristische Methodenlehre, Rn. 347 ff.

[30]Inter alia: *Herbst*, in: Kühling/Buchner, DS-GVO/BDSG, Art. 17 Rn. 47.

storage must be observed. The lack of inclusion in the final text of the Regulation can be argued against an obligation of the data controller.[31]

3.2.4 Teleological Interpretation

With regard to the teleological interpretation, it must be determined what the legislator's purpose was in creating the provision.[32] The rights of the data subject and in particular the right to erasure are based on the legislator's objective of giving the data subjects more control over their personal data.[33] The fact that the legislator assigns a prominent position to the rights of data subjects is made clear by the fact that the highest fines of the GDPR accompany their violation, Art. 83 (5) lit. b) GDPR.[34]

The GDPR has its origin in Art. 8 CFR,[35] which goes back to the same wording of Art. 16 TFEU,[36] and is thus an important aspect for the teleological interpretation. For the interpretation of data protection law, the European Court of Justice (ECJ) relies on Art. 7 and Art. 8 CFR. However, it is correct to assume that Art. 8 CFR takes precedence over Art. 7 CFR as lex specialis with regard to data protection law.[37] It is questionable whether it can be derived from this fundamental right which is also the origin of data protection law whether Art. 17 (1) DSGVO infers an erasure obligation without a request of the data subject. According to the Commission, the right of the data subject originates in Art. 8 (2) CFR.[38] This provision represents a legal barrier.[39] This can be agreed upon with regard to Art. 8 (2) sentence 1 CFR. With regard to sentence 2, it is more difficult to understand this regulation as a legal barrier. It rather clearly defines the right of the data subject which he can directly enforce from the obliged to observe the fundamental right, the State. This right then also applies to the controller through the indirect third-party effect of fundamental rights.[40] Due to the structure of Art. 8 (2) sentence 2 CFR, it will not be possible to derive an independent obligation of the controller from it. In this respect, it would not be possible to fall back to this provision in order to substantiate a simple legal

---

[31]Other view: *Meents/Hinzpeter*, in: Taeger/Gabel, DSGVO BDSG Art. 17 Rn. 85.

[32]*Reimer*, Juristische Methodenlehre, Rn. 357 ff.

[33]*Meents/Hinzpeter*, in: Taeger/Gabel, DSGVO BDSG, Art. 17 Rn. 19; *Peuker*, in: Sydow, DSGVO, Art. 17 Rn. 1.

[34]See also: *Peuker*, in: Sydow, DSGVO, Art. 17 Rn. 2 with further proof.

[35]Charter of Fundamental Rights of the European Union.

[36]Treaty on the Functioning of the European Union.

[37]In detail: *Michl*, DUD 2017, p. 349 (349 ff.). As a result as here: *Peuker*, in: Sydow, DSGVO, Art. 17 Rn. 7 f; *Leutheusser-Schnarrenberger*, in: Schwartmann/Jaspers/Thüsing/Kugelmann, DS-GVO/BDSG, Art. 17 Rn. 5.

[38]KOM(2010) 609 final (A comprehensive approach on personal data protection in the European Union) p. 8.

[39]*Kingreen*, in: Calliess/Ruffert, EUV/AEUV, Art. 8 EU-GRCharta, Rn. 3.

[40]In detail: *Streinz/Michl*, EuZW 2011, p. 384 (384 ff.).

obligation. The obligations that affect the controller rather originate in Art. 8 (2) sentence 1 CFR.

The systematics and structure of the rights of the data subject suggest that the legislator wanted to include the simple-law design of the fundamental right provisions of Art. 8 (2) sentence 2 CFR in it. The simple-law design of the legal barrier of Art. 8 (2) sentence 1, i.e. the reference to a processing including the principle of fairness, appears to be difficult when regarding the structure of the right of the data subject in the GDPR. If this approach is applied to the provision of Art. 17 (1) GDPR, it seems logical to see it as an exclusive right of data subjects because it does not restrict the fundamental right to data protection of the data subject. Rather, this fundamental right of the data subject is substantiated and developed. Thus, it can be concluded that Art. 17 (1) GDPR is based on Art. 8 (2) sentence 2 CFR. An obligation to erasure without a request of the data subject cannot be derived from it. The obligation to lawfully process personal data arises only from Art. 8 (2) sentence 1 CFR.

Another argument against erasure without a request could be the fact that the justification of such an obligation to erase simultaneously substantiates an audit obligation at the controller.[41] In this case, the controller would be obliged to erase the personal data the moment the erasure reason arises. He can only fulfil this obligation if he regularly checks the existing personal data.[42] However, this will not result in the assumption that an erasure obligation without a request cannot exist, since Recital 39 sentence 10 shows that such an obligation to audit was intended.[43] This, in turn, is contradicted by the fact that Recital 39 does not refer to Art. 17 GDPR.

Finally, the following consideration provides an argument against the understanding as an erasure obligation without a request: Assuming that Art. 17 determines an erasure obligation with a request from the data subject in addition to another erasure obligation without a request from the data subject, the condition "without undue delay" would have to be interpreted differently.[44] If assumed that Art. 17 (1) GDPR regulates the erasure obligation with a request from the data subject, the controller must erase the personal data directly after having received the request. However, if it is assumed that Art. 17 (1) GDPR provides for the erasure obligation without a request from the data subject, the term "without undue delay" refers to the period between the occurrence of the erasure obligation and the

---

[41]See also: *Meents/Hinzpeter*, in: Taeger/Gabel, DSGVO BDSG, Art. 17 Rn. 83.

[42]Concerning the obligation to check: *Herbst*, in: Kühling/Buchner, DS-GVO/BDSG, Art. 17 Rn. 47.

[43]See also: *Meents/Hinzpeter*, in: Taeger/Gabel, DSGVO BDSG, Art. 17 Rn. 83; *Krämer*, NJW 2018, p. 347 (350); *Leutheusser-Schnarrenberger*, in: Schwartmann/Jaspers/Thüsing/Kugelmann, DS-GVO/BDSG, Art. 17 Rn. 45.

[44]*Meents/Hinzpeter*, in: Taeger/Gabel, DSGVO BDSG, Art. 17 Rn. 86.

subsequent erasure.[45] Such a differentiation can neither be inferred from the text of the Regulation nor can it be inferred from the meaning and purpose of the provision.

3.3 Conclusion of the Interpretation of Art. 17 (1) GDPR

It can be deduced from these considerations that Art. 17 (1) GDPR does not establish an obligation for the controller to erase the personal data without a request from the data subject. Rather, a request by the data subject is necessary for erasure pursuant to Art. 17 (1) GDPR.

4 Other Legal Grounds for an Erasure Obligation Independent of the Request

However, it cannot be inferred from this result that the controller has no independent erasure obligation. Such an obligation could result from Art. 6 respectively 9 or Art. 5 GDPR.

4.1 Erasure Obligation Under Art. 6 and 9 GDPR

The data controller may be obliged to erase personal data if there is no legal basis for the processing of such data. The obligation to erase personal data could thus result e contrario from the absence or omission of the legal basis of Art. 6 or 9 GDPR. This could be supported by the legal conception of these legal bases. This is a so-called ban with permit reservation.[46] The processing of personal data is only permitted if Art. 6 or 9 GDPR or any other legal basis in the BDSG or in a special law permits it. Conversely, this could lead to the conclusion that processing is prohibited again at the moment when the conditions of the legal basis are no longer present. Personal data may therefore no longer be processed. At the moment the legal basis no longer applies, the personal data would have to be erased.

However, this result cannot be endorsed. Since the deletion pursuant to Art. 4 No 2 GDPR itself constitutes a processing of personal data, such an act is only permissible if there is a legal basis for it. The absence of the requirements of Art. 6 or 9 GDPR is not sufficient. Another argument in favor of this result is that the

---

[45]See also: *Meents/Hinzpeter*, in: Taeger/Gabel, DSGVO BDSG, Art. 17 Rn. 86; *Herbst*, in: Kühling/Buchner, DS-GVO/BDSG, Art. 17 Rn. 47.

[46]Probably predominant view: *Taeger*, in: Taeger/Gabel, Art. 6 Rn. 5; Plath, in: *Plath*, DSGVO/BDSG, Art. 6 Rn. 1.

exceptions under Art. 17 (3) GDPR would not be applicable, at least not directly.[47] The erasure obligation therefore does not arise directly from the absence of a legal basis in Art. 6 or 9 GDPR.

4.2 Obligation of the Controller Under Art. 5 GDPR

The question arises as to whether an obligation on the part of the controller to erase data can follow from Art. 5 GDPR. If this was the case, it would have to be clarified which action the controller has to take in order not to violate a possible obligation under Art. 5 GDPR. Both restricted processing and erasure can be considered here. With regard to deletion, however, it must be taken into account that there may be reasons that prevent erasure.

4.2.1 Establishment of a Legal Obligation

An erasure obligation could result from Art. 5 GDPR.[48] The basic prerequisite for it would be that Art. 5 GDPR does not only determine principles but also allows the derivation of a direct legal obligation. Only in this case it would be considered as a legal basis for erasure. In contrast to its predecessor, Art. 6 Data Protection Directive, Art. 5 GDRP is not only an orientation commandment, but a binding provision.[49] This results from the fact that it is the embodiment of Art. 8 (2) CFR.[50] Furthermore, the fact that, in contrast to the earlier regulation of Art. 6 Data Protection Directive, a violation of Art. 5 GDPR pursuant to Art. 83 (5) lit. a) GDPR is subject to a fine speaks in favor of this understanding. Art. 5 GDPR thus includes not only principles but also binding legal provisions. It is therefore a legal basis that regulates the requirements for the processing of personal data in conformity with fundamental rights. If the requirements listed in Art. 5 (1) GDPR are no longer available, the data controller is obliged to stop processing the data.

According to Art. 5 (1) lit. a) GDPR, personal data must be "processed lawfully." The prerequisite for "lawful processing" is that the data controller processes the personal data on a legal basis.[51] Conversely, processing is inadmissible if the legal

---

[47] *Kappeler/Berning*, ZD 2017, p. 134 (315).

[48] As well: *Voigt*, in: Taeger/Gabel, DSGVO BDSG, Art. 5 Rn. 37; *Kamlah*, in: Plath, DSGVO/BDSG, Art. 17 Rn. 6; *Peuker*, in: Sydow, Europäische Datenschutzgrundverordnung, Art. 17 Rn. 43; *Dix*, in: Simitis/Hornung/Spiecker gen. Döhmann, Datenschutzrecht, Art. 17 Rn. 1, restricting his comments to Rn. 6.

[49] *Schantz*, in: BeckOK Datenschutzrecht, Art. 5 Rn. 2; *Pötters*, in: Gola, DS-GVO, Art. 5, Rn. 4; *Roßnagel*, ZD 2018, S. 339 (343). Other view: *Frenzel*, in: Paal/Pauly, DSGVO, Art. 5 Rn. 9.

[50] *Albrecht/Jotzo*, Das neue Datenschutzrecht der EU, Teil 2 Rn. 1; *Schantz*, in: BeckOK Datenschutzrecht, Art. 5 Rn. 2.

[51] Recital 40 GDPR.

basis for the processing no longer applies. This will be the case, for example, if the data processing is carried out on the basis of the data subject's consent and the data subject withdraws his consent. Furthermore, processing will become inadmissible if the data subject objects to the processing (Art. 21 GDPR) or if the processing was unlawful from the outset. In addition, Art. 5 (1) lit. b) GDPR stipulates that personal data may only be processed if there is a specified, explicit, and legitimate purpose. Processing of personal data must therefore cease if the purpose for which the controller is processing the data has ended.[52] Additionally, Art. 5 (1) lit. d) GDPR expressly stipulates the obligation of the data controller to erase or correct personal data (. . .) if they are "inaccurate."

Consequently, the controller is subject to an audit obligation. Within this framework, he must check whether the processing of personal data is still lawful. The answer to the question concerning the scope of this audit obligation is difficult. The determination must be based, among other things, on the amount of personal data, and needs to take the existing interests in the individual case into account.[53]

4.2.2   Consequence of the Legal Obligation

If one of the reasons given above applies, the question arises as to what the controller must do to avoid violating a legal obligation. Both restricted processing in the form of separate storage and erasure can be considered. The argument in favor of restricted processing would be that Art. 18 GDPR assigns the data subject a right to choose between erasure and restricted processing in the specified cases. In this respect, it could be argued that erasure in these cases is only permissible if the data subject decides in favor of erasure. The consequence would be that the data controller would have to ask each data subject in individual cases whether erasure or limited restriction is desired. The structure of Art. 18 GDPR as a right of the data subject speaks against such a procedure. An obligation of the data controller, which would argue for a separate storage, cannot be inferred from the wording. Rather, according to Art. 12 GDPR, the controller only has to inform the data subjects of his rights. It is therefore sufficient for the controller to draw, at the time of data collection or change of purpose, the attention of the data subjects to their rights under Article 18 GDPR. In the present constellation, the data subject must therefore be informed as to when data will be erased, thus the controller fulfils his duty to provide information pursuant to Art. 13 GDPR. If the data subject is aware of it, he or she can exercise his or her right under Art. 18 GDPR before the end of the period. Therefore, the data subject does not normally have to be questioned again as to whether he or she wishes to make his or her right under Art. 18 GDPR applicable in the case of a specific act. It can be deduced that if the reasons outlined above are

---

[52] See also and with examples: *Peuker*, in: Sydow, DSGVO, Art. 17 Rn. 16.

[53] For this, but with a view to Art. 17 GDPR: *Herbst*, in: Kühling/Buchner, DS-GVO/BDSG, Art. 17 Rn. 47.

present, the controller must delete the personal data. This is also supported by the principle of data minimization as stated in Art. 5 (1) lit. c) GDPR.

4.2.3 Reasons Contrary to Deletion

However, deletion need not always and immediately to take place when the permissibility of the processing no longer applies. Rather, it must be examined in each individual case whether a legitimate interest precludes deletion. In particular, personal data may not be erased if one of the aspects listed in Recitals 50 sentences 3, 4, 5 GDPR exist. In this respect, the content of these grounds largely corresponds to the reasons given in Art. 18 (3) lit. b), c), d) GDPR. In addition, deletion must also be omitted if overriding fundamental rights or interests of third parties or interests of the public are opposed to erasure.[54] In particular, the fundamental rights of third parties of Art. 10 CFR, freedom of expression, and of Art. 11 CFR, freedom of opinion and information, have to be considered in this context. But also the freedom of economic activity in Art. 15 and 16 GRCh or the right of access to documents in Art. 42 GRCh may have to be taken into consideration.[55] However, this last opinion must be regarded critically.[56]

An erasure is also not to be carried out if the controller can show a justified interest in the further processing. This is the case, for example, when he needs the personal data to enforce his claims. In addition, the data controller will also be able to assert a legitimate interest in further processing if he can assume with a high degree of probability that the data subject needs the personal data in order to assert supposed claims against him. If he were to delete the personal data in this case, the controller would run the risk of being accused of thwarting evidence in a possible lawsuit, which would be legally disadvantageous for him.[57]

It will also not be permitted to erase the data if the controller is legally obliged to store it. Thus, it cannot be argued that the exceptions from Art. 17 (3) GDPR are not taken into account against the recourse made here to Art. 5 GDPR in order to substantiate an obligation to delete. The reasons of Art. 17 (3) GDPR, which contradict the erasure, must also be taken into account in the context of an erasure obligation under Art. 5 GDPR. These only do not arise, as described above, directly from the text of the Regulation, but also from the Recitals. During the time of the review as to whether deletion is necessary, the processing of that personal data must be restricted. The fact that this new processing purpose is permissible results from Recital 50 sentence 6 GDPR.

---

[54]Like here, but with view on Art. 17 DSGVO: *Peuker*, in: Sydow, DSGVO, Art. 17 Rn. 8.

[55]See *Peuker*, in: Sydow, DSGVO, Art. 17 Rn. 8.

[56]Regarding the criticism: *Leutheusser-Schnarrenberger*, ZD 2015, p. 149 (150).

[57]Overview of the legal consequences of "Beweisvereitelung" in civil proceedings: *Prütting*, in MüKo ZPO, § 286 Rn. 84 ff.

4.3 Time and Requirements for Deletion

If there is no reason why the data should not be deleted, the question arises as to "when" and "how" the personal data should be erased. The point in time at which the processing authorization no longer exists can be seen as the general timeframe for erasure. However, it gets difficult with categories of personal data for which a weighing of interests may become necessary in individual cases. In this case, the question arises how long the review is allowed to take place before a decision on erasure must be made. Whether the maximum period, as partly advocated, can be the monthly period of Art. 12 (3) sentence 1 GDPR[58] or even a further extension under Art. 12 (3) sentence 2 GDPR,[59] however, is to be assessed critically. These periods appear to be too long.

Finally, the "how" of the erasure must be determined. In § 3 (4) No. 5 BDSG-old the "how" of the erasure was defined. However, Art. 4 GDPR does not define the "how" of erasure. The question of the difference between erasure and destruction also arises in this context. Some argue that destruction is a (sub)form of erasure,[60] whereby destruction is the physical "elimination" and erasure is the technical obliteration, which can also be carried out by physical elimination.[61] This point of view cannot be accepted. Erasure and destruction are two autonomous "methods of disposal."[62] This does not mean that, as an exception, destruction is also necessary if deletion is actually not possible, for example, when personal data is stored on shellac-records. The difference between erasure and destruction can be seen in the fact that the destruction results in the irrevocable elimination of the personal data. Erasure, on the other hand, is only the technical obliteration which must be undertaken in such a way that the personal data becomes unusable for "normal use."[63] The differentiation according to the possibility of recovery is supported by the cases in which the regulation speaks of "destruction." Art. 32 (2) GDPR and Recital 83 cite "destruction" as an aspect for the assessment of data security risks. In particular, the following question should be asked here: Can the destruction cause physical, material, or immaterial damage? A damage can only occur if the personal

---

[58] *Dix*, in: Simitis/Hornung/Spiecker gen. Döhmann, Datenschutzrecht, Art. 17 Rn. 8.

[59] *Herbst*, in: Kühling/Buchner, DS-GVO/BDSG, Art. 17 Rn. 46.

[60] *Arning/Rothkegel*, in: Taeger/Gabel, DSGVO BDSG, Art. 4, Rn. 96; *Stollhoff*, in: Auernhammer, DSGVO/BDSG, Art. 17 Rn. 9. Seeing a more-less-relationship: *Nolte/Werkmeister*, in: Gola, DS-GVO, Art. 17, Rn. 8; *Ernst*, in: Paal/Pauly, Art. 4 Rn. 34.

[61] *Arning/Rothkegel*, in: Taeger/Gabel, DSGVO BDSG, Art. 4 Rn. 94 f.; 96; *Roßnagel*, in: Simitis/Hornung/Spiecker gen. Döhmann, Datenschutzrecht, Art. 5 Rn. 30, 33.

[62] As a result also: *Ernst*, in: Paul/Paaly, DSGVO/BDSG, Art. 4 Rn. 34; *Reimer*, in: Sydow, Europäische Datenschutz-Grundverordnung, Art. 4 Rn. 75; *Schild*, in: BeckOK Datenschutzrecht, Art. 4 Rn. 53 ff; *Meents/Hinzpeter*, in: Taeger/Gabel, DSGVO BDSG, Art. 17 Rn. 72.

[63] *Stollhoff*, in: Auernhammer, DSGVO/BDSG, Art. 17 Rn. 9. Other view: *Meents/Hinzpeter*, Taeger/Gabel, DSGVO BDSG, Art. 17 Rn. 74; *Leutheusser-Schnarrenberger*, in: Schwartmann/Jaspers/Thüsing/Kugelmann, DS-GVO/BDSG, Art. 17 Rn. 38; *Dix*, in: Simitis/Hornung/Spiecker gen. Döhmann, Datenschutzrecht, Art. 17 Rn. 5.

data are irrevocably removed, i.e. recovery is de facto impossible, because otherwise the recovery would be carried out to avert the damage.

It is therefore sufficient for the erasure if the controller "removes" the personal data in such a way that a restoration is only possible with a high technical effort. It is not necessary, however, that the personal data can no longer be recovered at all, as this can hardly be technically guaranteed. However, it is not enough to prevent personal data from being perceived.[64] If backups or backup copies of the personal data have been made, the obligation to erase also applies to these data, unless there is a reason that permits further processing by the backup or backup copy.[65]

5 Reasons for Deletion that Can Be Taken into Account for the Erasure Concept

With regard to the preparation of an erasure concept, the controller must therefore ensure that he can guarantee the erasure resulting from Art. 5 (1) GDPR. It should be noted in the context of the erasure concept that the personal data must in principle be deleted if the legal basis no longer applies, the original purpose of the processing no longer exists, the processing was inadmissible from the outset or the personal data are incorrect. In addition to answering the question as to whether there is any reason for deletion at all, it must also be ensured at the same time that it is possible to check whether personal data may exceptionally not be erased. For this purpose, a weighing of interests must be carried out on a case-by-case basis. The balancing of interests is always necessary when legitimate interests stand in the way of erasure. In addition to this erasure obligation without a request of the data subject (Art. 5 GDPR), there is also an erasure obligation with a request of the data subject (Art. 17 GDPR). Some of these are identical within the content. Only the erasure obligation under Art. 17 (1) lit. f) GDPR exists if a request has been made by the data subject. If there is a reason for erasure independent of the request and there are no conflicting interests, the controller must erase the personal data at the moment in which the reason for deletion arises. If he does not do so, a fine may be imposed on the controller. In both cases of the erasure obligation, in cases according to Art. 5 GDPR as well as according to Art. 17 GDPR, the amount of the penalty is determined by Art. 83 (5) GDPR.

---

[64] About this problem: *Kremer*, in: Laue/Kremer, Das neue Datenschutzrecht in der betrieblichen Praxis, § 4 Rn. 48. As a result as here: *Däubler*, in: Däubler/Wedde/Weichert/Sommer, EU-Datenschutz-Grundverordnung und BDSG-neu, Art. 17 Rn. 21.

[65] This would be the case, for example, if tax law or commercial law storage obligations exist.

References

Abel, R. (2017). Lösch- und Sperrkonzepte nach der DSGVO. In *PinG 2017* (pp. 177–182).

Albrecht, J. P., & Jotzo, F. (2017). *Das neue Datenschutzrecht der EU*. Düsseldorf.

Brink, S., & Wolff, H. A. (Eds.) (2018). *Beck'scher Online Kommentar Datenschutzrecht*. München.

Calliess, C., & Ruffert, M. (Eds.) (2016). *EUV AEUV, Kommentar* (5th ed). München.

Däubler, W., Wedde, P., Weichert, T., & Sommer, I. (Eds.) (2018). *EU-Datenschutz-Grundverordnung und BDSG-neu, Kompaktkommentar*. Köln.

Ehmann, E., & Selmayr, M. (Eds.) (2018). *Datenschutz-Grundverordnung, Kommentar* (2nd ed.). München.

Eßer, M., Kramer, P., & von Lewinski, K. (Eds.) (2018). *Auernhammer, Datenschutzgrundverordnung, Bundesdatenschutzgesetz und Nebengesetze* (6th ed.). Köln.

Gola, P. (Ed.) (2018). *DS-GVO Datenschutz-Grundverordnung, Kommentar* (2nd ed.). München.

Hennemann, M. (2016). Das Recht auf Löschung gemäß Art. 17 Datenschutz-Grundverordnung. In *PinG 2016* (pp. 176–179).

Hole, P. (2019). Datenminimierung und Löschkonzepte nach DSGVO. In *DSB 2019*, pp. 124–126.

Keppeler, L. M., & Berning, W. (2017).Technische und rechtliche Probleme bei der Umsetzung der DS-GVO-Löschpflichten. In *ZD 2017* (pp. 314–319).

Kodde, C. (2013). Die "Pflicht zu Vergessen" – "Recht auf Vergessenwerden" und Löschung in BDSG und DS-GVO. In *ZD 2013* (pp. 115–118).

Krüger, W., & Rauscher, T. (Eds.) (2016). *Münchener Kommentar zur Zivilprozessordung*. (5th ed.). München.

Kühling, J., & Buchner, B. (Eds.) (2019). *DS-GVO/BDSG Datenschutz-Grundverordnung Bundesdatenschutzgesetz, Kommentar* (2nd ed.). München.

Laue, P., & Kremer, S. (2019). *Das neue Datenschutzrecht in der betrieblichen Praxis* (2nd ed.). Baden-Baden.

Michl, W. (2017). Das Verhältnis zwischen Art. 7 und Art. 8 GRCh – zur Bestimmung der Grundlage des Datenschutzgrundrechts im EU-Recht. In: *DuD 2017* (pp. 349–353).

Piltz, C. (2016). Die Datenschutz-Grundverordnung, Teil 2 Rechte der Betroffenen und korrespondierende Pflichten des Verantwortlichen. In *K&R 2016* (pp. 629–636).

Plath, K.-U. (Ed.) (2018). *BDSG DSGVO, Kommentar* (3th ed.). Köln.

Paal, B. P., & Pauly A., D. (Eds.) (2018). *Datenschutz-Grundverordnung, Kommentar* (2nd ed.). München.

Reimer, F. (2016). *Juristische Methodenlehre*. Baden-Baden.

Roßnagel, A. (2018). Datenschutzgrundsätze – unverbindliches Programm oder verbindliches Recht? Bedeutung der Grundsätze für die datenschutzrechtliche Praxis. In *ZD 2018* (pp. 339–344).

Schwartmann, R., Jaspers, A., Thüsing, G., & Kugelmann, D. (Eds.) (2018). *Datenschutz-Grundverordnung Bundesdatenschutzgesetz, Kommentar*. Heidelberg .

Simitis, S., Hornung, G., & Spieker gen. Döhrmann, I. (Eds.) (2019). *Datenschutzrecht DSGVO mit BDSG, Großkommentar*. Baden-Baden.

Streinz, R., & Michl, W. (2011). Die Drittwirkung des europäischen Datenschutzgrundrechts (Art. EUGRCHARTA Artikel 8 GRCh) im deutschen Privatrecht. In *EuZW 2011* (pp. 384–388).

Sydow, G. (Ed.) (2018). *Europäische Datenschutzgrundverordnung, Handkommentar* (2nd ed.). Baden-Baden.

Taeger, J., & Gabel, D. (Eds.) (2019). *DSGVO BDSG, Kommentar* (3th ed.). Frankfurt am Main.

Trentmann, C. (2017). Das "Recht auf Vergessenwerden" bei Suchmaschinentrefferlinks. In *CR 2017* (pp. 26–35).

Wybitul, T. (Ed.) (2017). *Handbuch EU-Datenschutz-Grundverordnung*. Frankfurt am Main.

Printed in the United States
by Baker & Taylor Publisher Services